Withdrawn
University of Waterloo

SOCIOPOLITICAL ECOLOGY
Human Systems and Ecological Fields

Contemporary Systems Thinking

Series Editor: Robert L. Flood
University of Hull
Hull, United Kingdom

A Continuation Order Plan is available for this series. A continuation order will bring
delivery of each new volume immediately upon publication. Volumes are billed only upon
actual shipment. For further information please contact the publisher.

SOCIOPOLITICAL ECOLOGY
Human Systems and Ecological Fields

Frederick L. Bates
The University of Georgia
Athens, Georgia

PLENUM PRESS • NEW YORK AND LONDON

Library of Congress Cataloging-in-Publication Data

Bates, Frederick L.
    Sociopolitical ecology : human systems and ecological fields /
  Frederick L. Bates.
        p.   cm. -- (Contemporary systems thinking)
    Includes bibliographical references and index.
    ISBN 0-306-45653-2
    1. Social structure.   2. Social systems.   3. System theory.
  4. Social ecology.   5. Human ecology.   I. Title.   II. Series.
  HM24.B3637   1997
  306--dc21   97-29385
                                                                       CIP

ISBN 0-306-45653-2

© 1997 Plenum Press, New York
A Division of Plenum Publishing Corporation
233 Spring Street, New York, N. Y. 10013

http://www.plenum.com

10 9 8 7 6 5 4 3 2 1

All rights reserved

No part of this book may be reproduced, stored in a retrieval system, or transmitted in
any form or by any means, electronic, mechanical, photocopying, microfilming,
recording, or otherwise, without written permission from the Publisher

Printed in the United States of America

To HAROLD L. GEISERT

whose insightful teaching and personal friendship
inspired me to start on the long road to the writing of this book

Foreword

In the late nineteenth century, researchers encountered limitations to reductionism and physics. A counterposition in biology took on a coherent form by the mid-1920s. Scientists such as Walter B. Cannon (credited with homeostasis), Paul Weiss, and Ludwig von Bertalanffy (credited with open systems theory) came to the fore. Von Bertalanffy, for example, demonstrated that concepts of physics and closed systems were helpless in appreciating dynamics of organisms. Existence of an organism cannot be understood in terms of behavior of fundamental parts in an isolated system moving toward disorder (as suggested by reductionism and the Second Law of Thermodynamics). A whole organism is characterized by increasing or at least maintaining order; its behavior is more than the sum of its parts. Biology therefore required new concepts.

New concepts in biology focused on functional and relational criteria rather than reductionist analysis of fundamental parts. Organisms exist in relation to an environment, and their functions and structure are maintained by a continuous flow of energy and information between organism and environment. An organism is a complex system comprising many interrelated parts resulting in a whole with integrity. Key concepts here include *self-organization* by way of progressive differentiation, *equifinality* as the independence of final state from initial conditions, and *teleology* as the dependence of behavior of the organism on some future purpose "known in advance."

Open systems theory and other biological conceptions like homeostasis portray concepts of physics as helpless in appreciating dynamics of social systems as well as organisms. Rather, open systems theory observes social systems as complex systems made up of parts most usefully studied as a whole. Social systems are open to an environment. For organizations, action is taken to hold its critical variables in the steady-state. The primary aim is to ensure survival by transforming inputs and by adapting to changes when they occur.

This influential view of systems in the world has been challenged by Maturana and Varela in their theory of autopoiesis. Again, they argued, biology required new concepts. For example, autopoiesis is a theory of self-referential systems. This introduces a new notion of the capacity of living organisms to reproduce themselves and to maintain themselves as autonomous things. Autopoiesis is well presented by John Mingers in his volume, *Self-Producing Systems: Implications and Applications of Autopoesis*, in this series Contemporary Systems Thinking.

However, there remains a possibility, argues Frederick Bates in this volume, that Maturana and Varela's work may continue to lead people to conceive social systems as living systems or organisms of sorts. This "danger" is surely one that we have learned to avoid in recent years. I feel Bates's concern here resonating with R.D. Laing's worry that "we have had accounts of men [sic] as animals, men as machines, men as biochemical complexes with certain ways of their own, but there remains the greatest difficulty of achieving a human understanding of man in human terms." (The Politics of Experience and the Birds of Paradise).

In this intriguing book, Bates tackles this great difficulty with his own theory of self-referential systems in human terms. For Bates, these systems exist only as realities created by an observer through the use of "sets of cognitive rules." From this develops a constructivist theory of self-referential thinking yielding a view that society as a social entity consists of a set of such interrelated systems. These systems move toward closure, but closure sits in stark contrast to closed systems thinking referred to earlier in this foreword. Dangling these ideas before you, Bates offers an invitation to explore this and other notions with him in an intellectually stimulating engagement with his sociopolitical ecology. I recommend that you take up that engagement.

ROBERT L. FLOOD

Preface

This book is an extension and, to a degree, a reformulation of the ideas presented in *The Structure of Social Systems* and in the various journal articles that led up to and followed its publication. It arose out of my desire to clarify and promote the development of sociological structuralism as opposed to sociological individualism. It also grew out of a recognition that my previous work had not provided a satisfactory view of macrostructure and that it had failed to deal effectively with social change or morphogenisis. In addition, it had not dealt explicitly with the epistemological foundation upon which structural analysis rests.

The Structure of Social Systems, as well as the various articles I have written on social structure, assumed an empiricist view of "systems theory" as their theoretical grounding and, as a consequence, accepted rather uncritically the proposition that societies are, by definition, as well as by their observable nature, systems. Gradually, as my experience as an observer in research settings around the world broadened, I grew increasingly uncomfortable with this proposition, especially in light of my growing interest in social and economic development and the various well-known criticisms of functionalism and its failure to deal effectively with conflict and social change. It has always seemed apparent to me that the logic of systems theory is, in fact, antithetical to the idea of conflict and that attempts to accommodate systems theory to conflict theory have weakened rather than strengthened the internal consistency of the various propositions upon which systems theory rests. Even so, it has also been my conviction that, lacking a satisfactory alternative as a theoretical foundation, we were compelled to live with these inconsistencies while we were searching for a satisfactory resolution of the problems they represent.

In order to write this book, which was originally to be directed toward clarifying the meaning of the concept social structure and discussing the role of structural analysis in the sociological enterprise, I needed a new way of looking at social systems. I chose "self-referential systems theory" as this new approach. I first learned of this approach from my friend and colleague, Carlo Pelanda, with whom I was working on an international disaster study at the Institute of International Sociology in Gorizia, Italy. Like me, one of Carlo's central interests is in sociological theory as it relates to the structure and functioning of social systems. In conversations over a period of several years the subject of self-referential systems theory came up repeatedly, and Carlo attempted to explain to me what it was all about. I must confess that for quite some time I was unable to grasp the meaning and significance of what he was saying and was at first resistant to the idea that such systems are thought of as being closed and autonomous. My mistake was to think of them as closed in the sense that Buckley or Rappaport and others think of closed systems. My other difficulty was in understanding the significance of the notion that self-referential social systems exist only as realities created by an observer through the use of "sets of cognitive rules."

I remember sitting one night with Carlo on the balcony of my hotel in Trieste overlooking the harbor in which several ships were maneuvering toward the dock and asking him, "Is the crew of that ship out there a self-referential system?" Carlo, I am sure, was puzzled by my question, but nevertheless, in his usual good humor, answered, "Perhaps." I later realized he meant by this, "It depends on how you look at it." I was not then aware of the fact that I, an empiricist, was asking for an empiricist's answer from a rather radical relativistic contructivist. My question was directed toward the issue of structural boundedness, which I interpreted to be the same thing as closure, and I did not understand what is meant by closure in self-referential systems from a constructivist point of view. It seemed apparent to me that whoever was in command of the ship we were observing, and whoever was at the wheel and at the engine controls, were all taking information from their environment into account and responding to it by changes in course. This meant to me that the ship's crew was an "open system." Later, I realized that this is irrelevant in a constructivist's version of self-referential systems theory. What is relevant is that perhaps, as Carlo said, it could be demonstrated that there is an "independent system of cognitive rules" that governs the behavior of the ship's crew and that these rules have evolved as a set of rules separately from other sets of rules covering other activities in society.

I really did not grasp what Carlo was talking about until I heard him give a paper at a meeting of Italian and American disaster researchers at the University of Delaware's Disaster Research Center. Although the paper was about disasters, it was couched in terms of constructivism and self-referential systems theory. It suddenly came to me what this theory is all about. I could think of nothing else for the next two days and nights. I could not sleep as I reviewed in my mind everything I had written or thought in the past on the subject of social structure, and by the time I left the meeting, I had in mind the outline and many of the details of this book. Upon returning to Athens, I began to write and had completed a draft in about eight months. Meanwhile I was searching the library for articles and books on self-referential systems theory without success. It was not until after I had completed the second draft that I became acquainted with the work of Humberto R. Maturana and Francisco J. Varela on autopoiesis. In their book, *Autopoiesis and Cognition*, and in Milan Zeleny's edited book, which contains a chapter by Maturana and an historical review of the development of the theory by Zeleny (1981), I found a statement of autopoietic systems theory as it developed in biology.

Much of the terminology used by Maturana and Varela is quite different from that which I understood from my conversations with Carlo Pelanda and our associates in Verona and from my own extension of these ideas as I wrote the chapters included in the first and second drafts of this book, but the central theme was the same. What was important to me was the fact that on the basis of the ideas I had taken from Carlo, I had, using my own perspective toward social structure, arrived at similar terminology and at the recognition of the same theoretical problems discussed by Maturana, Varela, and Zeleny.

The ideas taken from Carlo were that (1) self-referential social systems consist of closed sets of interrelated cognitive systems that develop autopoietically as a population of people interact with an environment and attempt to render their relationship to it stable and predictable; (2) such sets of cognitive systems continue to evolve toward closure, which is reached when they achieve a stable predictable relationship to each other and to their environment; (3) such systems are separate, bounded, and therefore autonomous; and (4) society as a social entity consists of a set or population of such systems.

I saw my task in this book as creating a basis for applying self-referential systems theory to social systems by creating a structural language for applying such a theory. In the final draft of this book, I have not revised what I have written to conform to the ideas I found in Maturana's work for several reasons. First, because I originally wrote this material in complete ignorance of self-referential systems theory as defined by Maturana, I cannot claim dependence on his ideas except as they may have filtered through my conversations with Pelanda. Second, it may be of some value to others to see that scholars working independently on quite different topics arrive at similar conclusions, even similar language. This seems to me to give some weight to the utility of Maturana's thoughts. The third reason is that I do not agree with a number of particular details in his theory, which is fundamentally a biological and not sociological one.

First, he focuses heavily on the capacity of living organisms to reproduce themselves and to maintain themselves as autonomous living systems. I think it would be a mistake to begin again to think of societies and other social systems, as we have in the past, as "living systems" or as "organisms." There are fundamental differences that make this analogy misleading. In particular, the role of cognitive processes and of meaning in the sense of symbolic codes is of central importance in the case of human behavior systems and is quite different from the figurative sense in which the idea of nonsymbolic, noncognitive chemical codes is used in the sense of biological genetics. In the case of social systems, it is not so farfetched to think of the structure of a system as existing as a set of symbolically encoded, cognitive rules, but when this is done in the biological sense that genetic codes provide rules for structure, I have the uneasy feeling that we are anthropomorphizing biochemical processes. We should no more "anthropomorphize" an organism than we should "organicize" a society.

A second reason to let my own version of self-referential theory stand as it is, at least for now, is that I believe Maturana is incorrectly using the strategies of modeling and classification, a subject discussed extensively in this book. He distinguishes between organization and structure in a way that seems to me to use a classification strategy for defining organization and a modeling strategy to deal with structure. To him, the organization of an organism refers to the traits or characteristics it holds in common with its species that allow us to define it as a member of a class. Although it is not entirely clear to me, as a nonbiologist, Maturana treats this categorical organization as if it is real and has the capacity to function as a constraint upon individual living organisms. He thinks of structure as referring to the configuration of real elements in a particular case. He also sees both organization and structure as somehow operating in interaction in particular cases. To me, the thing called "organization" by Maturana is a classificatory abstraction (a metaphenomenon) having no substance and no independent existence in the real world and therefore is incapable of exercising constraints upon any empirical phenomenon other than the act of conceptualization in the mind of an observer.

In this book, the terms *structure* and *organization* are also used, but their usage derives from Raymond Firth and British social anthropology. I have been using these terms in roughly this manner for over 40 years. But it is interesting that a similar, yet independent, conceptualization was employed by Maturana to solve a similar problem. In my writing, however, the term *structural form* takes on the role of Maturana's *organization* and the term *social structure* is used to refer to the "rules of organization" that exist as a stored symbolic code in the minds of a particular set of actors. This leaves *social organization* as a term referring to the "structure of real behavior" as it occurs in the actual activities of those actors that are accessible to an observer.

There is a great deal more to this distinction than can be made of it in this preface, but it is important to point out that the structure of a system is specific to an exact system, that is, to a single empirical case, and not to a category of cases, as in Maturana's conception of social organization. Each particular case of a social system is therefore conceived of as being characterized by both a "social structure" and a "social organization" that can, but need not be, like any other case. Neither concept is therefore categorical but, instead, unit specific.

One of the central propositions of this book is that all societies are not necessarily systems. Whether a society is regarded as a system depends upon the structural characteristics we attribute to it by use of our cognitive apparatus. I am convinced that modern capitalistic societies are not usefully conceptualized as systems but are instead better understood as ecological fields comprised of bounded systems that are evolving and developing separately but in interaction with each other. Maturana at times seems to think of the whole universe as one system, and therefore of the "ecosystem" as a system. At other times, it is clear that he recognizes the possibility of another type of collectivity. For example, he uses the word *colony* to refer to a collection of separate organisms that do not themselves form an organism, a coral colony, for example. It is in this sense that I am using the concepts "social network" and "ecological subfield" to refer to communities and societies with capitalistic market economies. Sorokin's term *congeries* could as easily be used to carry the meaning of ecological field or social network in this book were it not for the fact that an ecological network is not a random or meaningless collection of social systems, but one that contains its own ordered set of contingent relationships. It displays an order, but that order is "probabilistic" and contingent. Parsons' "collectivity" could also have served this purpose if it had not already been appropriated by him as a collective noun referring essentially to many different types of systems. The term *ecological field* was chosen because of its neutral character with respect to the concept system. Here it is used to refer to an organized set of interacting systems that themselves may or may not be elements in a larger system. Thus, a contingency network becomes a nonsystem or ecological field, and a bonded network, a system.

I have been aware for some time of the work of Niclaus Luhman on self-referential systems theory but, being illiterate in German, have been unable to avail myself of the opportunity to study this work in detail. It was not until the 1988 publication of an article concerning this work in the *Journal of Sociological Theory* that I was aware of his dependence on Maturana's work and able to read in English a brief summary of his perspective. By that time, the basic ideas on which this book is based had taken their final form. Any correspondence between it and Luhman's work therefore has emerged either through my contacts with Pelanda or from the correspondence of our independently derived conclusions with respect to social structure, which owe their origin to Maturana, and earlier to Talcott Parsons and his followers.

The contents of this book are a result of my prior work when it was blended with the notion of self-referential systems and the epistomology of constructivism as I understood it from my association with Carlo Pelanda and our colleagues in the Social Systemics Group in Gorizia and later. Because it is quite likely that I have distorted these views considerably in the process of blending them with my own, my colleagues should not be held responsible. However, I would like to acknowledge my debt to Carlo and our associates in Italy for initiating the stimulating and challenging experience of rethinking and recasting my views on social structure.

One other very important source of influence over my current way of thinking must be added to this preface. In the process of writing it, I was "born again" philosophically, as a neoconstructivist. Up until the late 1980s, I regarded myself as an enlightened empiricist. By *enlightened* I mean that I had no respect for those who were raw empiricists, believing that the data would speak for themselves without the benefit of a prior theatrical foundation. I was an empiricist in the Karl Popper tradition.

After I had completed the second editing of this book, I asked Carlo Pelanda to organize a meeting of the Social Systemics Group of the Institute of International Sociology to criticize my work in light of their thoughts on self-referential systems theory. When the group met, it diplomatically but rather emphatically made the point that my work was still mired down in old-fashioned empiricism. Together they recommended a program of study that led me to von Glasersfeld, von Foester, Watzlawick, and other constructivists. It now became apparent to me that there was a natural cognitive affinity between the ideas of self-referentiality, constructivism, and cognitive science. For the next couple of years, I reworked the second draft to be more explicitly in line with a constructivist epistemology. In this process, I was immensely aided and encouraged by Davide Nicolini, Daniele Ungaro, and Marco Lombardi of the Social Systemics Group, and by frequent conversations with Carlo Pelanda. Davide Nicolini was especially helpful, spending several months going over the second draft, making specific detailed comments and suggesting bibliographic references. As usual, my long-term colleague and theoretical kinsman, Walter Peacock, made many useful suggestions for improving the manuscript, as did Daniel Rodeheaver and Joseph McCrary.

Out of all of this (that transpired over a 10-year period), the present book has emerged as a rather longish essay on sociopolitical ecology. It became ecological rather than strictly sociological when it became necessary to think of the relationships among systems in a common environment. Ecology had always been lurking back there behind my work ever since my article entitled "Institutions, Organizations and Communities" in the late 1950s and since the chapters in *The Structure of Social Systems* dealing with communities. There, the distinction was between the structure of an organization and that of a community. The distinction was made using so-called reciprocal and conjunctive relationships as the discriminating concepts. Communities were characterized as having contingent, categorical relationships among their parts and as being characterized by conflict and competition among their various component units. These are the characteristics used in this book as the distinguishing characteristics of the relations among units in an ecological field. In other words, the communities described in *The Structure of Social Systems* are the same as the ecological subfields referred to in this book.

The kind of ecology offered here is one that includes human systems on a par with biological organisms. An ecological image of the world is obviously weirdly incomplete without human beings, at present the dominant species on the earth. It is also rather bizarrely presented when it ignores the social life of various species and the social interaction among species. It is hoped that the ecology presented here allows for a truly comprehensive view of this planet as an ecological field.

Contents

The Design of a Cognitive System for Generating Structural Models of Social Behavior Systems and Ecological Fields

1.1 Introduction

1.1.1 A Constructivist Epistemological Foundation

This book is concerned with relationships between human systems and their environments. It is also concerned with relationships among the human systems themselves as they interact in an environmental context. Its objective is to present a theoretical orientation and a conceptual scheme for use by those interested in creating structural models of social systems and of their relationships to each other in the context of the ecological fields they inhabit. It will not offer a description of any particular society nor will it present models of particular social systems or particular environmental problems. Instead it will develop a cognitive apparatus that can be used for such purposes.

The plan is to begin with a set of assumptions that lay an epistemological foundation and then proceed to define the conceptual elements required to fill out a completely developed cognitive system that is capable of producing cognitive images of the relationships among human systems and between them and their social, biological, and physical environments. By a "completely developed cognitive system" we mean a conceptual apparatus that contains a set of cross-referenced, interrelated concepts and a logic that makes it possible to employ them together in a consistent fashion so that they make it possible for the user to construct mental models of phenomenological targets. Such a cognitive system can be employed by an observer to convert raw sensory experience into organized cognitive models of phenomenological targets, thereby making it possible for the mind to work with and upon them.

The conceptual apparatus presented here is a form of "human ecology" focused on the structural relationships among human systems and between them and their nonhuman environments. As shall be seen, the object that is comprised of populations of bounded social and biological systems interacting in a common space will be referred to as an *ecological field*. Because ecological fields are comprised of systems, in order to construct the cognitive apparatus under development, it will be necessary to take a close look at systems theory. When this is done, the result will be that certain types of societies will be modeled as ecological subfields operating in what will be described as larger ecological fields rather than as social systems. Such an approach will challenge many of the ideas that have dominated the social sciences for the past 50 years. At the same time, it is hoped that this perspective will open a new window of theoretical opportunity and lead to new approaches that are more appropriate to the world of the forthcoming 21st century.

At the outset, it should be understood that the ecological approach to societal structure to be presented in the book grew out of attempts to bring about conceptual clarity and interconcept consistency and not out of empirical observation. The objective of this work is to create a flexible and versatile set of cognitive tools, capable of creating a wide variety of structural models by use of an internally consistent language and logic. Also, its objective is to create a conceptual apparatus that can be expanded by others to include as yet unimagined conceptual tools that reveal unrecognized structural and ecological patterns. The hope is that the cognitive system developed here will be sufficiently complete and sufficiently integrated to sustain itself as a working cognitive apparatus, even as it generates additions and revisions to its own internal order. It is my hope that it will have the characteristics, figuratively speaking, of a "mental organism" capable of both growth and evolutionary adaptation, thereby becoming the basis of a new school of thought in the social sciences.

1.1.2   Philosophical Foundations

Every intellectual enterprise rests on a foundation of assumptions that furnishes a starting point and give a direction to the effort. In the sciences that purport to create new knowledge, there is always an epistemology in the background, either consciously recognized by the scientist as he or she works or lurking below the surface as a tacit beginning point influencing the direction taken by research and molding its outcome.

In the case of a theoretical endeavor aimed at supplying the cognitive tools through which scientific problems are framed, it is very important to be self-conscious about these philosophical foundations. This is so because they profoundly influence the way the enterprise is approached and how it is shaped as it moves toward completion. For these reasons, this chapter will be devoted to a self-conscious discussion of the epistemological foundations of the conceptual apparatus to be developed and to a discussion of the historical roots of the ideas taken as the beginning points of this work.

1.1.2.1 Constructivist Foundation

The philosophy of knowledge known as constructivism has been chosen as the epistemological foundation for this book. Constructivism, which has roots stretching back several centuries, has rapidly gained adherents in the second half of this century as biology and cognitive psychology have shed new light on how the senses, the nervous system, and the brain operate, and as we have come to learn more about the human "mind" and how it works (von Glasersfeld, 1987; Gardner, 1985; Bateson, 1972; Maturana and Varela, 1980).

Constructivism assumes that all "knowledge" and all the information and data upon which it rests is relative to the theoretical apparatus or conceptual scheme and linguistic code that was used to generate and codify it in a form that the mind can use in its internal operation. Because knowledge and information are mental phenomena and exist in the form of encoded "ideas" of one sort or another, and because the mind is the agent that organizes and gives meaning to the ideas it contains and works with, all information or knowledge is, in some way, generated by the mind itself.

This does not mean that nothing exists outside the mind in a so-called real world, but it does mean that an observer's contact with that world is guided, shaped, and filtered by the mental apparatus employed to create mental images in the form of encoded conceptualizations of that world. What an observer as a thinking subject sees through the senses, as far as the mind is concerned, is a cognitively constructed reality that always takes the form of an encoded abstraction that has been shaped by a priori mental constructs.

Although the senses do take in stimuli from the environment of the observer's organism, which stimuli are sought and attended to, and how they are perceived by the mind and what meaning is assigned to them depends upon the cognitive structure or ecology of the mind itself (Bateson, 1972b). The mind perceives the world by organizing and interpreting neutral stimulation by use of an organized cognitive code and by use of preformed mental strategies.

For this reason, constructivists regard all mental images said to represent "reality" in the mind of an observer as being constructed by the cognitive action that precedes and follows sensory stimulation. Knowledge or information is therefore seen as being the result of a transaction between a cognitive system or set of systems and sensory inputs derived from a world outside the mind, assuming also that sensory inputs are sought and filtered under the control of the cognitive apparatus itself (von Glasersfeld, 1987; von Foerster, 1984; Maturana and Varela, 1987; Bateson, 1972b; Pelanda 1989).

To the constructivist, the cognitive system employed to generate an image of a reality such as ecological or social structure consists of a set of cognitive conventions organized as a self-referential cognitive system (Maturana and Varela, 1980; Luhman 1984, 1986). That system is an organization of self-contained mental abstractions that are cross-referenced and interrelated to form an operating apparatus that functions in the mind as a bounded mental system. It contains within itself the rules by which it is able to generate an image of a mentally constructed reality out of facts it derives from a transaction between itself and an environment it filters and interprets. This set of conventional ideas maintains itself as a cognitive system by generating "facts" that feed back upon the generative structure that created them, thereby confirming and reinforcing its organization. Such self-confirmation is accomplished by referring all observations of things outside the mind that were, in the first place, cognitively generated by a conceptual apparatus working upon sense impressions, back into the generative mechanism that produced them, thus giving them meaning and locating them in the mind relative to other mental content.

This book rests on the assumption that all scientific theories or models, including those concerned with social or ecological structure, and all data generated by them, no matter whether their creators are empirical positivists or radical relativists, are of this nature. It rejects the utility of the empiricist tradition, which assumes the possibility of inductive knowledge gained through objective verification of the truth of a theoretical system by means of a methodology that brings that theory into contact with an independent reality. It further assumes that there can be no methodological strategy that infallibly recognizes the one true reality, or one that is capable of recognizing the falsity of particular images of so-called reality.

Instead, this book is founded on a cognitively relativistic foundation. It holds that any "truth" and all facts or data said to establish it are relative to the cognitive apparatus that generated it. It assumes that there is a "real world" outside the mind of the observer, but it also assumes that this world can only be encountered by the mind through the cognitive action by which it constructs its own world of experience using an organized cognitive code. According to this assumption, instead of there being no "reality" outside the mind, there are as many realities as there are cognitive systems to construct them (von Glasersfeld, 1987).

Such a prospective should not be interpreted to mean that "empirical" research is useless because it depends upon a circular process, and because, at any rate, it can result in as many realities as there are theories (cognitive systems) to generate them. Even assuming these things, it is not necessary to assume that all cognitive systems are equally useful or that they are equally capable of functioning continuously by confirming themselves through empirical observation. They are only assumed to be self-referentially circular and therefore truthful only within their own definition of truth.

From a pragmatic perspective, relative to the adaptation of human systems to an environment, some cognitive systems provide a means by which the user can solve a cognitively defined practical or intellectual problem and thereby adapt to a set of conditions that can only be "known" through cognitive action while others do not possess this quality (von Glasersfeld, 1987). Those cognitive systems that have utility have the capacity to survive as instruments of adaptation, and those that do not are likely to be negatively selected out of the ecologies of our minds. Such negative selection occurs when a cognitive system lacks the capacity to generate facts that can be absorbed back into its own organization in the form of "predictions" that confirm the utility of its own internal order. None of this means that the cognitive system that survives must therefore be metaphysically true and, as a consequence, must correspond to a part of "reality." It merely means that the theoretical apparatus has, up until this moment, worked as an adaptive mechanism and therefore is useful because it generates a "reality" with which it can contend without collapsing as a mental apparatus. To survive means to continue to function as an adaptive mechanism; it does not, however, have any further "metaphysical" meaning.

A map that is able to guide a person from Kansas City to Nashville can be supplied by many different conceptual apparatuses, none of which can be said to correspond in the sense of being a true representation of the earth's surface between these two points. Each one can be useful without, at the same time, being true. The utility of such a map is defined by its capacity to function from within its own rules as a guide between the points it conceptualizes (Bates, 1972; Korbyski, 1941).

This book will attempt to provide a cognitive apparatus and a strategy for its use that has the capacity to supply "maps" of the structure of social systems and of their relationships to each other in the context of their environments that can be useful to those who wish to know how to pass mentally from one place in an ecological field to another, without losing one's way. It is not, however, assumed that the "maps" thus created reflect a "true cartography" of an objective reality that exists independently as "real" ecological structure. Instead, it is assumed that the conceptual apparatus that will be developed in this book will supply one useful device for guiding the mind of an observer as it moves between a conceptualization of one part of a constructed reality conventionalized as ecological or social structure to another.

All that can be asked of a conceptual apparatus is that it works to achieve the purpose it was constructed to achieve. In von Glasersfeld's (1987) words, in order to open the door, the key does not have to correspond in the sense of matching the lock in order to function as a key. It merely needs to operate as a key. We are after socioecological keys to open socioecological locks but with the foreknowledge that the lock as a reality can only be known to us through fashioning the key. The key maker's responsibility is for unlocking the lock. He or she is not also responsible for fashioning a true and exact image of the lock itself. The lock must forever remain a mystery if we use it as a metaphor for ultimate, true, "natural" reality.

The most important message of the constructivist epistemology is *"Observer beware!"* When you, as a scientist, collect data, you are not gathering "natural facts" but creating relativistic information by the use of a cognitive apparatus that controls your senses and organizes every transaction you have with the environment of your mind. If you wish to observe and use the information you construct through observation to solve some problem, you will increase the probability of success if you know what you are doing and how you are doing it. You must self-consciously examine your cognitive apparatus. To improve the adaptation of your cognitive apparatus to its self-constructed environment, you must improve your cognitive system itself, so that it reorders the reality you perceive, thus supplying a more useful key to unlock the door you wish to pass through. The lock itself, as an independent reality, will not teach you how to fashion the key by "speaking the truth" in direct communication between your mind and reality. You, the observer, through care in controlling your cognitive apparatus, are responsible for creating your own reality as well as the keys that fit it!

1.2   The Cognitive Task

To follow a constructivist agenda in providing a cognitive system that conceptualizes social and ecological structure, as this book attempts to do, it is mandatory to be explicit and self-conscious concerning the foundation upon which the conceptual apparatus rests. There should be no hidden assumptions, nor should there be any evasiveness or obfuscation used to cover theoretical ambivalence or conceptual indecision. The constructivist approach recognizes that a cognitive apparatus designed to deal with a particular scientific problem is always a conventional system; that is, it consists of a set of linguistic and theoretical conventions that are constructed as an artificial mental device to interpret a phenomenological domain by imposing an order upon it through the mechanism of the conventional apparatus itself. Such a cognitive system (theory or model) creates a cognitive reality relative to itself alone. It operates, in Pelanda's (1989) terms, as an "artificial observer" as opposed to a "natural observer," since it conventionalizes the observation process according to its own rules. The world of "raw reality" is encountered only as a set of "artificial observations," codified and organized according to the rules of the cognitive system being employed. By "natural observer" we mean a hypothetical observer capable of seeing things as they really are; an observer with a godlike ability to know and recognize the ultimate truth. On the other hand, the "artificial observer" refers to a cognitive mechanism that has been built up in the mind of an observing subject on the basis of self-constructed experience. In almost all cases, it includes culturally derived elements, for example, a symbolic code or language, a belief system, values, and so on. It is artificial in the sense that it has been constructed as opposed to being "discovered."

Such a cognitive apparatus is useful as an artificial tool if it is able to generate information that allows it to predict the behavior of its environment and furnish useful responses to the "empirical environment" it creates through its own cognitive action. A cognitive system literally creates its own "facts" or "data" by selecting, interpreting, codifying, and processing "sense impressions" arising out of interaction between the cognitive apparatus itself and the phenomenological environment to which it relates or with which it interacts through observation.

In this statement, the term *sense impressions* refers to the neural stimulation received through the senses prior to the cognitive action that organizes and gives meaning to them. As Maturana and Varela (1980) have pointed out, the organic nature of the sensory system itself converts the external world into a neurological code, which is then further interpreted by use of a cognitive code. It is the results of these processes that the "mind" perceives (Maturana and Varela, 1980).

1.2.1 Evaluating the Cognitive Apparatus Being Constructed in This Book

To understand the reality that a cognitive system creates by generating and processing "facts" or "data," it is necessary to understand the cognitive "machine" itself and to know how it, itself, is constructed and what its rules of operation are. In the case of this book, the artificial construction that creates or organizes a particular view of "socioecological reality" supplies a kind of "thinking machine" or, in Pelanda's words, an "artificial observer" through which we, as scientific observers, can order our efforts to construct intellectual images of a relativistic reality called "ecosocial structure."

This cognitive apparatus must be comprehended and criticized from within itself. It is not appropriate to approach it as an empiricist would, by evaluating its correspondence with an empirically given, observationally verified reality and to criticize it because it does not "correspond" to perceptions of the critic. It is also not legitimate to criticize it by using another quite different and separate theoretical system as the basis of criticism, saying that it does not recognize or deal with problems associated with this other system, and therefore it is wrong or defective.

The cognitive apparatus constructed in this book is designed to deal *only with the reality it itself creates* and *not with other realities* brought to it by the reader or the critic on the basis of a belief in the ultimate correctness of other theoretical formulations. It, like all such systems, is entirely limited by its own cognitive code and its own internal organization, and should be evaluated on the basis of its capacity to operate as a cognitive tool with respect to its own particular domain, within its own language and logic.

Nevertheless, to evaluate the cognitive system to be presented here, it is necessary to know how it was constructed and how it limits itself by its own internal order. The task of criticism appropriate to evaluating such a relativistic cognitive apparatus is somewhat like the task of deciding whether a set of mathematical equations follows the rules of mathematics, or deciding whether a paragraph in English follows the rules of English grammar, syntax, and semantics. Here the issue is, "Does the cognitive system presented here for modeling ecosocial structure present a clear set of rules, and does it follow these self-generated rules without forcing us to abandon them because they are internally inconsistent, contradictory, indeterminate, or so obscure that they cannot operate as rules in a stable and meaningful fashion.

It must also be evaluated on the basis of its capacity to absorb the facts it generates without collapsing as an apparatus. Can an observer, using this apparatus, generate facts through observation that are predictable on the basis of the cognitive "machine"? Most of all, it should be judged in terms of its ability to furnish solutions to problems posed from within its own framework concerning phenomena falling within the domain it defines for itself, ecosocial structure. Ultimately, does it furnish a useful key capable of unlocking doors we wish to unlock?

With this understanding as a beginning point, it is time to go on to the task of revealing the foundations upon which this enterprise in constructivist ecostructural modeling rests. These foundations result from a set of consciously taken design decisions that determined the strategy for this constructivist endeavor. They will not necessarily be presented in an historical order representing the mental process of the author over many years but, instead, in an order that facilitates comprehension of the design of the apparatus under construction.

1.2.2   Basic Guidelines for the Construction of the Cognitive Apparatus

A set of strategic decisions has guided the construction of the cognitive apparatus developed in this book. These decisions resulted in the choice of certain existing cognitive systems already in use in sociology as beginning points for constructing a new theoretical or cognitive apparatus. Such an enterprise must inevitably begin with ideas already contained in the mind of the architect of the mental construction. In this case, it begins with concepts and theoretical perspectives contained in the mind of the author gained from 40 years of experience as a practicing sociologist.

It should be understood at the outset that the intended function of this apparatus is to provide a tool for constructing cognitive models meant to represent the relationships among human systems in the context of their environments. This choice of objectives served to suggest to the author the conceptual ingredients appropriate as beginning points for this task of cognitive construction. The basic ingredients selected as beginning points for the construction of a cognitive system defining a new field called sociopolitical ecology are given in Table 1.1

1.2.2.1   Atomistic Approach

The first strategic decision, as pointed out earlier, was to use a constructivist epistemology. The second was to use an "atomistic" or "hierarchical" approach in the process of theoretical construction, beginning the process of conceptualization of the structure of human systems and ecological fields at the microlevel, and then building a set of concepts upward from this base until the total conceptual apparatus contains a specification of how entire societies, intersocietal networks, and ecological fields are constructed out of the same basic phenomenon called behavior. The atomistic strategy requires that all concepts have to be defined in terms of each other so that there is no conceptual discontinuity as the mind passes from one level of scale and complexity in structure to another. This is like saying that the conceptualization of microstructural units such as the positions and roles that make up group structure must be compatible and translatable into the conceptualization of macrostructural units such as complex multigroup organizations or societies.

Once a cognitive system has been built up from micro- to the macrolevel and the various elements in the conceptual scheme have been defined in terms of a common language, this new apparatus may be used to generate mental images of phenomena thought of as existing outside the mind of an observer. The cognitive system being formed in this book is intended for use in constructing cognitive models of particular behavior systems and networks of such systems in the context of their environments. In other words, this particular cognitive system is intended to furnish the cognitive tools

TABLE 1.1
Components of Cognitive System under Construction

Type	Function
Constructivism	The epistomological foundation
Atomism	The construction approach
Behavior	The phenomenological domain
Structure	The organizing principle
System	The explanatory dynamic
Self-referentiality	The criterion for defining systems
Role theory	The language for describing system structure

through which an observer can create specific structural models of particular groups, organizations, communities, societies, and ecological networks set in the ecological fields they inhabit.

It should be understood as a general cognitive tool and not as a description of any particular empirical reality. It furnishes a method by which a user can construct structural models of particular cases. Later in this book, the implications of this method will be discussed, and examples of how this cognitive apparatus can affect the way we view modern societies will be given.

The user of this cognitive apparatus is forewarned that it creates a set of mental images by imposing its own "intellectual regime or discipline" on the observer who uses it by controlling transactions between the observer's mind and his or her environment. That environment, in this case, is the world of social behavior and the ecological context of such behavior. When this apparatus is used to generate, control, and order observations, the social world will take on the appearance it generates. We will never be able to say that the world is, in fact, as it appears to be when viewed through this cognitive lens. Perhaps, however, we will be able to say that seeing the world this way yields some useful results.

1.2.2.2 Behavior as the Cognitive Domain

Aside from selecting an epistomological position and a construction strategy, the first and most basic decision in an enterprise such as this is to select and define the phenomenological domain within which the cognitive apparatus will operate. In this case, behavior was selected as the target phenomenon for ecostructural modeling, and this decision requires careful specification of the meaning of the concept behavior and of its limits as far as this endeavor is concerned. Later chapters in this book will discuss this matter in detail. To do so here would obscure the broad outline of the overall design of this cognitive apparatus, and it is this design that must be made transparent at this point. At present, suffice it to say that the entire edifice of concepts to be presented as elements of the general ecostructural model being constructed will refer to the behavior of systems or networks of systems in relationship to each other in the context of their environment.

It is important to recognize that this decision rules out using "biological, social, or mechanical actors" as the units of analysis and selects the behavior or action of such actors as the target phenomenon. The implications of this decision are far reaching and, as shall be seen, permeate the entire edifice of concepts and theoretical propositions that are developed on the basis of it. Behavior was selected as the target phenomenon on the assumption that it is through behavior that active systems adapt to and impact upon each other and upon their environments. In addition, systems themselves may be regarded as behavioral (living or otherwise operating) mechanisms in the sense that they function within themselves on the basis of behaviors (actions) executed by their various component parts in relation to each other.

After pointing out the philosophical foundations of the cognitive apparatus under construction and pointing to its intended phenomenological domain, Table 1.1 shows that several already existing, separate but interrelated cognitive systems were used as basic "building blocks" or conceptual modules in constructing this general model. First, the idea of structure, as a general cognitive apparatus used in many different fields, was chosen as the central organizing apparatus of the cognitive system. Second, so-called systems theory, in particular the idea of a closed self-referential "system," was employed as the boundary-establishing criterion for using the concept structure. It was also used as the basis of a method of explanation.

The objective of this book is to create a cognitive apparatus that will generate structural models of behavior systems and of the interrelationships among behavior systems in the context of ecological fields. Because of this, the ideas *system* and *structure* are the central cognitive tools used in conceptualizing social units that are assumed, at the outset, to be phenomenologically comprised of behavior. It will, of course, be necessary to specify what interpretation of the concepts *system* and *structure* will be employed in this particular cognitive construction before the meaning of the term *ecological field* can be clarified. But now it is necessary to point out other broad cognitive decisions.

In order to employ the ideas of system and structure in conjunction with behavior, for example, it was necessary to select a "language" that could be employed to "operationalize" these concepts so that they could be employed to construct a cognitive apparatus related to the task at hand. So-called "role theory" was chosen as that language (Biddle and Thomas, 1966; Bates and Harvey, 1975; Merton, 1968; Gross, Mason, and McEachern. 1958). In other words, the language of "role theory" was used to furnish the terms necessary to implement the idea of structure as it applies to the phenomenological target "behavior system."

In order to achieve cognitive compatibility, several other strategic decisions were "forced upon" the design process when the elements of behavior, structure, system, and role theory were brought together and redefined. These need to be briefly mentioned here before going on to a more detailed discussion of how each of these cognitive ingredients was limited and modified to achieve conceptual integration.

First, it was decided that so-called "self-referential" or "closed" systems theory was the variety of systems theory most compatible with a constructivist epistemology and with the resultant awareness that a cognitive apparatus was to be constructed that would create its own view of reality (Luhmann, 1986; Maturana and Varela, 1980). Second, because "role-theory terminology" was to be employed as the language of construction, it was assumed that roles, and larger units constructed by the use of the concept role, would be treated as cognitive systems in and of themselves, that, by their own operation in the minds of human actors, produce a "reality" called "behavior."

Roles, as cognitive systems, were assumed to operate to organize an actor's relationship to a self-constructed social environment by providing a set of rules that govern the transactions between actors' minds and their perceived environments. Because self-referential systems theory, as well as cognitive systems theory, demands that the user think in terms of bounded systems that achieve closure, it was necessary to seek a means of dealing with a set of bounded and separate closed systems that nevertheless interact in a common environment. To supply this element in the cognitive apparatus, the idea of "social network" was employed, but with a particular theoretical "twist," namely, that of an ecological field.

The meaning of all of these decisions will be discussed briefly in this chapter as a kind of foreword to guide the reader through what is to come. Later chapters will discuss each of these elements of construction in much greater detail. For the time being, Table 1.1 presents a summary of the strategic decisions in diagrammatic form.

The term *cognitive system*, which has been used many times previously, was adopted from the work of Carlo Pelanda and from others. This term implies a mental apparatus comprised of "information" encoded in the mind by use of symbols and their associated semantic structures. Thus, it refers to the contents of the mind rather than to the brain as a biological organ (Pelanda, 1989; von Foerster, 1984; Bateson, 1979, 1972b, etc.).

By using the term *cognitive system*, we can refer to a wide variety of mental phenomena that are often covered by such words as *theory, model, paradigm, frame of reference,* or *conceptual scheme* and also to phenomena such as language or symbol systems, ideological orientations, technological systems or even to conceptualizations of political and economic systems such as capitalism and socialism.

As already stated, a cognitive system amounts to a set of interrelated ideas organized by use of symbolically encoded information. Information is understood to include information based on perceptions of a world exterior to the mind as well as "semantic information" in the form of concepts and symbols. It also includes "moral information" in the form of rules that furnish standards of evaluation and methods of operation. At the level of the individual mind, a cognitive system consists of a bounded, interrelated, cross-referenced, interdependent system of information that the mind uses to control its relationship to an environment that it experiences through the operation of its sensory apparatus. According to Pelanda and others, the mind of the individual is host to a whole population of cognitive systems, each of which has developed and continues to develop around an adaptive problem faced by the actor as a means of managing transactions between the mind and its self-perceived environment (Pelanda, 1989; Bateson, 1972b, 1979; Luhmann, 1986).

A "scientific" cognitive system represents a kind of "theoretical construction," meant to define and solve a "scientific problem" by building up a conceptual apparatus and rules for its use in "predicting" or "managing" data (facts) it generates by controlling the relationship between the mind of the scientist and a methodological operation through which the mind of the scientist encounters that sector of the environment under consideration. Scientific cognitive systems, as opposed to "folk cognitive systems," function in the mind of the user in the same manner and differ only in the rigor of their construction and the criticism and self-awareness to which the scientist subjects his or her cognitive apparatus.

In both cases, the host mind, in which a cognitive system is constructed and operates, creates a version of reality by cognitive action, thus ordering a sector of the mind's environment, which, itself, is a cognitively constructed empirical world. It is also true in both the cases of "scientific" and "folk" cognitive systems that the cognitive apparatus is usually shared (within limits) as an intersubjective "cognitive culture" acquired and developed through symbolic interaction among human actors. In other words, the cognitive systems employed by both scientists and laymen are in one sense built up in individual minds as they interpret the communicative behavior of others in their environment and "receive" previously constructed cognitive systems from others.

Because some cognitive systems may be regarded as cultural artifacts, we can think, at least figuratively, of some such systems as being somewhat independent of the minds of specific individual actors. To do so, we must be willing to refer to a "shared set of ideas" as a "cultural system," stored in the minds of a population of individual actors, be the culture that of a scientific field or of "lay culture." This view is useful if we remain aware that any cognitive system can only operate to generate cognitive action, and therefore behavior, if it has a "host mind" within which to be "housed" and within which it can function to construct its own interpretive reality.

The point of this discussion as far as this book is concerned is as follows: The culture of sociology and of associated sciences contains a set of cognitive systems, some of which will be employed in this book as the "raw materials" for constructing a new cognitive system. These existing cognitive systems include those named in Table 1.1 under the labels (1) structure, (2) system, (3) role theory, and (4) ecological relationships. These shared ideas, as they are constructed in the mind of this writer from intersubjective interaction with colleagues, will be used as "building blocks" to construct a general model of human systems and their relationships to each other in the context of ecological fields.

The cognitive task is to "force" these separate systems into agreement so that they form a single cognitive apparatus whose internal order is transparent, both within the mind of the constructor, this writer, and I hope, to an intersubjectively communicating audience. To accomplish this task, we must begin by specifying the broad outline of these separate cognitive systems, and then later, by becoming more detailed and precise concerning them, as they are revised in relation to each other. Accordingly, the next few pages will be used to set the stage by discussing briefly each of these cognitive system components at a very general level.

1.2.2.3 Structure as a Cognitive System

The concept *structure* is a rather complex set of interrelated ideas that form a bounded cognitive system. Of course, our minds are not always aware of this complexity, nor of the rules that organize the subcomponents of the cognitive system called *structure* into a bounded mental apparatus. As a matter of fact, as a later chapter will show, there is considerable variability among users of this conceptual apparatus, and a good deal of intersubjective noise and confusion occurs as users attempt to communicate about it. This book will argue that the cognitive system called *structure* is one of a set of strategies the mind employs in ordering itself and its sensory relationships to its environment. The structural strategy works by use of the ordering principle of connectedness or relationship in space through time. It can be reduced to its simplest form by thinking of it as a process whereby the mind forces itself to perceive its environment in terms of configuration and bounded wholeness. The "wholeness" of structure is one where separate bounded elements are conceived of as being within and a part of a larger whole, where they are joined or related to each other by a relationship system. Thus, structure as a mental-ordering strategy constructs a kind of "gestaltist" reality or a reality based at the same time on separation and on juncture, or connectedness (Bates and Peacock, 1989; Bates and Harvey, 1975).

For purposes of illustration, this mental strategy (or cognitive system) may be contrasted with a strategy called *classification*, which uses an entirely different ordering principle for creating its "reality." In classification, the ordering strategy is that of similarity and difference, not connectedness or juncture. In classification, objects whose identity is assumed to be separate are compared and grouped in the mind according to similarity and difference. Objects that are alike on criteria selected by the cognitive orderer are placed in the same category and given a common symbolic label, and objects that are different on these criteria are placed in different categories according to the criteria of classification. A cognitive code is built up on the basis of comparison and contrast among separate units using the mental criteria that define the code.

Both cognitive systems "structure" and "classification" are actually complex sets of ideas that supply an "ordering mechanism" that organizes a way of thinking of a phenomenological domain by use of a cognitive strategy that imposes itself on both perception and cognition. We cannot say there are natural structures "out there" in the real world, nor can we say that there are natural classes or categories: It is not a question of discovery but of cognitive construction.

Nevertheless, both strategies can prove useful if they provide the user with a means of adapting to the environment they work upon. Pragmatically, a conception of structure can help the user mentally construct an object or a system outside the mind, for example, a chair, an automobile, or a corporate organization such as a college or a hospital. Likewise, it can furnish a means of selecting a line of behavior that adapts the user to a part of his or her environment, for example, an adaptation to the behavior of bureaucrats in an organization. Similarly, classification can help the user adapt to a world outside the mind by reducing its complexity in terms of a finite number of classes, and thereby generalizing adaptive strategies that work for whole categories of objects, events, or forces.

As noted earlier, a cognitive system employed by the mind need not be regarded as yielding a true reflection of a kind of "God-given reality" to be useful. To be useful, it need only function as an adaptive mechanism that permits the survival of the user and, therefore, of the cognitive system itself.

To employ the basic idea of structure as a cognitive strategy in connection with a particular phenomenological domain, it is necessary to make many decisions that supply the general strategy with the cognitive particulars it works upon, and limit or bound its use in particular cases. A search for these particulars in the case of ecosocial structure will be the subject of later chapters, but now it is time to specify the principal limiting assumption that will guide the search. That assumption is that it is the structure of *systems* that is of central concern to sociologists when they attempt to model social structure and its relationship to the environment using the strategy inherent in the cognitive system called *structure*.

1.2.2.4   The Cognitive System Called *System*

The concept *system* consists of a complex set of interrelated ideas that themselves make up a bounded cognitive system that operates to organize or order the way the mind functions in its transactions with an assumed empirical world. Systems thinking forces the user to employ a particular type of structural strategy for ordering ideas and perceptions. The idea of "system" rests upon a structural base, but it places restrictions on how the structural strategy is employed by assuming a position with respect to "causal explanation." The objective of systems reasoning is to concentrate attention upon how a phenomenological target "works" or "operates" to produce the internal behavior of its component structural elements, and in the case of certain types of systems, how the system produces its outputs, obtains and transforms its inputs, or even on how it preserves its boundaries and revises its internal order.

Essentially the idea of *system* assumes that the structure or organization of an object and the relationship of that structure to its environment "explains" how the object operates. Explanation and understanding lie in the mind being able to specify the organization of the system in terms of a dynamic set of relationships among its parts or elements in such a way as to specify its mechanics or principles of operation. Systems reasoning does away with simple cause-and-effect reasoning and substitutes a complex notion of ordered or structured interaction among structural elements that are "shaped" in terms of each other to form a "total systemic mechanism."

Systems are regarded, consciously or unconsciously, as "machines" or "organisms" in which the elements are interdependent, coacting, interrelated units, regulated in their behavior by their ordering in the mechanism of the whole. By using a cognitive apparatus, systems are thought of as operating or active structures that function to produce the phenomena we observe by furnishing an ordering mechanism.

Furthermore, because they are thought of as being structured, systems are assumed to be nonrandom and nonchaotic in their internal operation. By imposing a mental ordering strategy in the form of a cognitive apparatus on a phenomenological domain that takes a particular stance toward structure and toward "explanation," systems are seen in the mind as bounded, self-contained, self-controlled objects.

This book will take the position that all systems are by definition closed. They constitute self-contained mechanisms whose internal order functions to seal them off from their environment, except under conditions that are controlled from within the system itself. The idea that systems are closed is an assumption meant to facilitate the construction of a cognitive apparatus designed to model ecosocial structure. This assumption is not to be taken as an empirical generalization but as an arbitrary conceptual decision. The basis of this decision will be explained in detail in later chapters because it involves a rather complex argument and cannot be given here.

Because the object of analysis in this book will be social or behavioral systems, a particular version of closed systems theory was selected. That version is called *self-referential systems theory*. It refers to systems that, although closed, are capable of responding to self-defined environments by (1) changing their internal operation in response to perceived environmental events and (2) changing their own internal organization in order to adapt to their environment. Such systems take in stimuli from the environment and transform them into information to which they can respond. For this reason, they would ordinarily be called "open systems" by scholars such as Buckley. They are also morphogenic systems in the Buckley sense (1967). However, this book will take a view of systems that is based on the work of Maturana and Varela, Luhmann, and Pelanda. These scholars are part of the "closed system" movement that has developed along with the constructivist "cognitive revolution" (Maturana and Varela, 1980 and 1987; Luhmann, 1984, 1986; Pelanda, 1989).

Self-referential systems are closed systems or systems that close upon themselves because they are able to control their relationship to their environments through internal mechanisms. This is not the same type of closure referred to in discussing theories such as Newtonian mechanisms. There, the closure is based on a set of assumptions that rule out all elements not specifically included in the language and logic of the theory. Here, closure refers to a boundedness that separates an operating system such as an organism or a social system from its environment except as that environment is "perceived" or "defined" (constructed) by the system itself.

In this book, the concept self-referential systems will be applied to social systems in order to recognize the fact that social systems, as behavioral phenomena, generate their own images of their environments and, on the basis of them, construct their own behavioral responses to them. In this book, ecological networks will be defined as webs of relationships among sets of separate, closed, self-referential systems, where separate and independent systemic mechanisms generate the functioning of the individual systems that form the ecological network. The ecological field itself will be seen as a contingent or probabilistic behavioral conglomerate and not as a system, but as a nonsystem comprised of interacting systems.

These decisions necessitate a clear recognition that the cognitive apparatus being developed as a theoretical device includes the idea of cognitive systems within itself. Social systems and individual actors employ cognitive systems as central elements in their operational mechanisms. Through their use, they construct the realities to which they construct responses.

At the same time, this model includes the idea of behavior in the sense of action. For example, social roles that are regarded as units of social structure will be thought of as cognitive systems stored in the minds of actors as sets of rules for behavior. But actual behavior in the performance of a role will also be included as a conceptual element in the theoretical (cognitive) apparatus in order to deal with the problem of how systems adapt to, draw resources from, and impact upon their environments.

1.2.2.5   A Note on Networks and Fields

Because *self-referential systems theory* employs the idea of bounded or closed systems, and therefore systems cannot themselves be regarded as components in a larger, more inclusive system, it is necessary to create a conceptualization referring to an object comprised of the relationships among many separate closed systems. To think of all the bounded systems that interact in a particular environment as forming a still larger system in which they act as subsystems would negate the concept closure and by so doing sacrifice the advantages of the concept system and of self-referentiality. *If systems are closed and separate, then they cannot at the same time be parts of another system.* Furthermore, the idea of system implies a completeness in the structure that allows the system to operate independently of its environment. This means that to regard systems as being part of a larger system negates the principle of completeness and separation. More will be made of these points in a later chapter, but now it is time to define what is meant by ecological networks and fields.

The concept *ecological network* has been chosen to allow us to think of a web of relationships among separate interacting systems, so that our cognitive apparatus can handle the problem of interrelationships among separate, bounded, self-referential systems. Ecological networks are conceived of as consisting of a web of contingent relations among a population of bounded, self-referential systems that are operating in an ecological "field." The conceptualization of an ecological field is generated by the idea of the interdependence among species of systems or types of biological or social systems in a biological or social division of labor. In an ecological field, the interactions among specific individual systems are mediated by a set of contingencies arising out of the structure of the field where separate self-referential systems operate as autonomous actors.

This statement cannot be made more specific here without getting ahead of ourselves. Suffice it to say at this point that the ideas of ecological network and ecological fields will become conventionalized elements of the cognitive system under development. Their use, like the use of all cognitive conventions, will create their own version of the reality called *society*.

1.2.2.6   Role Theory as a Language of Construction

A "language" is needed to refer to the behavioral phenomena upon which this enterprise in structural modeling will operate. This language must be compatible with both cognitive and self-referential systems theory, and it must lend itself to an "atomist" or "hierarchical" approach to constructing structural models of social systems and ecological fields. It is this language, when infused into the separate cognitive systems discussed earlier, that will be used to bring them together into a single, internally consistent, cross-referenced, cognitive apparatus.

In many respects, the language of role theory as used in sociology is ideally suited for this task if it can be expanded and modified to give it more precision, therefore expanding the possibility of greater intersubjective meaning. Role theory has always had both an implicit cognitive-systems and constructivist approach through which its founders, Mead and Cooley, pointed to the mental operations whereby human actors construct their behavior by building up self-conceptions and role definitions that fit their behaviors into environmental situations. Roles in one sense or another have always been regarded as "cognitive systems" or "subsystems," although often without explicit recognition of the idea of cognitive systems as such. Furthermore, roles have always been regarded as "behavioral" phenomena, referring to an organization of symbolically meaningful behavioral expectations organized into a configuration of action patterns that display a stability through time.

In addition to this, the concept role has been associated with the concepts status and position since Ralph Linton's 1936 *Study of Man*. Although confusion has developed over the relative meaning of the concepts *position* and *role*, the two concepts have long been used as conceptual building blocks for modeling larger units of social structure (Bates and Harvey, 1975; Linton, 1936; Hiller, 1962; Biddle and Thomas, 1966; Nadel, 1957; Merton, 1968). This means that, without too much revision in definitions, role-theory concepts may be used to furnish a language by which models of social or ecological structure may be built up using an atomistic approach.

When we refer to roles as cognitive systems, we must recognize two levels of meaning of the *concept cognitive system*, one referring to the mind of the "scientific analyst," for example, this writer, and the other referring to the minds of the actors in "society," who are regarded as being outside the mind of the scientist but known to him through the cognitive action. The "scientific cognitive system" being constructed in this book contains a construction called the "actor." The actor, according to this cognitive construct, contains within his or her mind a set of cognitive systems, themselves assuming a conventional status in the apparatus. Among these cognitive systems is a set of roles, which are themselves regarded as constructs within the cognitive apparatus of the scientist. Therefore, we are constructing a theoretical or technical cognitive system that itself contains the idea of "folk cognitive systems" as a conventional element inside itself (von Foerster, 1987).

This same scientific cognitive apparatus will also contain the idea of a position and networks of positions as conventional concepts used to organize the topological structure of roles as they are arranged in relationship to each other. In other words, the scientific cognitive system will contain a set of conventions by which to conceive of the interrelationship among roles in clusters called *positions* and networks of positions called *groups, organizations, communities,* and *societies*. All of these terms will assume a conventional status in the "logic" of the cognitive apparatus and will generate a conventionalized reality called *social* or *ecological structure*. This whole apparatus will be built up step by step from the level of the act, norm, and role by a set of cognitive decisions, thus implementing an atomistic agenda.

Also included in the apparatus will be the concept *behavior* or *action*. Behavior as action is also a conventionalized concept. It allows the cognitive apparatus to incorporate not only the cognitive systems contained within the minds of "conventionalized actors" but also the actions or behaviors of these actors that are related to the cognitive systems in their minds. The link between actual behavior and the cognitive system related to it will be attained by assuming that the actor, in behaving, is constructing a reality called *behavior* and thereby exposing the actor's cognitive apparatus to revision or reinforcement by its environment in a self-referential cycle.

To solve the dilemma introduced by defining the actor both as the generator of action, that is, as a set of cognitive systems, and the actor as the performer of behavior, an additional set of conventions must be generated within the cognitive apparatus, called *social structure*. One of these involves a distinction between the positions actors occupy, the cognitive systems that define them, and the actions performed at the structural locations represented by the positions. Such conceptual differentiation makes it desirable to distinguish at a more general level between social structure and social organization as did Radcliff-Brown (1977) and Raymond Firth (1963).

When such a distinction is made, social structure is regarded as the potential or latent structure of action stored in the form of a complex web of cognitive systems, in other words, as "culture." Social organization, on the other hand, refers to the organization of action or behavior in the sense of the actual responses of actors to an environment they construct cognitively through the use of conventionalized cognitive systems. Thus, this cognitive apparatus distinguishes on the one hand between the actor and the position occupied by the actor, and therefore between a population of actors and a population of positions. On the other hand, it distinguishes between the structure of positions and networks of positions, defined as *cognitive systems*, and the organization of positions, and networks of positions, conceptualized as behavior.

The link maintained between these seemingly incompatible views will be furnished by the assumption that in acting, the actor is creating an interpretation of his or her relationship to the environment by "speaking" in the language of behavior with a world he or she has constructed by cognitive action. This means that, in a sense, behavior itself can be regarded as a kind of cognitive system generated on the basis of the rules and language of another set of cognitive systems stored as symbolically encoded, self-referential systems of rules in the mind of the actor. The trick is to think of the behavior system called *social organization* as the language with which the cognitive systems in the mind of an actor communicate with themselves through emitting behavior on the basis of their own self-constructed reality and receive feedback from that behavior, thereby updating and revising themselves or confirming their own internal order.

1.3   Conclusions

In order to construct a fully developed cognitive system called *ecosocial structure*, there is an enormous amount of work that needs to be done to flesh out these bare strategic bones. The task is to formulate a set of precise and explicit conventions that work consistently together to form a kind of "thinking machine" that can repeatedly generate consistent models of social structure, without falling apart in disarray when an unexpected problem is encountered. The apparatus should be such that when a new problem arises out of attempts to use the system as a guide to observation and explanation, it can be easily incorporated into the apparatus without abandoning its foundation and starting all over again. In the process, it is important to remind ourselves that this enterprise is directed only at constructing a conventionialized reality that calls itself *ecosocial structure*. It does not, and cannot, deal with problems outside this domain. This is not a general theory of society or of social behavior that pretends to deal with every aspect of human life in society. Moreover, it provides only one way to deal with so-called social or ecological structure. Obviously, there are many alternative ways to construct images of these phenonenological targets.

The cognitive system presented here does not pretend to be a reflection of an empirical reality by saying this is the "real way" societies are put together. Instead, this is a cognitive apparatus through which a certain type of structural reality may be constructed, and its designer claims that it works if you will follow its rules. With it, you can "see" some things you cannot see without it, and with it, you are blinded to things that it cannot help you to see. But please remember that in any case, the reality you see, regardless of the cognitive apparatus you use, is one you are constructing yourself by cognitive action. If you would like to see what I see, use my machine, but if you prefer a different image of the world of ecosocial structure, use another one. The test of each will be whether they yield results that open doors or solve problems.

1.4   Summary

The general plan for constructing the theoretical system to be developed in this book is summarized in Table 1.1. This table shows that the concept behavior is the phenomenological domain of this theoretical system. It employs an atomistic or hierarchial approach to building concepts, using a structural strategy and the language of role theory to built conceptualizations of systems, in particular, self-referential systems. Finally, it conceptualizes the relationships among systems by employing the concept *ecological network* and its accompanying notion of an ecological field.

2

Behavior as a Phenomenon

2.1   *Introduction*

The cognitive apparatus under development in this book takes human social behavior as its phenomenological domain. In doing so, it assumes the existence of a phenomenon known as *social behavior* that takes place in the "real world" outside the mind of the scientific observer. At the same time, however, it assumes, from a neoconstructivist perspective, that this phenomenon cannot be encountered directly through the senses "as it is" but must be constructed in the mind of the observer by use of a cognitive apparatus. This means that the term *social behavior*, especially in the context of a scientific theory, inevitably refers to a conventionalized abstraction that builds a reality called *social behavior* by means of cognitive action.

The conventions that construct a mental image seek and give a particularized meaning to observations made on an empirical world and, by so doing, create social behavior as a cognitive experience or event. Social behavior literally becomes what the cognitive apparatus, through which it is constructed as a sensory experience, defines it as being. The user of the apparatus therefore encounters behavior not as a pure, natural phenomenon but as a phenomenon the mind generates by cognitive action. For this reason, observers can never make a legitimate claim that the conception they use to operate as a surrogate for behavior in their minds as they think about it, corresponds to a true reality independent of any cognitive action they have taken.

Because social behavior is the target phenomenon for structural modeling in this book, and because it must be viewed as a conventionalized concept, it is important to specify the attributes to be employed in constructing the concept and to reveal its limits because only then can the cognitive system built upon this foundation be evaluated and criticized intelligently.

2.2   *Beginning Assumptions*

The mind of every social scientist will normally contain a variety of interpretations of the concept *social behavior*, and more often than not, these interpretations will have evolved as parts of many, separate cognitive systems in many social and linguistic contexts. The mind of any thinker can be compared to a kind of cognitive *garbage can* or *trash bin* into which many ideas have been dumped after they have been formed and used for the great variety of particular cognitive purposes pursued by all human actors. The cognitive garbage filling the mind may, like any disorderly conglomeration, contain many different ideas that go under the same label. The idea called *social behavior*, when it is retrieved from the memory, is therefore apt to carry with it many inconsistent connotations and many irrelevancies as far as the cognitive task faced by the user at a particular time is concerned (Bateson, 1972b).

We, however, wish to use the term *social behavior* as part of a cognitive system meant to create rather precise images of human social systems and ecological fields. It will be employed in connection with other concepts that also must be given very precise and restricted interpretations. For example, social behavior as a concept will be used along with ideas such as structure, systems, ecological network, position, role, group, organization, community, society, and so forth. This means that the concept *social behavior*, when it emerges from the *garbage cans* of our *natural minds*, must be *purified* or *pared down* to fit the particular cognitive apparatus being developed. It must be cognitively cleaned up and reshaped to fit the purpose at hand. At the same time, we must recognize that we begin with a disorderly set of preconceptions pulled from the storage bins of our undisciplined minds that contain all of the rich linguistic overtones of the words *social behavior*.

The original act of cognition that brings the idea of social behavior into our consciousness will inevitably affect later cognitive actions taken in constructing a theoretically purified and disciplined cognitive apparatus. However, we inevitably begin the task of formulating a precise concept called *social behavior* with a rather confusing conventionalized reality, already constructed on the basis of our cultural biases and our educational and experiential backgrounds. We must then, by critical cognitive action, attempt to assert control over the tools we will use in the process of theoretical construction. For this reason, cognitive construction is always more properly thought of as cognitive reconstruction, because we never begin the task with a clean slate.

Furthermore, because we wish to communicate, this reconstruction is limited by the necessity to use a common language and a common set of metaphors that cannot be entirely reshaped without putting us in danger of losing the capacity to interact with colleagues. The hope to communicate influences and shapes even our strongest efforts to think systematically in a completely disciplined and purposeful or pragmatic manner, and limits our capacity to exert total cognitive control over any enterprise of cognitive reconstruction.

In the case of this book, the term *social behavior* will be defined using the English language and the theoretical traditions of sociology, both of which were originally formed for other purposes. This will be the beginning point from which we will start to define the meaning of the concept *social behavior*, realizing as we do, that the words we use carry semantic "impurities" as they emerge from the garbage cans of our minds. They also carry a burden of traditional cultural meaning and considerable reference to sometimes unrecognized ideological biases.

In addition, the very words used in writing this book, no matter how carefully defined, will evoke unintended connotations and cognitive associations in the minds of readers. All that can be done to solve this problem is for both reader and writer to be aware of these cognitive traps and attempt to avoid them by exercising as much caution as possible in threading their ways through their respective mental mine fields.

2.2.1   Behavior as Opposed to Organism and Social System

Behavior, as a term in the cognitive apparatus being constructed here, will be used to refer to activities carried on by an organism or by a corporate social body (such as a small group or a complex organization) in relation to their environments or in relation to themselves as actors. In the case of organisms, it excludes reference to the normal life processes taking place within the organism as part of physiological functioning. Such phenomena as breathing, the operation of the heart and circulatory system, and other vital biological organs will be regarded as nonbehavioral, constituting the substrata upon which behavior as a process rests. In the case of corporate social bodies (e.g., social groups or organizations), it is necessary to suspend judgment concerning the boundaries of the concept at this point.

Behavior will be thought of as the means by which organisms and social bodies as bounded systems adapt to their environments by attempting to control their interaction with that environment through processes involving cognitive action. By using this definitional condition, we mean to rule out of consideration actions of the organism that are mere reflexes or that involve other operations of the nervous system that do not involve cognitive processes.

Behavior from this point of view is always directed toward or in response to events or conditions outside the biological or social system, or toward the system as an object in and of itself. This latter point means that in the case of organisms, such activities as personal grooming, eating, dressing and undressing, and so forth may be thought of as behavior involving the operation of the mind as the actor performs actions toward itself.

When we say that behavior is the means by which an organism or a social system adapts to its environment, we mean to include the ideas that it is the means by which these systems (1) obtain resources from their environments; (2) utilize resources in internal behavioral processes to produce outputs; (3) return outputs, including waste products, to the environment; (4) reshape or reconstruct their environment by making alterations in it; and (5) defend themselves against threats from their environment. Given these assumptions, it is apparent that the concept *behavior* is essential to the construction of a cognitive system that can deal with the relationships between systems and their environments or between and among systems in the context of a common ecological field. Without the concept *behavior*, we would lack the capacity to conceptualize the relationship between human systems and their environments. This will be particularly true if we assume systems to be bounded entities whose internal operation is autonomous and self-referential, as will be the case in this book.

In order to clarify the meaning of the concept *behavior*, it is necessary to make a clear distinction between it and the system or systems that generate it. In particular, behavior must be distinguished from the concepts *organism* and *mind*, which, in turn, must be differentiated from each other. The organism and mind of the actor are defined here as the generators and executors of action. They constitute the actor as a system with the capacity to perform behavior in the same sense that an already programmed computer (which is turned on) is in a state of readiness to respond to imputs by performing computer functions.

In these statements, the term *mind* is not meant to refer to the brain and nervous system of an organic actor, but to the socially acquired content of the brain, which is organized as a complex cognitive apparatus containing its own symbolic codes and its own rules for operation (Bateson, 1972b). It is thought of as the set of mechanisms that inhabit the brain as the "vocabulary, semantics, and grammar" of cognitive action and furnish the organism with files of information constructed through previous cognitive actions.

Although the mind operates on the basis of organic processes that are a function of the brain and nervous system, it is assumed that the mind itself is built up as a cognitive apparatus or set of apparatuses out of interaction between the organism and its environment. On the basis of this assumption, it follows that the contents of the mind and its organization depend upon experience. Although the mind depends upon the organic structure of the organism to develop and operate, its contents and organization may be thought of independently of the organic system it inhabits. This is like saying that to operate, a computer program depends upon the "circuitry" of the computer and is limited by this "circuitry," but at the same time, many different programs are possible within the same computer. Furthermore, using the same analogy, the output (or behavior) of the computer depends upon the program, as do the events occurring within the computer as it operates upon inputs to produce its outputs. Behavior is like the *operation and output processes of the human computer* and must be distinguished from the computer itself and its capacity to operate.

The mind here will be thought of as being constructed out of many separate but cross-referenced cognitive systems or subsystems that themselves have evolved out of the history of organism–environment relations (Pelanda, 1989). It will be viewed as a kind of mental ecological field in which separate, bounded cognitive systems operate internally and interact with each other to form a kind of "ecology of the mind" (Bateson, 1972b). The point at this juncture is to think of behavior as the output of an organism that is generated by the functioning of the cognitive systems that comprise the architecture of the organism's mind.

Because it is assumed that behavior is a process involving cognitive action, and because cognitive action is always a symbolic process, behavior itself must be viewed as a symbolic process. Indeed, it must, in this context, be thought of as a kind of *language by which the mind of an organism "communicates" with itself about the organism's relationship to its environment.*

2.2.2   Behavior as a Language

Each action taken by an actor may be thought of as a kind of symbol, or figuratively, as a "word" in a behavioral sentence or larger linguistic output. The perpetrator of an act gives meaning within a cognitive system to that act in relation to internal states of the organism as these internal states relate to a cognitively constructed image of the environment. Behavior thus can be thought of as a kind of "spoken language" that is based on a cognitively stored latent language that exists in the form of a behavioral vocabulary and grammar in the mind of the actor. From this perspective, behavior consists of meaningful actions of the organism, which derive their meaning from the cognitive systems stored in the mind of the actor.

It therefore follows that *meaningless action* is ruled out of consideration, because it is defined as *nonbehavior*. Accordingly, the cognitive system under construction is intended to deal only with human actions that constitute a kind of "communication" between a human actor or a social system and an environment constructed by it through a cognitive process that is reflexive and symbolic in nature (Blumer, 1969; Blumer and Mead, 1980; Goffman, 1974, 1983; Fine, 1993).

When we say that behavior is the language by which the human organism or a social system communicates with *itself* concerning its relationship to its environment, we mean to point to the idea that as the organism acts, attributing meaning to the act it performs, and then interprets the response of the environment to its action, also on the basis of cognitive action, it receives "feedback" messages that convey information (also created by cognitive processes) back into the cognitive apparatus of the actor. The organism or social system thus tests or evaluates its capacity to exercise cognitive control over its relationship to its self-defined environment through a process that outputs meaning in the form of behavior and inputs meaning in the form of self-interpreted feedback. The organism's or social system's interpretation of the effects of its own behavior on its self-defined environment acts as a kind of *self-generated or reflexive communication process* that, in the long run, builds up and revises the "language" itself. This autopoietic process, in other words, constantly builds up and revises the actor's cognitive apparatus in a continuous cycle of reflexive or recursive interactions (Maturana and Varela, 1980; Pelanda, 1989).

The foregoing discussion of behavior as a process that involves cognition does not imply rationality as a defining mental attribute of human action. Behavior may be accompanied by either rational or irrational cognitive processes. Neither does it imply a deliberate, fully conscious, self-controlled process under the guidance of an independent human will. Instead, a natural, automatic, self-regulating reflexive process that joins cognitive action and overt behavior to each other as an ongoing operation of the organism in relation to its environment is envisioned. Behavior is seen as an expression of the organism's need to draw vital resources from the environment and to adapt to environmental conditions and events in order to survive and function. The organism survives and operates as an organism through the use of its behavior as a set of adaptive mechanisms. Cognitive action in relation to overt behavior is a natural expression of the requirement that the organism be able to *predict* its environment and the impact of its behavior upon itself in order, in the long run, to survive and operate as an organism. The necessity to predict the consequences of its own behavior in turn requires the existence of mechanisms that allow prediction, at least within limits that permit survival. In the case of human beings, it is posited that cognitive systems comprised of learned patterns of behavior, stored as a symbolically coded repertoire of action, or as a kind of *behavioral language*, perform this function.

It is assumed that the behavior of the human organism is an expression of the functioning of a cognitive apparatus that has evolved within the organism according to natural processes that tie the brain and nervous system to a complex set of sensory mechanisms in such a way as to make learning and, therefore, the development of cognitive systems and of the so-called *mind* (as opposed to the brain) inevitable. Along the same line, learning is regarded as a process that is oriented by the very nature of the organism toward rendering the relationship between the organism and its environment predictable within survival limits by assigning meaning to objects and events by use of a symbolic code, thus maintaining the viability of the organism (or social system) by structuring its behavior.

This statement should not be interpreted to mean that survival is inevitable or that adaptation will constantly improve with time, or that it will result in ideal or perfect adaptive patterns. It does mean, however, that if behavior and, therefore, the system of meaning that is attached to it, fails to fit within the limits of viability, it will result in the eventual negative selection of the organism and thereby of the cognitive apparatus associated with that organism.

2.2.3   Behavior as a Multidimensional Phenomenon

The word *behavior*, as it is used here, is meant to include several categories of activity, some of which may not be thought of as being covered by this term in ordinary language. First, in the case of individual organisms, it refers to observable activities that involve movements in the various parts of the body (walking, grasping, pushing, pulling, striking, chewing, biting, working, playing, etc.). Second, it includes vocalization and, along with it, speaking, singing, shouting, crying, and so on. Third, and perhaps less obviously, it includes the actual process of perceiving when this process is thought of not merely as the receiving of neurological stimulation but as the process of encoding sensory stimulation as information by joining it to a cognitive system that assigns it meaning. The decision to include perception as behavior is necessary, because it is assumed that behavior is a process that involves the operation of a cognitive apparatus, and because perception involves the attribution of meaning that is derived from cognitive action, it must also be regarded as a form of behavior. In addition, perception is a process that flows through time as the organism encounters its environment and adapts its behavior to it.

Finally, the thought or cognition processes that transpire as the mind operates to control the relationship of the organism to its environment are also classified as behavior. This is necessary because thought itself is a process that flows through time, and as it does, the cognitive action occurring in the mind changes in content and form as the organism adapts to a perceived environment by emitting overt behavioral responses.

Thus, behavior as a total process contains cognitive or mental action, perceptual action, and bodily activity as interrelated subprocesses. It is possible that even a more diffuse and more difficult to define subprocess called *emotional behavior* should also be considered as part of this conceptualization. This will be true if we can think of the emotions experienced by the organism as occurring in a temporal stream and as being mediated by the cognitive apparatus of the organism that gives meaning to them. For example, insofar as an emotional state such as fear can be seen as being an episodic occurrence that is a function of a cognitive apparatus that defines the objects of fright and the behavioral expression of fear, as it mediates between the perceived environment and the organism, the experience of actually feeling emotions such as fear should be regarded as a form of behavior.

The attempt here is to separate the organism as a kind of "machine" with a prepared organization containing the capacity to act from the action the organism actually performs. It is a distinction like that between a computer already programmed and capable of receiving data and processing it, and a computer in the process of actually taking in data, or in the act of processing it on the basis of a program and producing an output that can be examined by an observer. Behavior is comparable to the process of receiving and storing input, processing input according to a program, and outputting the results. All are "computer behavior" as opposed to the computer as a programmed machine capable of this behavior. The inclusion of thought and perception, as well as overt muscular activity, as aspects of behavior follows this same sort of distinction.

This means that behavior as a concept refers not only to the overt, observable actions of human actors, but also to the active operation of their cognitive apparatus as distinguished from that apparatus viewed as an entity in a state of readiness to perform. Having made this assumption, it is important to be clear in pointing out that it is *not assumed* that cognitive action is being thought of as the master and behavior the slave. To do so would impose a "rationalistic" orientation, because such an assumption would lead to the conclusion that thought or cognition always precedes and controls action, as the orders of a master precede the actions of the slave. Thought, as a behavioral process, is regarded here as one that may as easily be provoked by overt action as to think of overt action as being provoked by thought. Without such an assumption, perception as a process could not operate to allow an organism to adapt to an environment outside itself. The process of perception must be conceived of in such a way that although ending in a cognitive process of meaning attribution, it begins with the events and objects outside the organism that elicit cognition through evoking neural stimulation. Thus, cognitive behavior may be "evoked" by environmental conditions or events, and thus the slave acts first and the master perceives and thinks later, as well as the reverse.

It is also necessary to recognize that an action taken by an organism that evokes a response in the environment, and in which the environmental response is then perceived as "feedback" by the organism, can stimulate further cognitive action. This sequence must also be classified as a behavioral episode. Thus, overt action may be seen as evoking or, in a sense, controlling the cognition that occurs further down the action stream of the actor as well as the reverse sequence. From this, it seems apparent that behavior must be regarded as a continuous recursive process in which perception, cognition, emotion, and overt action occur both together and in various sequential orders in a more or less seamless flow of events.

2.3   Behavior, Time, and Space

Behavior as an idea has a distinctly temporal underpinning in almost all uses of the term. The actions or behavior of an organism, or the behavior of a social system, *flow through time* in the sense that behavior unfolds as a series of events, one following another in a progression (Bates and Harvey, 1975; Barker, 1963). At any given instant, we can conceive of a living organism or an active social system as being in the process of performing some particular action or set of actions. As time passes, an actor performs other actions as it perceives itself facing new contingencies. If the actor (an organism or social system) is thought of "out of time," it becomes a kind of "inoperative machine," perhaps capable of action but not acting. Action is the "use of time" in the sense of operation, operation itself being a "time-ladened" concept.

Unlike the organism or social system, which may persist more or less unchanged as a physical form through relatively long intervals, the essence of behavior is that its "content" or "form" changes as time moves on. An actor performs an action, and once the action is performed, it is replaced by another, and another as time progresses. Behavior is therefore not only a "time-laden concept," but also it refers to a phenomenon that is "time bound" in the sense that once a behavior, that is, a specific act, is performed, it disappears and can no longer be observed. Behavior is therefore "perishable" in the sense that once it has transpired, it no longer forms part of the environment of the observer (i.e., occupies space) or, for that matter, a part of the behavior in the process of being performed by the actor. From this, it can be assumed that behavior in the case of an individual actor can be represented graphically as a linear progression in which the "content" of behavior changes as time progresses. The concept of an *action stream*, as used by Barker, can be employed to represent this idea. The basic idea can be presented as follows (Barker, 1963).

If symbols such as the letters *a b c . . . z* are used to represent particular actions defined by their content, then an action stream representing the behavior of an individual actor would look graphically like the following:

Time I (*a b x z c y m n . . . r s t x*) Time *n*

This conception implies that behavior consists of a stream of discrete acts that take place in a temporal sequence, so that acts are like so many beads strung together to form a string in which each individual bead is identifiable as having boundaries. Another analogy is to think of the behavior of an actor in linguistic terms. Acts are like words in a long linguistic utterance. Each act, like each word in a sentence, is identifiable as a unit by its capacity to convey or carry meaning. Similarly acts are strung together in a sequence according to rules of syntax and grammar, to convey larger meanings. Once one word in a sentence is spoken, it is followed by another and another. At any given instant, only one word is in the process of being actually uttered. Nevertheless, once uttered, their occurrence is fed back into the "machine" that uttered them, where they are filed in the memory as others emerge as occurring events.

There are "methodological" problems associated with applying the assumption that behavior consists of strings of discrete acts (Barker, 1963). However, at the moment, we are dealing with theoretical problems and cannot deal with these issues in detail. Suffice it now to say that human actions as discrete units, like words in a language, are distinguished from each other by the meanings attributed to them by the actor performing them. This means that the cognitive apparatus built up in the mind of the actor that operates to attribute meaning must be conceptualized in such a way as to make it possible to distinguish acts from each other in terms of the criterion of meaning.

Before leaving this part of the discussion, it is important to point out that cognition, perception, emotion, and overt action all can be represented as action streams and that it is necessary in the long run to think through how this conception will be treated in relating these forms of behavior to each other. It is apparent that several alternative sets of assumptions concerning the relationships between cognition, perception, emotion, and overt action are possible and that each conception will construct its own distinct image of behavior as a process. Although a detailed discussion is impossible here, this problem can be illustrated as follows. One assumption is that there are four simultaneously occurring streams of behavior that, in some way, interact and affect each other, each being represented by a continuous flow of action as shown in Table 2.1.

An alternative assumption is that there are four separate streams but that each stream is discontinuous because the various forms of action occur in spurts, with gaps occurring between acts while the other forms of action are taking place. Thus, an actor does not "think continuously," but while

TABLE 2.1
Types of Action Streams

Type of act	Time 1 ... Time N
Perceptual stream	$P1\ P2\ P3\ P4 \ldots Pn$
Cognitive stream	$C1\ C2\ C3\ C4 \ldots Cn$
Emotional stream	$E1\ E2\ E3\ E4 \ldots En$
Overt action stream	$A1\ A2\ A3\ A4 \ldots An$

TABLE 2.2
Action Streams

Type of act	Time							
	1	2	3	4	5	6	7	8
Perceptual stream	*	P1	*	P2	*	*	*	Pn
Cognitive stream	*	*	C1	C2	*	*	Cn	*
Emotional stream	E1	*	*	*	*	*	E2	En
Overt action stream	*	*	*	A1	*	*	*	An

TABLE 2.3
Single Stream of Action

Time	T1	T2	T3	T4	T5	T6	T7 . . . TN
Action	P1	C1	E1	C2	A1	A2	P2 . . . quit

overt action is occurring, the thought process stops, waiting for feedback from perception, as seen in Table 2.2.

A third conceptualization might represent the process as a single action stream with permutations of cognitive, perceptual, action, and emotional components occurring in sequences such as in Table 2.3.

This is not the place to deal with this issue in detail. These examples are offered only to illustrate the fact that this book will regard behavior as a concept representing a multidimensional process. It further illustrates the assertion that however defined, behavior as a term refers to a set of conventions that operate in the mind to define symbolic surrogates for the phenomenon. These conceptual surrogates guide and limit both perception of the phenomenological world outside the observer's mind and the cognitive action that takes place within the mind of a theorist, as the concept *behavior* is employed as a cognitive tool.

2.4   *Social Behavior*

So far, the discussion has centered on the term *behavior* itself and has more or less ignored the adjective *social* attached to it at the beginning of the chapter. There, we stated that the target phenomenon of structural modeling in this book will be *social* behavior. What, then, does the word *social* mean in this context?

As a beginning point (again drawing a term from the "garbage cans" of our natural minds) the term *social behavior* will be used to refer to any behavior that is regulated in part or in whole by aspects of a cognitive apparatus built up in the mind of the actor in a cultural context as a consequence of interaction with other human actors. In other words, social behavior is behavior that is generated by social rules, *rules* being broadly defined to include any symbolically encoded aspect of a cognitive system that defines an act as being expected, appropriate, or useful in relation to a set of perceived circumstances.

Under this conceptualization, so-called cognitively stored rules can be related to all four forms of behavior discussed earlier, and certainly can apply to the rules that establish linguistic and other codes used by the organism to process information. It would include socially mandated behavior performed by an actor in actual interaction with other people, but it could also include action performed in solitude, when no other actor is involved because many solitary actions are "social in nature." For example, as I write these lines, alone in my office, I am engaged in social behavior because what I write is in accordance with a set of shared linguistic rules and because the product I am producing is intended for communication with my colleagues. It is also social because it will be acted upon as a manuscript by other actors, who will treat it as a kind of "raw material" to be processed and eventually delivered to still others.

As a matter of fact, it is difficult to conceive of "nonsocial" behavior in the case of an actor who has been "socialized" through contact with other actors. However, this definition leaves open the possibility that some behavior may be thought of as nonsocial and still qualify as action if it involves some form of individualistic. nonsocially derived cognitive control.

Social behavior at the level of the individual, according to this theoretical scheme, can be either solitary or interactive, but it must always be behavior that is related to some aspect of a cognitive apparatus that is derived from social contact. This does not mean, however, that behavior is only social when it conforms to a common social standard. It is not implied that only "norm-conforming" behavior is social.

There are several reasons not to make this assumption. First, individual actors, as we have said, never encounter their environment directly but only through a cognitive apparatus that constructs an environment on the basis of cognitive action. This means that no actor can be in direct contact with the behavioral rules of another, but like all environmental phenomena, the norms of others must be constructed as cultural or normative "reality" by cognitive action. Such a perspective leads to the inevitable conclusion that each actor's construction of the "rules for behavior" depends upon the unique cognitive apparatus of that individual, and this means that there can never be any assurance that the rules for behavior of any two people are, in fact, identical. An actor may learn a completely different lesson from interaction with another person than that which was intended. The same actor may then act on the basis of this lesson, appearing to others to be acting in an idiosyncratic or deviant fashion, even antisocially. Nevertheless, the claim may be defended that the rule being followed was derived from social contact and that the behavior is norm conforming.

It is apparent therefore that the socially derived cognitive content, implicated in the behavior of an actor, may be nonconformist or highly individualistic and still be social. Even antisocial behavior in the terms used by researchers on *deviant behavior* may be social. According to the perspective presented here, such behavior may involve the operation of a cognitive apparatus derived from interaction between an actor and a social environment. After being formed, this apparatus functions to adapt the actor to an environment that itself is defined by the actor's own cognitive action. Even deviant or antisocial behavior may be regarded as behavior that was intended to be adaptive because it was performed by an actor in order to adapt to self-defined social situations.

2.5   Higher Levels of Social Behavior

This is a book on ecosocial structure and not one on individual behavior. It must, however, rest on assumptions about the individual and individual behavior. This is why the discussion so far has been focused primarily on consideration of behavior at the level of the individual actor. Now it is time to step up the discussion to include more complex considerations.

In the long run, the objective of this book is to treat whole societies, even global ecological fields, as behavioral phenomena. This, of course, implies that small groups, complex organizations, and communities will also be treated as instances of social behavior. For this reason, it is necessary to discuss social behavior at higher levels of scale than the individual actor. This requires the introduction of new defining qualities to the idea of social behavior, so that we know the whole phenomenological arena within which this cognitive system for modeling the structure of social systems and ecological fields is being developed. This discussion should sensitize us to the qualities of the phenomena that are important to the development of other parts of the overall cognitive apparatus.

2.5.1   Group-Level Behavior

Although it is assumed that all behavior is performed by individual actors, it is necessary to recognize that actors often interact and behave together or jointly in interdependent streams of action. At the lowest level of scale, above the individual level, there is the level of the dyadic social relationship. Here, we can conceptualize two separate actors whose individual actions are performed in relation to each other. As each acts toward and reacts to the actions of the other, the other also acts and responds. Taken together, the behavior of the two actors can be considered to be a form of "social behavior."

Although it is true that each actor "contains" a cognitive apparatus separate from the other and each acts according to internally occurring cognitive processes, these processes cannot be thought of as being entirely independent of each other. This is true because, as we have said, each cognitive system is built up and constantly under revision as the actor containing it uses it to guide behavior toward an environment he or she constructs through cognitive action. Because, in a social relationship, another actor, alter, is in the environment of ego, ego and alter can be thought of as the source of sense stimulation and of feedback to each other. This is true even though ego and alter construct their own images of each other. As ego interacts with alter, ego's cognitive apparatus is exposed to the possibility of revision by the actions of alter. Even though ego constructs a cognitive image of alter's behavior, that behavior may or may not be predicted by ego's cognitive apparatus. When it is not, ego's perception of it will operate as negative feedback for ego's cognitive system. When it conforms to self-generated expectations, perception of it will operate as positive feedback. On these grounds, there is a basis for asserting that the cognitive systems of ego and alter are interdependent, and so long as ego and alter continue to interact, will tend to (but not inevitably) develop in a direction that will produce a predictable behavioral dialogue that can be seen by an observer, assuming that the observer is equipped with a cognitive apparatus that allows him or her to model that behavior.

All of this means that the operation of the cognitive systems of ego and alter are interdependent, not only for the reason mentioned above but also for others. For example, the behavior of alter may act as a meaningful cue that "communicates" with alter and activates aspects of alter's cognitive apparatus that otherwise would have remained inactive or latent. It also means that the process usually defined as *thought* or *cognition* in the "mind" of ego is not completely under ego's control because actions by alter may bring thoughts to ego's mind. An overt behavior on the part of ego can produce a cognitive response in alter, sometimes even the response desired and predicted by alter. It is even sensible to say that, at one level, the behavior of ego and alter make up a single behavioral conglomerate that makes no sense to either actor or to any observer unless considered as a whole. In social relationships, the behavior of ego has meaning within the mind of ego only in terms of its relationship to the behavior of alter. An episode of interaction between ego and alter therefore can be considered a more complex level of social behavior (than individual behavior) that is associated with a complex web of cognitive systems that are stored in the minds of distinct actors.

It can even be argued that a process such as thinking, which is usually considered to be a process that goes on only at the individual level, because it requires the brain as an organic mechanism, can, under some conditions, be thought of as a "group-level" process. Because ego and alter stimulate and affect each other's cognitive action and because out of this costimulation, thoughts arise and decisions are made that would not occur otherwise, is it not reasonable to entertain the notion that at least a form of social cognition takes place at the group level? Such an idea only requires that we be willing to assume that each actor contributes a part to a larger cognitive process that itself creates interdependent cognitive events not possible under conditions of individual isolation.

It is also necessary to recognize that the culturally based cognitive systems that human actors use to store the behavior patterns they use to manage their actions in relation to the environment, and therefore to other actors, are not totally independent of each other. In the relationship between ego and alter, for example, between a husband and a wife, or a teacher and a student, the cognitive apparatus that defines and gives meaning to the role that ego plays contains symbolically encoded rules for behavior that depend upon the existence of complementary rules in a cognitive system stored in alter's mind. The behavior of ego is given meaning to both ego and alter by and in relation to an environment in which alter is included as an interacting party, and in which ego is able to predict and understand alter's behavior on the basis of a cognitive program.

In a sense, therefore, the cognitive system that defines ego's action as a husband, and alter's action as a wife, is a single cognitive system, comprised of interrelated elements even though the total system, to produce behavior, must be contained within more than one mind. On this basis, we can say that ego's and the alter's interactive behavior comprises a larger behavioral episode with its own unity and its own boundaries. We can also say that there is a larger cognitive object than those that exist at the individual level that constitutes a more complex cognitive apparatus at the group (or relationship) level and stores the design for this interaction as a program for joint action. This is like saying that while the "minds" of ego and alter are separate, as are the "brains" that contain them, the cognitive materials they contain constitute fragments of a single, larger cognitive system that requires more than a single mind to allow it to function or operate.

This idea can be illustrated by an analogy using two computers that have been programmed to interact by responding to each other's output. The program contained in computer A is written so that it performs a set of operations when it receives input from computer B, which itself has been programmed to emit output understandable to computer A as input and vice versa. The programs in the two computers must be written as a "total" program that defines the terms of interaction and coordinates the separate operations of the two machines. The two machines operate as if they were performing one operation organized into two interacting parts, whereas the actual machines are separate units. In other words, they act as if they were performing a single, complex task that can only be performed when the two operate in interaction. The point is that not only must we think of the operation of the two as a single operating "system" involving active interaction, but to do so we must also recognize that the program upon which the joint operation is based, itself, forms a unity.

On this basis, we will broaden the concept of social behavior beyond the individual level to the level of the dyadic social relationship, the group, and the multigroup system. In other words, when we say that behavior is the phenomenological domain of the theoretical system under development here, we mean to cover behavioral systems and behavioral networks in which the actions of many individuals are embedded as fragments of a larger, more complex behavioral whole. To use another metaphor, we intend to include the whole performance of a play as behavior, not just the performance of isolated actors. Similarly the play, for example, *Hamlet*, can be viewed not only as a live performance witnessed by an audience as observable dramatic action, but may also be viewed as a script that organizes and controls the action, that is, as a cognitive apparatus. The play in both senses is a bounded, unitary whole, comprised of separate parts or elements such as roles or verbal utterances, and bodily actions that take on their meaning from the context of the total play in which they are embedded.

2.5.2   Group- and Multigroup-Level Behavior

Higher orders of behavioral complexity introduce new attributes to the problem of constructing an image of behavior as a phenomenon. These characteristics must be taken into account in formulating a cognitive system meant to allow us to construct mental representations of the structure of human behavior systems, and of networks comprised of such systems. These attributes must serve as keys to organizing other parts of a complex cognitive apparatus, for example, for defining the concept "social structure" itself. When used as defining characteristics, they will result in the construction of a particular way of perceiving social reality. It is important to realize that, conceivably, we could focus on alternative attributes, and that we are therefore selecting a set of guidelines that will, at the same time, allow us to perceive a particular kind of social reality and also bias us against perceiving other possible realities through use of this apparatus. It cannot be claimed that this way of looking at things truly and accurately represents the way the social world actually is, even if, when we look at it this way, we seem to confirm our preconceptions. This same experience of self-confirming validity would be encountered if we were to build an entirely different perspective. With this in mind, it is time to move on to revealing other aspects of social behavior that will function as key elements in constructing an image of ecosocial structure in this book.

2.6   Time, Individual and Group Behavior

Behavior is a process, and this means that time is a key element in conceptualizing it. As noted, the behavior of the individual may be represented as a temporal progression or an action stream (Barker, 1963). This conception implies that for the individual organism, behavior is a continuous process that begins at birth and ends with death. This is true, however, only if we are willing to think of such things as sleeping or dreaming, as well as resting in a more or less motionless state as behavior. If we classify cognitive action or thought, perception, and possibly emotion, as well as overt action as behavior, it seems apparent that we must also assume that the behavior of the individual constitutes an uninterrupted stream because it is hard to imagine a time during which one or more of these activities are not in progress. There is, of course, the possibility that individuals in a comatose state would be excluded. Furthermore, as shall be seen in later chapters, there are theoretical advantages to the assumption that behavior is continuous for the individual.

Such a decision is an arbitrary one, made for purposes of theoretical construction, and it is not a matter of factual accuracy when we say the behavior of a particular individual is continuous. Instead, it is a matter of cognitive convenience, meant to facilitate the construction of a theoretical system. Making this assumption means that we will think of the living human being not only as being continuously functioning as an organism in the physiological sense, but also as continuously in the process of engaging in some form of behavior. This is like thinking of a computer as being continuously "turned on" and operating and never actually being inactive merely as a piece of machinery with stored programs and data stored in its memory.

According to this conception, there are no gaps in the stream of behavior for the individual. What differs from one point in the stream and another is the content and form of the acts that are being performed. The content of behavior changes as time progresses but behavior as a total process ceases only at death.

Because, however, content changes, and because we must be able to represent this content symbolically in a theoretical system, we are compelled to introduce the term *act* and to think of particular acts as being bounded and discontinuous. Even though we refer to a single particular action as occurring at a particular time, the same content may be observed with respect to many separate acts occurring at different points in an action stream. For example, let us suppose that we are willing to call "tooth brushing" a type of act. Every morning, ego performs the behavior of tooth brushing. Each occurrence is a separate act but the acts have a similar behavioral content. Each episode of tooth brushing is bounded as a behavioral performance and is therefore discontinuous. Yet the behavioral content occurs over and over again and, when cognitively constructed by an observer, it may be recognized as being repetitive. This is like the word *behavior* as it has occurred in this book. It has occurred many times, and when it passes into the reader's consciousness, it evokes a meaning, but it occurs as a discrete symbolic unit at a particular location in a long linguistic stream. The point is that while the stream flows on and is itself continuous, the units in the stream are discrete, but many discrete units may display the same form and content.

Groups as examples of behavior at a higher level of complexity are not like this. Social relationships, and the groups based on them, as behavioral phenomena are, like individual acts, episodic. The behavior that constitutes a group as a performance is discontinuous. Group behavior is like the performances of a long-running play acted out each night on a stage. The actors assemble at curtain time and perform their roles in interaction before an audience and then disperse. Each performance of a given play is a discrete behavioral episode bounded from other performances by entirely different behaviors performed by the actors in other settings.

This means that group behavior must be represented in time as a discontinuous sequence of episodes, each episode being bounded and separate from the next. Unlike the analogy to a theatrical performance, however, all of the forms of behavior that are associated with a group do not normally take place in one discrete episode. Ordinary groups such as families or work groups are more to be compared to a television soap opera having multiple unfolding episodes. In other words, the expression of most human groups as behavioral entities in all of their structural complexity does not occur as behavior within the boundaries of a single, temporally bounded episode. Only part of the behavior patterns that go into the makeup of the behavioral repertoire of a group occurs in a single bounded interval of time.

To represent this idea, we will later introduce the ideas of activity and latency. The individual, specific groups that are parts of the behavior that comprises a society as an operating entity pass through active and latent phases. In the latent phase, groups as "behavior systems" will be thought of as being stored in the form of a complex, socially organized cognitive apparatus that provides the "script," so to speak, of the "play" which, when performed, becomes the *active* group as a performance (Blumer, 1969; Blumer and Mead, 1980; Goffman, 1974, 1983; Fine, 1993). This is not meant to imply that the "script" of group behavior contains a precise set of instructions to the members but, instead, that there is a kind of symbolically encoded storage mechanism that permits the performance of a series of behavioral episodes among actors that have a larger meaning than the separate behaviors of individual members.

Groups turn on and off, and appear as behavioral episodes separated by time periods when the group is inactive. This view is necessary because, in most societies, individual actors may belong to many separate groups. If the behavior of individuals is continuous and at the same time the individual belongs to many different groups, the behavior constituting a particular group must be discontinuous. The only way that group behavior could be continuous would be if every actor contributing behavior to a group as an interactive social system belonged to one and only one group and at the same time we assumed that the behavior of all actors is continuous.

It is obvious that if we are to think of particular groups as being part of larger networks or systems, such as organizations, communities, and societies through relatively long intervals, it is necessary to posit a means of conceptualizing groups that does not require them to be comprised of active or transpiring behavior to be thought of as an existing element of social structure. If a particular group exists as a part of a larger behavior system only when it is active, then we are faced with the conclusion that such a group ceases to exist when an episode of that group's behavior dissolves into episodes of other sorts. Each episode would therefore represent a different group springing into being spontaneously and then dissolving. Using such a view, we would have trouble thinking of the sociology department at the University of Georgia, where I work, as the same group on Tuesday that operated on Monday, or more to the point, it would be illogical to think of the University of Georgia as having a department called sociology as part of its structure continuously since that department was founded in the 1920s.

It is essential to the conceptualization of society as a total object of structural modeling to be able to think of the various parts of the whole as persisting together through time as elements that operate in relationship to each other even though they may pass through active and latent phases. Even when the U. S. Congress is not in session, we must be able to think of it as being part of American social structure. Even when the New York Stock Exchange is closed on Sunday, we must still be able to think of it as a part of the economic structure of American society. Indeed, all units of social structure turn on and off in such a manner, passing through phases when they are active as actually transpiring behavioral action, and phases when they are inactive, latent, or dormant. In this state, they exist as a commitment to future action, in the form of complex sets of behavior expectations stored as cognitive systems comprised of socially constructed "rules for behavior." In order to think of the component units of social structure as persisting through time, we will be compelled to posit the existence of a mechanism that maintains groups and multigroup systems as elements of social organization even during periods of inactivity. This will be done by using the idea of cognitive systems in connection with other concepts such as culture in later chapters.

At this point, it is only necessary to make explicit that we assume that social relationships and the networks of social relationships constituting groups persist continuously through time even though they express themselves as transpiring behavior only on an episodic basis. Thus, although group behavior is discontinuous and episodic, the group as a part of the organization of society is continuous within the period between its formation and dissolution. This means that the conceptual apparatus being developed must provide the symbolic means by which a group can be represented as an identity during both periods of activity and latency.

2.7   Groups and Group Membership

If behavior is taken as the phenomenological domain for modeling ecosocial structure, such social units as groups and organizations are thought of as being comprised of behavior and *not* people. A group is conceptualized as an "action system" and not as a collection of actors viewed as biological organisms or as "personalities." Such a view allows us to think of a group or multigroup system as persisting as a part of social structure even as its members change.

This is a very important advantage of using behavior as the phenomenological basis for defining ecosocial structure because it permits us to think of the parts of social structure as persisting through time and operating continuously as parts of social structure even though the people who perform the behavior, or who store and use the cognitive apparatus upon which it is based, come and go. It would be logically impossible to think of a group such as the sociology department at the University of Georgia as existing as a part of the structure of the university year after year, decade after decade, unless we were to define it as an object consisting of behavior or behavior patterns and not of the particular actors who perform the behavior. Today, there is not a single person on the faculty of that department who was a member in 1950, but the department as a working group, performing behavior within the organization called the University of Georgia, has operated continuously as a "behavior system" since the 1920s. Professors, students, and office workers come and go. They change positions within the structure of the group. The group also changes its internal organization. It expands in size and contracts. It elaborates or simplifies its activities. Yet the group as a behavior system goes on.

If we are to think of groups and of networks of groups such as organizations, and for that matter, of human communities and societies, as persisting through time, especially through long periods of time, it is essential that we use a conceptualization that allows for changes to take place in group membership. Obviously, almost all conceptualizations of the term *society*, although rarely explicitly, assume that societies may persist for many generations. To make such an assumption implies that a society may persist as an organized object even while the population of actors who are its "members" changes generation by generation as people are born and die. If this is true, then it is apparent that turnover must also occur in the personnel who make up the various smaller component parts of society. For example, the workforce of bureaucratic organizations and the members of other components such as schools and churches must be thought of as changing even as these parts remain intact as elements in the organization of society.

For these reasons, it is necessary to avoid making the assumption that society and its various parts are made up of human actors as particular people, and to make some other assumption. Otherwise, we cannot think of societies as entities persisting through time. As suggested here, one way to solve this problem is to think of society and its various parts in behavioral terms. Behavior can be conceptualized in terms of persistent patterns of action that have the capacity to go on in a stream of episodes that repeat or reproduce themselves in time and space by constantly replacing their members.

This shift in orientation toward behavior and away from people is also necessary to contend with the activity latency problem discussed earlier. If we assume (1) that societies and their various smaller parts are behavioral phenomena, (2) that behavior is an episodic phenomena, and (3) that behavioral systems may persist even when the actors performing the behavior change, we are able to solve the problem of "historical" continuity. That problem can be defined as the need to represent social systems such as groups, organizations, and societies as entities capable of persisting through time. Unless we see them in behavioral terms, we are faced with having to think of such units as disappearing or dissolving into nonexistence when (1) they are inactive and/or (2) their membership in terms of human actors changes.

If we wish to think of social units either in terms of stability through time or as changing as they pass through time, we are faced with this same problem of continuity. To speak of a unit as having a stable organization even though it passes through active and latent phases, we have to define it in terms of a phenomenological reference that permits such a conception. This means that we must be able to identify a social unit, whether it is active or latent, as an object of observation and to think of it as being the same unit observed on previous occasions. Thus, to study the sociology department of the University of Georgia through an interval of several years, we must be able to assume that the social object we observed in 1995 is the same object we observed in 1960, even though it may have passed into a state of latency thousands of times during this period, and even though the actors who are members of the department have turned over completely in the interim. It is also necessary to be able to claim that it is the same object, even though it may have changed structurally.

2.8   Behavior and Space

Before leaving this discussion of social behavior as the phenomenological target for structural modeling in sociology, a few words need to be said about social behavior as it relates to space. This is particularly important because we are building a cognitive system that defines a new kind of ecology meant to deal with the relationships among human systems and between them and their environments.

Obviously, like all observable phenomena, behavior takes place in physical space. But, as pointed out, particular actions occur in discrete time intervals, at which time they are locatable in physical space. Once an action is completed, however, it ceases to "occupy physical space" and is replaced by another act. Units of behavior are not like physical objects that may occupy the same location through long intervals of time. They are temporally bounded and transitory.

Suppose we were to think of the individual bricks that form the smaller units in a brick wall as being comparable to the individual acts that make up a unit of social structure. In the case of bricks in a wall, their physical location relative to each other and relative to other objects in physical space remains more or less fixed through a relatively long interval. In contrast, the acts making up the structure of a social unit not only appear and disappear from physical space, but also they may occur in one physical location at one time and at different locations at other times. For example, the actions making up the behavioral episodes comprising a particular family may occur at home, in an automobile driving down a highway, at a shopping center, or anywhere that actions that relate family members to each other as family members take place.

Neither behavior nor the structures formed out of behavior are "physical objects," even though they are observable in physical space, and even though behavior is executed by physical objects called *organisms*. Physical space is not, therefore, the best grounding for thinking of ecosocial structure when that concept is applied to behavioral phenomena. As shall be seen in the next chapter, structure as a concept requires the use of the idea of space as a grounding, but in the case of behavioral phenomena, the space needed is a kind of behavioral or social space, not physical space. The various actions making up the organized repertoire of behavior that forms the structure of a particular family must be located in social space, where the actions of group members are performed in relation to each other to form family structure.

We must recognize that behavior flows not only through time but it also flows through physical space. Even as it does, the parts of social structure that are made up of social behavior may remain intact, sometimes relatively unchanged even though they pass through active and latent phases, change their members, and move about in physical space. When we say they remain intact, we mean that they continue to occupy social space and maintain a stable pattern. To think this way about behavioral systems and networks, it will be necessary to formulate a conception of structure and of the space it occupies that is appropriate for behavior as a phenomenological target. In doing so, we are not merely using an analogy to physical space and physical structure, but we are constructing a new and quite different reality, *social reality*, whose ontological status is no different than that so-called reality consisting of physical structures seen in physical space. Both are constructed by cognitive action and lead the mind that uses them to view its environment in a way determined by a cognitive apparatus.

2.9   Summary

This chapter is meant to reveal the defining characteristics of the phenomenological domain within which a cognitive apparatus or theoretical system that represents ecosocial structure will be built in later chapters. Certain attributes of social behavior have been selected as crucial elements for shaping the theoretical system being developed. These elements were identified by drawing them out of the more or less disorderly set of ideas and concepts already stored in our minds as a result of past experience. The objective has been to focus our attention on those already formed conceptions of the phenomenological target, social behavior, and use them as a basis for creating a more controlled and precise artificial image of the structure of human behavior systems and networks in our minds. We do not claim that these selected defining characteristics correspond to a true reality called *social behavior* but only that their use will result in the construction of a mental image that can prove useful in guiding our behavior with respect to one important target of sociological analysis.

The critical attributes of social behavior selected as guides to constructing an image of social structure may be summarized as follows:

1. Behavior consists of the actions of an organism toward the organism's environment or toward itself as an object or of the coaction of organisms toward each other and toward their common environment. Physiological functioning and reflex actions are not included in the category *behavior*.

2. Social behavior consists of actions that involve some form of cognitive processing that uses the socially acquired cognitive content of the mind in guiding action and giving meaning to it.

3. Behavior is regarded as an adaptive process whereby an organism or a social system draws the resources it needs or wants from an environment perceived through cognitive action, or through which it adapts to events or conditions in that environment by controlling its own actions. Behavior is the process through which human systems impact upon their environment and defend themselves against environmental threats and hazards.

4. Behavior, in the case of the individual, is a continuous, uninterrupted process between birth and death and can be represented as a linear progression or action stream.

5. An action stream consists of units of behavior called *acts* that are bounded and vary in content as time progresses.

6. Behavior is like a language in that acts and sequences of acts are given meaning by the cognitive apparatus of the actor or actors involved. Behavior is the means by which the organism or group of coacting organisms reflexively "communicate" with themselves concerning their relationship to a self-defined environment.

7. Social relationships and the larger networks comprised of them consist of the interrelated actions of two or more actors joined into common behavioral episodes in interdependent streams of action.

8. Social relationships, social groups, and multigroup systems are episodic phenomena in which actual behavior occurs in interrupted, discontinuous streams. Thus relationships, groups, and multigroup systems pass through active and latent phases. They may exist through long intervals of time continuously as elements of social structure, even though the actual performance of behavior is episodic, by maintaining themselves through periods of latency as cognitive systems or sets of interrelated cognitive systems.

9. Even though individual acts in the action stream of an individual are bounded and occur in discrete units of time, and even though episodes of group behavior are also temporally bounded, similar acts and episodes may occur repeatedly and in association with similar environmental contexts.

10. In order to account for this repetition and also to defend the idea that social units such as families or work groups persist through time even when their occurrence as behavior in the process of being performed is episodic, it is necessary to assume a storage mechanism that preserves the form of behavior during periods of interaction, or during the latent phase.

11. The storage mechanism is assumed to be found in the cognitive systems stored in the minds of human actors and in the organization of these systems in relationship to each other. These cognitive systems together constitute the content of culture as well as the content and structure of the minds of the individual actors, who store parts of the total culture of a society as cognitive material.

12. The term *social behavior* refers both to the actions of the individual and the coactions of multiple individuals organized into groups and multi-group systems.

13. Behavior as a concept refers to four types of adaptive operations of the organism: (a) overt action, (b) cognitive action, (c) perceptual action, and (d) emotional behavior, all of which are assumed to form part of a continuous, interrelated stream of events involving the interaction between an organism or an organized or interrelated set of organisms and an environment.

14. Social units may persist through time as behavior systems and networks by replacing the organisms (individuals) who perform the behavior. This is a logical assumption because it is also assumed that society (and the various smaller units that make it up as a larger object) is comprised of behavior and not of organisms, and societies persist beyond the life spans of their individual members.

3

Structure and Structural Analysis
As a Cognitive Strategy

3.1   Introduction

Chapter 1 pointed out that the idea of structure will be employed as a guideline for constructing a cognitive system useful in forming mental models of social systems and ecological fields. This statement is meant to point to the fact that a generalized conception of structure as a mental construct used with reference to a variety of phenomenological targets, in this case, will be used to guide thought with respect to complex systems of social behavior. As a conceptualization, structure may be regarded as a generalized cognitive system in and of itself, independent of the phenomenon to which it is applied. This cognitive system consists of a complex interrelated set of subelements that, taken together, guide the mind in creating mental images of a variety of objects.

Structural analysis is a process by which the mind follows a set of rules to construct a particular type of symbolic model that it then uses to represent a phenomenon as it thinks about it. This form of analysis creates an interpretation of "reality" on the basis of a set of cognitive procedures that force the mind to think of some bounded whole as being comprised of a set of interrelated parts, units, or elements. Structure is imposed upon the environment of the mind by cognitive action and is not "discovered" as an attribute existing in nature, independent of the mind of the observer. The mind creates structural models or images by following a mental strategy that assigns meaning to sense impressions and organizes them according to a cognitive plan.

To think in terms of structure, it is necessary for the mind of the observer to (1) select and interpret a limited set of sense impressions out of all those potentially available with respect to an object of observation, and (2) to ignore or strip away those sense impressions that are irrelevant to the rules of structural analysis by regarding them as so much perceptual or cognitive noise.

When the mind engages in structural analysis, it creates a *structural model* of an object that by the use of a cognitive code, then, represents that object in the mind of the analyst. This model does not represent the "full true" object in all of its possible perceptual or cognitive ramifications, but only those features of the object of analysis that conform to the analyst's cognitive preconceptions of structure. Because structural models are symbolic, being constructed by use of an abstract code, the choice of elements entering into the symbolic code profoundly affects the mental image conveyed by any structural model. The mind therefore "sees" what the code allows it to see, and those aspects of nature falling outside the code are perceived as noise or go unnoticed.

In this book, a language for the structural modeling of social systems in the context of the ecological fields they inhabit will be created. This language, which will consist of a terminology and an associated set of definitions forming the concepts behind the symbols, will be employed as the code used to form structural models. It will also include a set of rules for employing the concepts in relation to each other, so that the total conceptual apparatus can operate as a kind of "thinking machine" that functions according to a structural strategy. It will constitute a thinking machine in the sense that when its rules and its code are followed, it will produce structural models and will allow the user to reason according to a specific form of structural logic concerning still unstated aspects of social systems and ecological fields. In other words, it will allow the user to deduce from its logic, structural properties, and relationships that lie beyond the stated rules and concepts that are already part of the cognitive apparatus presented in this book.

3.2   *The Essential Ingredients of Structure as an Idea*

Structure as a general concept constitutes a complex set of interrelated ideas that have come down to the social sciences historically from the field of architecture through the physical sciences. In architecture, structure was meant to refer to the stable arrangement of elements that go into the makeup of a building and preserve it as a constructed object. Structure, in the technical sense, rather than as a synonym for a building, refers in architecture to the basic, underlying physical framework of a building, through which the integrity of the building as an object is maintained by a balance of forces or by the bonding together of elements in such a way as to resist forces that might cause the building to collapse or fall apart.

Thus, architects interested in the "structural engineering" of buildings are concerned with (1) the configuration of architectural elements going into the makeup of an edifice, (2) the forces operating through the relationship system that binds the elements together to form the configuration, and (3) the impact of external forces on the building as a configured system of elements. Structural analysis in the architectural sense does not focus on esthetic elements except insofar as they represent loads, or supports, or "structural features" in the sense of being involved in the maintenance of the building as a stable configuration. In a gothic cathedral, it does not matter structurally which saint is represented in the adornments over the portal, nor does it matter whether the saint is male or female, smiling or frowning, or otherwise represented. What counts is what the saint weighs and how that weight is placed with respect to the supports that bear the weight. Matters of symbolism and esthetics, although extremely important in giving meaning to a building and to its users, are simply not of concern structurally. They constitute a kind of noise that must be ignored or stripped away in order to get at those elements of a building that are regarded as structural.

This characteristic of the idea of structure carries through to its use when applied to other fields of science. In creating a structural image of the solar system, scientists ordinarily ignore the "surface appearances" of the planets and their various satellites to focus upon attributes such as their mass, their distances from each other, the shapes of their orbits, their velocities, and their gravitational relationships. Newton was interested in what preserved the solar system as a more or less stable configuration of operating elements and not in the color of Mars or Earth as seen from space, or for that matter, in the geography of the planets' surfaces or their climates and their populations of organisms. All of these latter attributes were ignored to get at the structure of the solar system.

These examples are given to point out two important features of the idea of structure. First, structural analysis, that is, the cognitive action required to formulate an image of structure, depends upon the idea of configuration, pattern, or form through which some bounded whole is thought of as being comprised of interrelated parts or elements. Second, it depends upon the idea of stability, order, or the persistence of the pattern through time for the criterion used to separate structure from the noise surrounding it. Those things that serve as the parts or units of structure, and those relationship concepts that represent the arrangement of those parts or units in a configuration are selected in order to reveal the structural mechanisms that allow an object to persist through time as a patterned, ordered whole, without disintegrating into its environment and becoming a random pattern of unrelated elements. The central question of structural analysis is the question of how pattern or configuration is produced and maintained, and not simply the question of how it may be represented as a pattern or configuration (Alexander, 1984).

3.3 Statics and Dynamics

Although it is possible to describe an object of structural analysis in purely spatial terms that result in a "static image," such an analysis represents only a first step in the full use of a structural strategy. Because the idea of structure involves the notion of stability or order, and because stability implies persistence in time, structural models must always apply to an object viewed through a temporal interval. Furthermore, since the purpose of structural analysis is to reveal not only the pattern that persists but also the mechanisms that allow the persistence of the structural pattern, there is always an implied search for the mechanisms that defy structural entropy. Because structural analysis is almost always applied to objects either with "moving parts" or to objects within which there are forces operating and stresses and strains present, or in which processes are occurring, useful structural models can rarely be "static, frozen images." They must provide a means of symbolizing both the patterned motion or behavior of the parts of structure and the forces, stresses, or strains operating among the parts, as well as the mechanisms that counterbalance or resist these forces.

Structures may operate or behave. The idea of structure does not, as many mistakenly believe, imply a frozen or static image. Symbolic representations of structure in the form of structural models may build processes such as patterned motion and the patterned operation of forces into the model as part of its symbolic cognitive apparatus. Once formed, a symbolic model or a structural image of a particular object may be regarded as being static, even though it includes patterned motion or stress in the sense that the model of an object's structure may not provide for change in the configuration itself; that is, the model may not provide a means for conceptualizing change in structure or for structural transformation or morphogenesis. Thus, the model may be static in the diachronic sense without being static in the synchronic sense.

In this book, it is assumed that structural models are constructed images of phenomenological targets produced by a cognitive system in the mind of an observer in order to help that mind understand how an object is assembled or put together, and how it is able to function or operate through time without falling apart. Thus, the cognitive apparatus that produces structural analysis is a mental tool designed to deal with the problem of ordering sense impressions and of conceptualizing a particular type of order thought of as existing in the world outside the mind of the observer. It is a method the mind uses to impose order on a world outside the mind that can nevertheless be encountered only through cognitive action. It presents the observer with the possibility of many alternative cognitive possibilities.

3.4   Subelements of Structure as a Cognitive System

The idea of structure actually consists of a complex set of interrelated ideas that together form a cognitive system with its own internal organization or order. Taken together, these subconceptions furnish a mental strategy for constructing mental images of phenomena chosen as the objects of observation. The subconcepts making up structure as a cognitive system include the following ideas, each of which, itself, may be comprised of subelements.

1. Space
2. Time
3. Parts or units
4. Relationship or relationships
5. Boundary

In the following paragraphs, each of these separate definitional elements will be examined and its role in structural analysis discussed. It must be remembered, however, that each subelement of the idea of structure takes on its meaning from its relationship to the other elements, because each is defined reciprocally in terms of the others. (For other uses of the concept structure, see Parsons, 1951; Merton, 1968; Bates and Harvey, 1975; Blau and Merton, 1981; Nadel, 1957; Katz, 1976; Firth, 1963).

3.4.1 Space

Structure as a concept employs the notion of space as a grounding. Structures are thought of as occupying space and of being comprised of elements that form a pattern or configuration. Both of these ideas imply a spatial arrangement through which a bounded whole object is conceived of in terms of an arrangement of smaller parts or elements.

Space itself is defined by the objects that occupy it and by their relationship to each other in forming a configuration. It is the background against which the parts of a whole are differentiated mentally from each other by conceptual boundaries, and against which they are thought of as being arranged in relationship to each other. Space, as an idea, in other words, is generated by the idea of separateness or boundary and by the idea of relationship. To have an idea of space, it is first necessary to conceive of at least two objects that are distinct, or bounded. The concept *space* is necessary to the idea of separation or boundary and comes into being in the mind as a natural outcome of drawing boundaries between objects or phenomena. It is also an automatic creation of the idea of relationship. All of these related ideas coemerge in the mind and give meaning to each other in a cross-referenced set of concepts. Separation into distinct elements and the conceptualization of relationship generates the companion idea of space, which constitutes the mental grounding of the very ideas that generate it.

The properties of space are not inherent in nature itself but are a product of the concepts employed to represent bounded objects and of the relationships among objects. Conceptions of physical objects and of physical relationships generate an idea of physical space, whose properties are regarded as being appropriate to objects comprised of matter. Geometric space is generated by a set of abstract concepts that relate cognitive "objects" such as points, lines, and surfaces to each other by relationship concepts such as distance, direction, and angle. What is important here is that the idea of bounded social objects generates the idea of social space and of a set of properties appropriate to conceptualizing how they are arranged in relationships to form configurations. Social space is not a mere analogy to physical space but is a separate idea, useful in its own right, because it is defined in terms of its own concepts and dimensions.

As we proceed to create concepts to represent social objects, for example, social roles and positions or bounded groups and organizations, and as we introduce concepts to refer to social relationships, we are simultaneously creating the properties that define social space. They coemerge in the same act of cognitive formation. We do not first define the concept *space* as an independent abstraction and then independently posit the properties of concepts meant to represent the objects that "inhabit" space. Instead, when we create concepts referring to social phenomena, for example, the concepts *social position* and *social relationship*, we simultaneously begin to create an idea of space, with its own special "geometry" or "topology." The acts of cognitive creation are totally interdependent!

As the concepts necessary to symbolize social objects and social relationships are introduced later in this book, the effect will be to create a complex notion of social space as part of the cognitive grounding for formulating structural models. Now, however, it is important to make clear what the other conceptual ingredients of the idea of structure are.

3.4.2   Time and Social Structure

Because the idea of structure includes the notion of stability, and because stability implies the persistence of a pattern, *time* as a concept underlies the concept *structure*. In thinking about structure, the mind organizes or orders its image of a phenomenological target by conceptualizing a pattern of elements or parts that are arranged into a relationship system that persists through an interval of time.

Time is a conception, necessary to differentiate structure from nonstructure, that is, from randomness in the relationships among objects of observation. Indeed, the idea of structure is the conceptual antithesis of randomness or chaos, both of which are taken as the definition of nonstructure. In the case of total chaos, no two objects or elements are thought of as having any predictable or stable relationship to each other. Each particle or element in a chaotic world behaves separately and independently of all others, except for instantaneous, temporary, chance encounters. There is no way for the mind to predict the relationships among the elements in a chaotic or random phenomenon because there are no stable relationships that can be used as a basis of prediction. Each instant sees a different arrangement of elements from the last, and each is different from future instances.

Structure is the opposite of this. In structures, the parts or elements of a whole maintain a set of relationships to each other, so that it is possible to predict future relationships on the basis of the past. *Structural entropy* is defined as the breakdown of the pattern of relationships among the parts of an object into randomness and chaos. This means that *structure* as an idea implies an entropy-defying mechanism as a feature of structure itself.

The point here is that to distinguish structure from nonstructure, it is necessary to think in terms of an interval of time within which it is possible to distinguish a persistent, nonrandom pattern from randomness. Without the passage of time, it is impossible to distinguish a chance arrangement of elements from one that involves an entropy-defying mechanism. To be able to think in terms of structure, it is necessary to be able to predict a set of relationships among elements from one instant to the next.

As a consequence of these considerations, time is always an element in the cognitive system that generates the concept structure. There is, however, no rule that specifies how long a time interval is necessary. Structural models may be created for objects that are very short lived, existing only for microseconds, and others may be formed for objects that are almost eternal. The time frame used to conceptualize structure is relative to the phenomenological target, and to the theoretical problem being faced by use of structural analysis.

3.4.3   Synchronic and Diachronic Time

It is useful in thinking about structure as an idea to think in terms of *synchronic* and *diachronic* time. Although the actual time periods referred to by these terms are relative to the problem being examined, they can be defined more exactly relative to each other. Synchronic time, in the case of social structure, refers to a time interval during which a structure may operate as a pattern *without the pattern itself* changing. Thus, in the synchronic sense, a structure may exhibit patterned behavior, or motion, among its various parts or elements. The solar system conceptualized in terms of planets in orbital motion in annual cycles includes the idea of motion or behavior with respect to the parts (planets and the sun) relative to each other through *synchronic time*. A factory building automobiles opens each morning after being idle at night, and the various workers execute behavior patterns that more or less repeat those that occurred the previous day. Thus, the concept *structure* may incorporate within its conceptualization an image of patterned behavior through an interval of time, during which the structure itself remains unchanged. This is a synchronic time interval.

In contrast, diachronic time is a conception made necessary as a basis for conceptualizing change in structure. It refers to a time period sufficiently long to conceptualize the transformation of structure itself. In diachronic terms, the synchronic pattern changes. Without a synchronic image, the conception of change would be impossible because change is defined as an alteration in that pattern.

It is important at this juncture to recognize that change itself implies the persistence through time of an object that maintains its *identity* in the mind of the analyst, even as it undergoes some form of transformation. Therefore, change is different from the idea of structural entropy. In the case of entropy, an object loses its identity, or dissolves, and therefore no longer is thought of as existing as an object. Change, on the other hand, implies that an object is transformed without experiencing structural entropy. Indeed, some objects may be thought of as changing as a means of defying entropy. This is what is ordinarily meant by the concept *adaptation*.

The concepts *operation, change,* and *time* are another example of coemergent constructs that so depend upon each other for meaning that each is meaningless without the others. Without something operating, moving, or changing, there is no time. Timelessness, that is, a reality without time, can only be conceptualized in a completely static world. Synchronic time and operation or behavior are tied cognitively to each other like Siamese twins born at the same instant. Similarly, change and diachronic time are inseparable.

3.4.4   Structure and Process

There has always been confusion among sociologists over the relative meaning of the concepts *structure* and *process*. This confusion stems from a failure to think through the relationship of the concept *structure* to the idea of time, and also to a failure to recognize that structure as an idea implies a nonrandom pattern, which by definition includes a dynamic mechanism that defies entropy. If one conceives of structure as a stable arrangement of parts in which the parts operate in relationship to each other in a synchronic pattern, then much of what is referred to as process becomes an element in the definition of structure itself. Structure is patterned synchronic process. This leaves the idea of *process* as a term appropriate to diachronic analysis. Process becomes change in structure. Such a distinction leaves open a whole field for conceptualizing forms of change processes through which structures are built up, differentiated, elaborated, and otherwise transformed as they pass through diachronic time. Under such a conceptualization, the operation or functioning of a structure is seen as a part of the structure itself and as emerging from the dynamic relationships built into the structure.

As can be seen from this discussion, the cognitive system symbolized by the word *structure* includes a rather complex notion of time as a conceptual ingredient. This temporal dimension of structure introduces into the cognition apparatus such ideas as stability, randomness, chaos, process, and change. It also implies a relativistic view of time, which itself is symbolized by the consideration of synchronic and diachronic time intervals. Again, it is apparent that all of these ideas are cross-referenced in a complex cognitive web in which each idea takes on its meaning from its relationship to the others. This being true, it is of utmost importance to structural analysts to be self-conscious and aware of what is being implied by these ideas, because it is through them that artificial images are constructed of a phenomenological domain.

3.4.5 Parts or Units

Structural analysis breaks down some object of investigation into a set of component parts or units. This is done by creating a symbolic code for use in referring to the fragments of a whole. It is important to understand that this is a cognitive action taken by an analyst and not a discovery arrived at by pure observation. The mind creates the idea of parts by an analytic procedure that itself is based on a conscious or unconscious objective. What the mind chooses to represent as parts depends upon the goal being pursued and, of course, on the preconceptions already present in the cognitive apparatus being employed. We cannot defend the statement that nature contains objects whose parts are given naturally and therefore can be observed as "natural units" without cognitive action. We cannot say, for example, that it is only natural to think of a tree as being a large object comprised of parts called root, trunk, branch, twig, and leaf. The fact that we see trees this way is a consequence of a linguistic apparatus that contains traditional symbols and a conception of tree structure that employs this code to construct trees as a certain type of reality in our minds.

An alternative view might use concepts such as atoms and molecules, cells, and cellular linkages to construct a different image of the same tree. One image may serve a microbiologist better, and different ones, foresters or ornithologists. Even so, each set of concepts used to represent the parts of a larger object must in the long run be regarded as arbitrary because each is the product of a set of cognitive decisions. Furthermore, each produces a different view of structure and, therefore, of the "reality" structural analysis is intended to represent.

All structures are thought of as being comprised of smaller elements that for purposes of this discussion will be called parts. Parts are themselves bounded objects or units that are thought of as being separate and distinct from each other. These boundaries are between and among parts and within the boundary of the larger whole, where they are created conceptually by the mental act of analysis; that is, the boundaries of parts are created when the mind of the analyst pulls the larger object apart and assigns a conceptual identity to the differentiated elements or units comprising the whole.

In a case in which a set of cognitive conventions already exists in the mind of the analyst, parts are thought of as separate, bounded units when they are assigned an identifying label as part of that cognitive code. For example, suppose the object being structurally modeled is a chair; then already existing designations such as leg, back, seat, arm, rung, and so forth would simultaneously operate as guides to perception and cognition, and therefore to identifying the parts of a chair.

It is important to recognize that an object can be regarded as a part of a structure *only* when it is included within the configuration that constitutes the whole of which it is a part. If a leg is removed from a chair and set aside in space from the chair from which it was taken, it cannot properly be thought of as a chair part, or for that matter, as a chair leg. At best, it can be thought of as a "former leg" or "former chair part," possibly even a "future chair part." To be a part of a structure means to be actually included in the structure as an element in relationship to other elements. Parts cannot exist in isolation. Part and whole are coemergent constructs!

The concept *part* takes on its meaning from the concept *whole* and cannot be cognitively separated from it without losing its meaning. It follows from this statement that the meaning assigned to the symbol used to refer to a particular part of a particular whole takes on its meaning from its placement in a larger conceptual apparatus that represents a particular whole object. For example, the meaning of the concept *leg*, as it applies to chairs, is not only associated with the code word *leg*, but also with a notion of where legs are located vis-à-vis backs, seats, arms, and so forth. In this case, there is an additional functional meaning with anthropomorphic overtones also associated with the symbolic designation. Legs, like the legs of an animal, support the weight of the chair and its occupant!

The point is that simultaneous with the act of identifying parts and their boundaries, a cognitive meaning is given to the parts in relation to each other and therefore to the whole. In fact, it is this meaning that is decisive in so isolating the part from its structural context. Thus, when the object of observation is a university and the observer gives the designation dean to one position in the structure, the concept *dean* is understood as a unit of structure only as it is related to other concepts applying to the same whole, for example, department head, professor, college president, and so forth, and only insofar as it carries some meaning that places it in a larger meaningful context.

To be a part, a unit must be defined in terms of its relationship to and placement in the whole where it functions as a part. This implies that each concept referring to a part must be defined in terms that are compatible with and reciprocal to the other concepts making up the set that refers to all other units making up the whole and also in terms of a conceptualization of the whole as an organized assemblage of parts. Thus, the terms employed as the symbolic tools used in a particular structural analysis to construct a structural model form a cognitive system. They are a system in the sense that they are cross-referenced and interrelated in such a manner as to operate according to a bounded logic in which the terms "interact" in the mind of the analyst, thus producing a larger, more complex meaning in the form of a cognitive model. If one term and the associated concept out of the total set is unrelated or contradictory to others in the set, or if it fails to "interact mentally" with others in the system, then the cognitive process involved in using the conceptual apparatus will be disrupted and fail to reach logical closure, thus constructing a model that will not work or function properly in the mind. It will produce a faulty model by use of which the logical operation of the mind will be unable to pass from one part of the conceptual apparatus to other parts without changing the meaning of other concepts within the total set away from their original form. There will, in other words, be a theoretical or cognitive ambivalence that destroys the utility of the whole apparatus. It will be like a computer program with a "bug" in its logic. Another way to think of it is in terms of a logical definitional trail that can be followed from one concept to another, so that the mind can pass through the entire system and return to its starting point without getting lost or being diverted from its path, or passing beyond the boundaries of the cognitive system and entering an entirely different one.

This does not mean that a given user of the conceptual apparatus will automatically recognize a "bug" in a cognitive system. Indeed, the user may continuously redefine concepts in isolation from each other, as is the case for much of the conceptual apparatus used by sociologists today. When it is used in connection with empirical data or with a theoretical problem, the consequence will be a loss of utility in the conceptual apparatus. It simply will not furnish a mental tool that allows the user to predict and control the results either of observation or the cognitive action directed toward explanation. The conceptual apparatus will remain open to uncontrolled changes according to the whims of the observer or to the idiosyncrasies of the relationship of the observer to his or her empirical environment.

The objective of this book is to design a terminology that is systematic and therefore reciprocally cross-referenced. This terminology will consist, in part, of a set of terms and associated concepts referring to the parts of social structure graduated in levels of scale according to an "atomistic principle." This principle is used as a logical tactic to keep the mind from losing its way as it reasons about the problem of modeling social structure. It accomplishes this by following the structural principle that larger objects are comprised of smaller parts or units, and that even larger objects can be constructed using these as parts. Thus, to proceed according to an atomistic principle, the conceptualization of each progressively larger unit of social structure must be

TABLE 3.1
Levels of Scale

Levels of scale	Unit
1	Act–norm
2	Role
3	Status
4	Position
5	Group
6	Organization
7	Community
8	Society
9	Intersocietal network
10	Ecological fields

accomplished by using prior conceptualizations of smaller units as conceptual elements *without* changing these prior conceptualizations as we pass from one level of scale to the next. Thus, prior wholes become parts at the next higher level of scale.

In this book, the terms shown in Table 3.1 will be employed to refer to the parts of social structure at different levels of scale. The progression will begin with the "sociological atom," the unit act, and end with the intersocietal networks and ecological fields, the largest whole formed out of progressively nested larger parts. All of these terms except the last refer to the parts of social structure viewed at a specific level of scale. They are like so many Chinese boxes, all nested within a larger box, in which each box contains a smaller one until we come to the penultimate microbox. However, in the structural model of each box, it is necessary to introduce relationship concepts through which the larger boxes are conceptually constructed.

3.4.6   Relationship Concepts

The structural strategy employs concepts representing relationships as the cognitive tools used to construct a model of the configuration of the parts that form a whole. These concepts are, of course, created by cognitive action and lead the user to view the world in a way determined by their own logic. They, too, are not discovered in nature as an ultimate reality but fashioned in the mind to serve a particular purpose. Accordingly, the choice of relationship concepts will depend upon the purposes they are intended to serve, and upon the prior biases of the mind that fashions them.

Relationship concepts intended to deal with social structure, along with concepts referring to parts, will create a geometry or topology of social space. If constructed in a certain way, they will create a kind of *structural ecology*, in the sense that they will make it possible to see human systems in relationship to their human and nonhuman environments, thereby creating a conception of an ecological field.

It is one of the primary objectives of this book to formulate a structural basis for modeling such ecological fields and for distinguishing between ecological fields and the systems that interact within such fields. At this point in the discussion, such a statement must be left somewhat vague and mysterious, because it will require many pages to clarify its meaning, and this work is still to come. As shall be seen in the discussion to follow, however, the distinction between a system and an ecological field will rest on the type of relationship that exists among the units of structure forming them.

In this book, several types of relationships will be conceptualized and employed to model the way the parts of ecosocial structure are configured with respect to one another. The following list enumerates these forms of relationships:

1. Spatial relationships
2. Bonds, ties, or attachments
3. Exchanges, transfers, or input–output relationships
4. Interactions
5. Functional interdependencies

Each of these forms of relationship needs to be discussed briefly here.

3.4.6.1 Spatial Relationships

As pointed out, structure is by nature a spatially grounded concept. Structural analysis locates the parts of a whole in relationship to each other in a spatial pattern represented by concepts defining relationship patterns. Even so, there are various potential ways of thinking about space. One way is to define relationships in terms of a formal geometry or topology that employs abstract "content-free" concepts. Such concepts refer to formal geometric properties and do not specify the phenomenological content found in particular "real-world" objects. This means of defining space lays out abstract spatial dimensions and defines them in terms that allow quantification, no matter what the phenomenon they are used to describe.

The social sciences have not progressed to this stage as yet. Even so, sociologists have been accustomed to referring to social structure in terms of a "vertical" and "horizontal dimension." They have also frequently spoken in terms of structural distance and social mobility. In addition, they use concepts such as *size* and *growth*, both of which have a connotation of volume. In almost every case, however, such spatial concepts are tied heavily to notions of phenomenological content and fail to define a precise geometry independent of a particular phenomenological application.

Using such a terminology nevertheless creates a purely spatial image of social structure in the sense that it refers to a kind of purely geometric pattern. The parts chosen to represent the units comprising the structure of a whole are conceptualized as being arranged in relation to each other along horizontal and vertical dimensions, along which they may vary in size and in distance from one another as they form a total configuration. The difficulty is that such spatial concepts have never been formalized into an integrated, logical system. As things now stand, these spatial concepts are part of a "general cognitive garbage can," containing a disorderly conglomeration of more or less unrelated ideas that exist in a rough form, unpurified by the discipline of rigorous systematic cognitive action in which all concepts are forced to relate to each other according to an underlying logic. As a result, separate users of spatial concepts create idiosyncratic structural models for which there is little or no theoretical defense.

Problems also arise because a given dimension of space is measured or quantified quite differently depending on the phenomenological target chosen for study. This would not be a serious problem if it could be claimed that all that is involved when this occurs is that different scholars are using different metrics to measure the same dimension of social structure. This would be like one person using feet and yards to measure physical distance, while another is using centimeters or meters. But when one sociologist measures the vertical dimension of society using prestige points on a prestige scale, and another uses income, while still another uses power, the situation is quite different. One can translate feet into centimeters by a well-known operation based on an underlying conception of distance, and this translation results in a more or less perfect agreement among measurements. In contrast, how do we translate prestige points into dollar income or power and arrive at a satisfactory level of logical correspondence? The problem is not one of precision in measurement. It is one of conceptualization concerning the meaning of distance along the vertical dimension of social structure.

The properties of social space must be derived from a model that places objects in relationship to each other using concepts that are, at first, nongeometric. Only then can a system of measurement appropriate to that conceptualization be derived. Such concepts as *direction, distance,* and *volume* should be made dependent on the set of concepts used to "populate space" conceptually, so that they are made consistent with a larger conceptual apparatus.

The plan in this book is to proceed step-by-step to define elements of social structure by dealing first with small social objects and then moving to larger units according to an atomistic strategy. By preceding in this way, it will be possible to define a set of concepts that refer in a very abstract way to dimensions of social space and how they can be quantified. In this manner, a concept such as *structural distance* can be derived logically from the prior concepts fashioned to place the parts of social structure in relationship to each other in forming larger social objects. This procedure requires the use of concepts that are not strictly spatial in character to form the foundation for the spatial concepts derived from them. One such essentially nonspatial idea is the notion of bonds, ties, or attachments.

3.4.6.2 Bonds, Ties, or Attachments

One way of thinking about how two parts of a larger structure are joined to each other is in terms of how they are connected, tied, or attached to each other so that they remain connected. This sort of relationship will be referred to as *bonds*. Using a physical analogy, one piece of wood used in constructing a piece of furniture may be screwed, nailed, or glued to the other, or they may be joined by a dovetail or mortise and tenon joint. By such means, they are "bonded" together in an attachment that fixes their relationship to each other through a time interval, assuming no forces intervene strong enough to break the bond.

The parts of social structure may also be thought of in terms of the "social bonds" that attach various parts of social structure to each other. For example, in a university, the position Dean of the College of Arts and Sciences is bonded in a relationship system to other positions such as Department Head and Vice-President. In other words, the position of Dean is fixed in a structural network at a certain location relative to other positions in the network.

The bond, however, is accomplished by social means and therefore must be conceptualized in social terms. This task is one to be undertaken in later chapters, but the point here is that one way to think of the relationships among the social units making up the structure of a larger social whole is in terms of bonds. Positions are bonded to each other to form structural networks, such as the work groups in a factory, which are themselves, in turn, bonded to each other to form the multigroup system comprising the factory as a complex organization. In a university, the sociology department is bonded to other departments comprising the College of Arts and Sciences, and this college is bonded to other colleges to form a particular university. Bonds imply a static fixing of elements in relationship to each other. To move toward a more dynamic view of structure, it is necessary to introduce other relationship concepts. Such concepts can be used to specify what occurs among parts that are joined to each other by attachments such as bonds. For example, transfers or exchanges may be thought of as taking place among the parts comprising a larger whole.

3.4.6.3 Exchanges, Transfers, and Input–Output Relations

A second way to conceptualize the relationships among the parts of a structure is in terms of exchanges or flows that take place among them. Something flows from part A over a channel to part B, thus relating the two parts to each other. The flow may involve the transfer of energy or of physical products, or it may involve information. The flow may be one way or two way, or it may be constant or intermittent, regularly scheduled or irregular.

Often such flows are thought of as input–output relations through which the parts of a structure exchange resources used in their individual internal operations. Thus, part A produces an output that flows into part B as an input where it is used as a resource for internal operation. Conceptualizing such flows among parts leads to an image of structure that is not purely spatial but one in which definable exchanges are thought of as taking place. The image is one of interdependence among parts in terms of the resources they employ and the sources from which these inputs are obtained. In a structure so conceptualized, there is a dynamic image of the parts behaving in relation to each other in a pattern of interdependencies. A purely spatial image locates parts in relationship to each other, but a relationship concept involving exchanges symbolizes one or more aspects of what transpires between and among units located in the spatial pattern. There is another way to think of what transpires among the parts of a structure. This way involves the idea of interaction.

3.4.6.4   Interactional Relationships

Certainly input–output relationships constitute a form of interaction among the parts of a structure but only one particular type. Input–output relationships are concerned with the flow of various things from one place in a structure to another. The parts of structure may impact upon each other without anything flowing out of the boundaries of one unit and into the boundaries of another. Part A may behave in such a manner as to affect part B without an input–output relationship taking place. For example, part A may produce a negative impact on part B. One cogwheel in a clock may be made of harder metal than the one its teeth mesh with and, as a consequence, wear out the teeth of the one made of softer metal. One work group in a factory may get into a conflict with another over the availability of resources, such as increased salaries or wages, and sabotage the operation of the other group. In these cases, it is not inputs and outputs that are the concern but the impact of one part on the other.

The parts of a structure may be conceptualized as interacting, that is, as impacting upon each other in a wide variety of ways. In such a case, an image of structural reality is created in which the behavior of the parts of a structure is viewed as affecting each other through relationship networks. The result in the long run is a conception in which the behavior of the parts of a structure is seen in terms of how the parts interact as they form the whole, and the behavior of the whole is viewed as arising out of the interaction of the parts. Such an image introduces a strategy for "explanation" into the idea of structure. It shapes the way the observer views the operation of an object by providing a means of "explaining" how the structure works. The object is no longer seen as a simple spatial configuration or static pattern but as a functioning mechanism whose operational characteristics are included within the structure itself.

3.4.6.5 Functional Interdependencies

Both the ideas of input–output exchanges and of interaction, but especially the former, imply an idea of functional interdependence. They imply that one part of a structure is dependent upon the other parts of the same structure either for the resources they utilize internally for their own functioning or that the behavior of one part cannot be explained, understood, or predicted without knowledge of the behavior of other parts in relation to it. This is what is normally meant by functional interdependence.

Another way to think of the relationships among the parts or units of a structure is therefore to conceptualize their interdependencies. In so doing, the analyst seeks to define the role or function of each part of the system relative to the others and to the system as a whole. This amounts to isolating the contribution that each part makes in a division of labor that organizes the mechanism of the whole. In this case, the division of labor is thought of as the division of the whole into separate parts or elements that contribute particular suboperations in the total mechanism of a bounded whole.

Such a structural image is useful in dealing with certain types of phenomena and not necessarily useful in conceptualizing others. In particular, objects thought of as machines or organisms, or as systems, make appropriate targets for this tactic because they can conveniently be thought of as consisting of an organized set of "functionally" differentiated parts that are interdependent and operate as a system. This same view would not provide any particular advantage to the analyst attempting to conceptualize an inert object such as a chair or a mountain range.

The point is that the type of relationship concept employed profoundly affects the image created in the mind and leads the observer to select observations to fit a preconceived mental apparatus. If the object of analysis is assumed at the outset to be a system, then relationship concepts such as exchanges, interactions, and functional interdependencies are appropriate, because they shall be seen in the next chapter as part of the idea of systems. If the object of analysis is not viewed as a system, they are, perhaps, inappropriate.

3.4.6.6 Boundaries

The boundaries of a structure are defined by the relationship system built up as a means of representing the relationship among parts. Boundaries are arbitrarily established by the cognitive action of defining the configuration that comprises the whole. They are not given in nature as an empirical attribute of an object. It is tempting to think, for example, of an organism as being bounded naturally by its skin. This seems obvious and self-apparent. To a biologist, however, this may not appear after careful thought to be so obvious. For example, are the microorganisms that inhabit the stomach part of the organism as a biological structure? Is the oxygen molecule captured in a blood cell, a part of the cell or is it in its environment? Is the food contained in the inside of the intestines part of the organism or in its environment? The answers to these questions depend upon the cognitive apparatus that models the organism relative to its environment, thus establishing conceptual boundaries. Conceptual boundaries and "empirical boundaries" are one and the same, because it takes cognitive action to perceive boundaries in the world outside the mind.

In order to create a structural model, it is necessary to establish a means to define the limits of the structure, because only then can we determine what to treat as the parts of the whole and define their relationships to each other. This requires a rationale that enables the analyst to integrate a conceptualization of boundaries with the set of concepts employed to define parts and relationships. As shall be seen, this proves to be a difficult logical task when the object of structural modeling is a social phenomenon. How can we, as observers, tell where one group or organization ends and another begins? How can we decide when it is appropriate to model a phenomenon as if it is one system comprised of two or more subsystems or as two or more bounded systems that are interacting with each other? Whatever the choice, it will always be one that rests upon a set of cognitive decisions and not upon the results of observation.

3.5   Summary

The idea of structure constitutes a rather complex cognitive system, consisting of a number of subconceptions that operate together as a mental apparatus. This apparatus produces mental images called *structural models*. Such models, once formed according to the rules of structural analysis, function in the mind as mentally encoded surrogates for a particular set of attributes of objects that are thought of as observed phenomena.

Depending upon the choice of concepts used to represent parts, relationships, and boundaries, and the space they occupy, a particular type of order will be imposed upon "reality." It will lead the observer to see the phenomenological world in a particular way, peculiar to the idea of structure and to the particular conceptual ingredients employed to encode it symbolically. Without such cognitive action, the phenomenological world will remain either inaccessible to the mind of the observer except as a buzzing confusion, or it will be organized or ordered by those cognitive tools contained within the mind that are derived from the general culture. Structural analysis, when conducted according to a rigorously developed set of rules, imposes a discipline on the cognitive process of ordering observations and creates models that have a known origin. This means that they can be criticized for their internal consistency, and different cognitive systems can be compared according to a known set of rules. Although we can never be assured that any structural model corresponds correctly to reality, we can test its utility in solving problems, and we can examine it for logical consistency.

4

Systems and Systems Theory

4.1   Introduction

The term *system* refers to a complex cognitive apparatus that organizes or orders an image of empirical phenomena in the mind of an observer according to a structural strategy. As a cognitive apparatus, the concept *system* consists of a cross-referenced set of ideas that produces a certain type of mental image used to represent phenomena thought of as being external to the mind. It operates in the mind as a kind of artificial "thinking" machine that imposes an order on the mind's transactions within itself and between itself and a world encountered through the senses.

Accordingly, systems do not exist in nature as pristine realities prior to conceptualization to be discovered by an observer and recorded according to a self-evident symbolic code. Images of objects seen as systems are artificial creations that exist as a result of a set of mental operations through which the mind orders itself and thereby its environment. Systems as "entities" are the consequence of following a structural strategy that itself has been limited and fashioned in such a way as to permit the mind to predict the operation or behavior of a structure on the basis of a kind of deterministic or causal logic. The idea of system, in a very crude sense, can be thought of as the result of joining together the cognitive strategy of structuralism with a cognitive apparatus that places an idea of a "causal mechanism" within a structural model, so that the behavior of the parts of a structure are explainable from knowledge of that mechanism.

At the most general level, the concept *system* employs the idea of structure as a means of supplying the basis for an explanation of how a phenomenological target works or operates. As shall be seen, this is accomplished by inserting relationship concepts into the formulation of structural models that have the capacity to yield predictions concerning how the elements of a structure operate in relationship to each other within the mechanism of the whole.

In order to clarify the concept *system* as a cognitive apparatus and to pare away the irrelevancies that have accumulated around it as it has been employed almost indiscriminately in the social sciences for the past 50 years, this chapter will examine the concept as it now occurs in different contexts. This will be done as a critical exercise meant to "purify" the concept *system* for use as part of the cognitive apparatus being developed in this book for purposes of modeling social structure. The objective is to reveal the core conceptual elements that enter into the cognitive system represented by the term system. This is *not* intended as an exercise in discovering the true meaning of *system* by examining its use by leading scholars, or by drawing inferences from empirical cases. Instead, it is meant to make transparent to the reader the meaning of the concept as it will be employed in this book, and also to make clear the reasons for the theoretical choices being made. In fact, the intention is to reconstruct the idea of system as a cognitive apparatus by deliberate, self-conscious cognitive action, so that it may be employed as a guide to conceptualizing social structure.

4.2   General Background

The difficulty in understanding the meaning of the term *system* lies in the tendency in recent years to apply it to virtually every conceivable phenomenological target and, at the same time, to employ it in connection with a wide variety of explanation problems with respect many different phenomenological domains. This has meant that in order to fit their intellectual projects, scholars in some fields emphasize certain attributes as defining characteristics of systems, whereas others emphasize different ones. But even as there has been a developing divergence in the meaning of the term within and among various disciplines, there has also been an attempt to formulate "systems theory" as a general approach applicable to all fields. General systems theory, and also cybernetics, have attempted to develop an abstract notion of systems that transcends individual fields of study and to formulate general principles that apply to all things considered to be systems (von Bertalanffy, 1968; Ashby, 1956; Klier, 1969; Lazlo, 1972; Miller, 1978). As a part of this effort, there have also been attempts to classify systems and to define more precisely how separate types of systems differ from and are similar to each other. Thus Walter Buckley's (1967) discussion of system types and of their evolution represents an attempt to "systematize" systems theory by providing categories into which various phenomenological targets fit when approached from the point of view implicit in the general notion of system. For the most part, these efforts (von Bertalanffy, 1968; Miller, 1970) have been guided by an empiricist's epistemology that thinks of systems as empirical entities in their own right and of the task of the systems theorist as the creation of a conceptual apparatus that corresponds to the nature of "real-world phenomena." Thus, most attempts at the classification of systems may be seen as attempts to represent empirical variability, while preserving the abstract notion of systems as a particular form of reality.

Although these efforts have at times been both helpful and important, they leave certain crucial questions unanswered. In particular, they do not address the question of what the limits of systems theory are and instead seem to imply that the term is useful in dealing with almost any phenomenological target. This is perhaps due to the belief that systems theory is, in reality, an intellectual approach to conceptualizing an explanation problem rather than a statement concerning the exact phenomenological attributes of particular empirical targets. This may be interpreted to mean that there is not just one kind of system out there in the empirical world, but there are many phenomena that may be understood by use of a "systems approach." It is therefore not a question of whether a phenomenon *is or is not* a system, but rather a question of how it must be conceptualized to take advantage of systems theory by using the idea of systems as an abstract model for phenomena that vary in empirical details (Churchman, 1969).

The question to be addressed in this chapter is concerned with the criteria used to establish the limits within which systems theory as a cognitive strategy is useful and therefore appropriate. Are there phenomenological targets for which systems theory is inappropriate as a useful tool of cognition? Are there explanation problems that cannot be fruitfully approached by use of systems theory because they lie outside the assumptions or symbolic code of systems theory? In particular, what are the limits of systems theory?

It is important to realize at this point that we are not speaking about correspondence when we ask these questions. The issue is not concerned with the possibility that there are empirical phenomena that do not match the idea of systems. The issue involves the logic of systems theory itself as it exists in the form of a cognitive apparatus. Our argument will be that the cognitive system called *systems theory* is a bounded, self-referential mental apparatus that limits itself by its own internal order and, by so doing, creates for itself a cognitive environment containing, among other things, the ideas of a nonsystem and of an ecology of separate systems. This environment is itself a cognitive artifact but, even so, calls into question the unlimited use of the concept system.

The questions posed here are intended to go beyond the issue raised by the view that systems theory is an intellectual approach and not a question of the "nature" of empirical objects. They cannot be answered by simply saying that if a phenomenon is not considered to be systematic, this is because the analyst has decided not to use a systems approach, and a different presumably more enlightened investigator could just as easily have used systems theory to deal with the same problem.

The issue is whether it is reasonable to assert that there are potential phenomenological targets that lack the basic attributes assumed to be present in a system and therefore are not understandable by use of the assumptions and theorems of systems reasoning. This is like asking, "Are there objects that may be thought of more usefully and more faithfully with respect to systems rea-soning as "nonsystems?" What would a nonsystem be like? After all, one can-not give meaning to a term unless it has boundaries that separate it from other terms, and this requires that it be defined against the background of negative examples. Even if we were to assume that all things that exist in na-ture can be usefully understood as systems, even if we must think of them as being enfolded as parts of a larger universal system, there still remains the necessity of specifying what the hypothetical negation of the idea of systems would be like. In systems theory as it exists within the empiricist tradition, the nearest approach to providing limits to the application of the idea of systems has been to contrast types of systems on the one hand, or on the other, to con-trast them to chaos or randomness.

If the first approach is used, open and closed systems, or morphogenic and morphostatic systems, are posed against each other as in the case of Wal-ter Buckley and Karl Popper (Buckley, 1967; Popper, 1972; von Bertalanffy, 1968; Katz and Kahn, 1978). If the latter approach is used, then the idea of systems and the idea of order as opposed to chaos become virtually synony-mous. The word *system* becomes just another term for order but one that uses a certain type of structural vocabulary as a basis for discussing it. Thus sys-tem, structure, and order blend into each other, and systems theory becomes a matter of using a certain symbolic code employing words such as interde-pendence and feedback to describe order as it is displayed in the case of par-ticular phenomena.

Such a point of view means that when a sociologist assumes society to be "orderly," at the same time, he or she is assuming it to be "a system" and is left only with the question of what type of systems model is appropriate. From this perspective, therefore, one could never arrive at a conclusion that societies cannot be considered systems without also assuming societies to be chaotic or to be nonphenomena. In the long run, the answer or answers given to the question posed must come from specifying the attributes of "systems" as a cognitive apparatus and then by using them as criteria that are applied in examining target phenomena such as social groups or human societies as constructed realities.

4.3   Interaction, Multilateral Causation, and System Theory

An examination of the broad range of phenomena to which systems theory is applied by general systems theorists will reveal that it is illustrated using widely differing examples. For instance, the thermodynamics of hot gases enclosed within a "jar" or a soap bubble is used to illustrate closed systems and the concept of entropy (Rappoport, 1968; Popper, 1972). At the same time, "natural" physical phenomena such as the solar system or atoms and molecules are given as cases of systems with a more patterned "structure" than that implied by the random behavior of gas particles in relationship to each other when enclosed within a boundary. On top of this comes the case of man-made machines that are incapable of self-regulation, and then those capable of self-guidance. Next come cases of individual organisms or aspects of organisms that are thought of as subsystems. Examples of "ecosystems" and "species as systems" are also added to the list. This latter step inevitably requires an introduction of behavioral phenomena because, to relate individual organisms and species to each other, especially in the case of animals, it is necessary to introduce behavior and "social" or at least "ecological interaction" to the growing list of phenomena to which the term *systems* is applied (Buckley, 1967; Popper, 1972; Boulding, 1968; Pondy and Mitroff, 1979).

This leads naturally to the application of systems theory to phenomena such as human communities and societies on the one hand, and to more abstract and specialized phenomena associated with them, such as language and communication systems or economic and political systems on the other, or for that matter, to culture and socially formed personality as systems (Parsons, 1951; Leach and Udy, 1968; Lazlo, 1972, 1986; Miller, 1978; Koestler, 1967; Flood, 1990). As part of the general application of systems theory to virtually every type of phenomenological target, there is the notion that there are orders or hierarchies of systems that can be traced along several dimensions and that "nature" is evolving in such a way as to develop higher order systems on the basis of lower order ones (Popper, 1972; Rappoport, 1968; Buckley, 1967). In sociology, as well as other fields, this sort of idea is as old as Spencer (1900) and Comte (1893) and stems on the one hand from Darwinism, and on the other from the physical determinism that arose out of Newtonian mechanics (Popper, 1965; Leach and Udy, 1968).

The direction along which this "evolutionary path" travels is from simplicity to complexity, from randomness to order, from passive to active, from insentient to sentient, and from nonintelligent to intelligent systems. This long list of target phenomena for systems analysis, the associated classification schemes, and the traditional ordering of systems in hierarchies of development leaves us with the question of what basic defining characteristics justify calling all of these cases systems.

Most of the literature on systems theory, it must be remembered, has been developed from the perspective of empiricism (von Bertalanffy, 1968). The implication is that the idea of systems corresponds to discovered characteristics that occur naturally in the real world. The agenda followed by much of the literature is therefore to codify, in terms of a conceptual apparatus, the organization of phenomena in relation to each other, as if they occur in nature. Systems are real-world entities. Systems theory is a reflection of our understanding of their inherent ordering and operational principles. The underlying belief is that many widely diverse phenomena display a certain form of organization. Because this is true, they can be approached from a common viewpoint toward "causation" or explanation. Systems theory from this perspective is no more or no less than an empirically based way of thinking about the problem of explanation that has been substituted for earlier, more simplistic views that sought to explain empirical phenomena in terms of such things as ultimate or efficient causes and in terms of purely physical determinism (Hempel, 1951; Lilienfeld, 1978).

Empiricist systems theory, although it was attacked by the more extreme neopositivists, rests on the assumption that every phenomenon that "exists" is part of a unified whole that can be viewed as having "levels" of phenomena. These levels begin with theoretically irreducible, ultramicrophenomena, even below the level of matter, and perhaps below the level of what we now understand as energy, and culminate in the complex ultramacrophenomenon seen as an evolving limitless universe. There seems also to be the assumption that every phenomenon has its place in a hierarchy of organization or structure, where it is based upon all of the lower levels beneath it, and fits into a place where it is affected by all of those levels above it (Boulding, 1968). The differences in observed characteristics among different phenomena are ultimately seen as an outcome of emergent properties stemming from the "level of organization" characteristic of that phenomenon as it exists in nature, this "organization" implying an ordering of more microphenomena layered one upon another.

Organization or structure, qualities that exist as natural characteristics of phenomena, and which are discoverable through observation, thus become the source of explanation for systems behavior because they refer to the way phenomena are constructed as empirical entities and therefore how they are naturally ordered. Organization or structure implies a pattern of relationships through which aspects of phenomena are produced through forces and elements that lie below their surface, where they interact at a lower level of scale that, itself, is also real and a part of the way nature organizes itself.

It appears that the irreducible aspect of the systems idea as it is applied to multiple phenomena at various levels of scale is that of interaction among the parts or elements comprising the microstructure of the phenomena (Marchal, 1975). The "behavior" of the phenomena under study is explained by (1) the properties of their inherent organization, and therefore the arrangement of the ingredients that go into their makeup in relation to each other and (2) by the nature of the interaction among these ingredients. The interaction can be conceptualized in terms of energy transfers, transfers of matter or substance, or even in terms of the transfer of information or meaning. No matter what the vehicle of interaction, the essential idea seems to be that the behavior and observable attributes of a macrophenomenon are explainable by the manner in which it is put together or organized, organization implying units and relationships at a minimum.

Matter or pseudomatter furnishes the source of units, parts, or elements out of which the organization is constructed, and energy or pseudoenergy furnishes the source of relationship because larger units in infinite regress are comprised of smaller units structured in terms of energy or pseudoenergy transfers of one sort or another. By pseudomatter, we mean things that perform the theoretical function of matter when dealing with a phenomenon that is nonphysical, for example, languages or social systems. In such cases, "particles" such as phonemes and morphemes perform similar theoretical roles to physical particles in physics, or in the case of sociology, roles and positions may perform this function. With respect to pseudoenergy, we have in mind symbolic transfers of meaning in a form called *information* that may be used as the vehicle of interaction in social systems occupying the theoretical place of energy or physical force with respect to physical phenomena.

It appears that the most general idea underpinning systems theory may be the idea that virtually every phenomenon in nature can be viewed in terms of a complex of parts or units that interact. Because interaction is conceptualized in terms of energy or pseudoenergy relationships, understanding, explanation, and prediction amounts to constructing the abstract rules that can "reproduce" the phenomena in the form of a theoretical model. Such a model is meant to correspond to nature and symbolically reproduce the properties of energy and the properties of the units upon or between which it operates as the elements of the model.

Multidimensional, interactive, relational causation operating among elements seems to be the key to regarding an objective phenomenon as a system if we include all of the cases listed earlier as systems. If, however, this is all there is to systems theory, we will be unable to distinguish the empiricist view of causation from what is called a system. Even from an empiricist perspective, the question arises, "Are there other criteria that must or should be added to make the term *systems* more useful as a concept that can be differentiated from the modern view of causal explanation?"

One way out of this dilemma is to take a constructivist rather than an empiricist perspective and say that any phenomenon thought of in terms of multidimensional, interactive, relational causation becomes a system when we cognitively construct it in these terms. Systems are therefore not types of objects having certain characteristics, but instead, there are in fact no objects that can be shown empirically to be systems but merely objects that are viewed from a systems perspective by use of a cognitive apparatus of a certain sort. We do not discover systems and the qualities that characterize them, but we impose the idea of system on an empirical world we construct by use of systems theory.

This conclusion still leaves us with the question of whether it is sensible or silly, enlightening or unenlightening, to apply systems theory to all phenomena that come under our scientific scrutiny. Surely, there must be some phenomenological targets that cannot be fruitfully approached from the perspective of systems theory without, at the same time, violating its defining principles.

From von Glasersfeld's (1987) perspective, certainly there must be some puzzles we wish to solve, some doors we wish to unlock, for which systems theory does not supply the key. Especially from the constructivist perspective, there remains the problem of understanding the limits of systems theory and, within it, understanding the problem of locating the boundaries of particular systems. Thus, even if we assume that everything in nature may be regarded as a system, a subsystem, or an irreducible part or element in either, there remains the question of how we conceptualize the boundaries implied by such terms as *system, subsystem,* and *part* or *element,* as opposed to *whole.*

For example, it is possible to think about societies in two quite different ways and still employ the notion of system. One is to think of a whole society as a system, and therefore of its parts as subsystems and sub-subsystems. In this case, the various subparts of society such as social groups, complex organizations, and communities are all regarded as elements enclosed within the boundaries of, and functioning or operating as parts of a single system. On the other hand, it is possible to view separate groups and complex organizations as systems that function or operate as bounded wholes, which are *not part* of a larger system called society. Instead they can be conceptualized as parts of a larger, more general ecological field in which their relationships to their environment are *not* mediated by an overarching system called society. Under this perspective, society is viewed as a "nonsystem." It is seen as a population of systems in interaction within a common field. If this is done, then it will become necessary eventually to ask, "Does this mean that under such a perspective societies are nonentities, and are regarded as fictitious or imaginary phenomena, or can this mean that there are objects that 'exist' that are not fruitfully conceptualized when they are thought of as systems?"

If this is a sensible question, then there is a need for additional criteria to use in determining when the systems perspective is useful as a tool for building structural models of social phenomena. We shall argue that there is, or should be, more to the systems perspective as a cognitive apparatus used to organize images of phenomenological targets than the view of multivariate, interactive causation associated with it. In particular, the ideas of structure or organization, and therefore of a certain type of cognitive ordering, must be added to the notion of interaction among elements or parts before we can separate one system from another and before we can cognitively separate systems as constructed objects from their environments.

4.4 Organization, Order, and System

We must think of systems as being "structured or organized" if we are to regard their properties or behavior as operating entities stemming from the organized interaction of their constituent elements. This, of course, implies that systems are conceptualized as assemblages comprised of units or parts that interact in a definite pattern. If this is true, then systems *cannot be thought of as being comprised of randomly behaving elements*, because the very idea of systems implies some form of organization and order. The ideas of chaos (Gleick, 1987) or randomness and the idea of systems are conceptually the antithesis of each other.

The concept *system* is akin to the concept *organization* because system implies structure, and as we have said, structure implies a bounded, relatively stable pattern of relationships (Ashby, 1956). It therefore follows that there can be no such thing as an unorganized or unstructured system comprised of randomly interacting but separate particles or units. If this is granted, then the question of what is or what is not to be modeled conceptually as a system becomes one that asks what kind of structure or organization is required to make the notion of system useful in modeling a phenomenological target in a manner that takes full advantage of the theoretical posture implicit in the cognitive apparatus that constructs systems as models for real phenomena. Will, for example, any type of structure, regardless of its characteristics, serve the purpose of separating systems conceptually and theoretically from nonsystems?

If we follow what was said about structure as a general idea in the preceding chapters, we will proceed from the assumption that all structures are described in terms of the parts, relationships, and boundaries associated with them and represent constructed images of patterns formed according to a set of cognitive rules. This being true, then the question concerning systems is whether there are any logical restrictions on the types of parts, relationships, and boundaries implicit in the idea of systems, because systems reasoning also includes a conception of "causal explanation." Classification schemes for systems such as that presented by Buckley (1967) have used differences in these elements of structure to define open and closed, as well as morphogenic and morphostatic systems. Even so, the characteristics of parts, relationships, and boundaries have not been explicitly used to define systems as opposed to nonsystems.

4.5 Systems Boundaries

A strategy for defining boundaries must be added to the notion of interactive causation, and the idea of structure viewed simply as a stable pattern of relationships among parts. All systems are thought of as having boundaries that set them off from objects or phenomena that are not included within the structure of the system itself. This implies that a system exists within an environment that is outside the system's boundaries, although it is by no means certain that the environment of a system is always significant in terms of the system's behavior, or that the environment consists of more than what could be termed the "nonsystem."

This ambivalence with respect to the importance of environment is apparent when the conceptualizations of closed and open systems are compared. Closed systems have traditionally been conceptualized as entities that are sealed off from their environment and affected by it only passively. As far as closed systems are concerned, knowledge of phenomena outside the boundaries of the system contribute nothing to understanding either the structure of the system or how that structure operates. In effect, the environment does not exist conceptually except insofar as it is necessary to define the boundaries of the system. It is for this reason that entropy is a necessary concept for use in dealing with closed systems. They are "self-contained," yet as systems, they operate. Because operation implies the use of energy, and the energy enclosed within their boundaries is always finite, closed systems are destined to run down. Entropy and closure are coemergent concepts in the case of systems reasoning.

It is important, however, to note that a distinction must be made between running down and falling apart. A wrist watch is a closed system that runs down as it uses up its energy supply, but it does not fall apart simultaneously with its running down. Instead, it becomes an inoperative system whose structure remains, at least temporarily, intact but no longer incorporates motion or behavior. Without the capacity to repair itself so as to maintain the boundary between it and its environment, such a system will also eventually "fall apart" and become indistinguishable from its environment. This falling apart also dissipates energy and represents "structural entropy" as opposed to "functional entropy." Structural entropy occurs when the elements of the system are so disaggregated that the relationships among them must be described as "random" or "chaotic," or indistinguishable from the environment.

An object with an inoperative structure, which lacks the energy to function, and is therefore still or "dead" in the strictest sense of the idea, cannot be regarded as a system. To be regarded as a system, an object must be operational, not merely capable of operating or the "dead" remains of a once functional apparatus. The dead body of an animal may retain the structure of a system but lacks the "animation" necessary to qualify as a system. In short, the idea of system includes both the notion of a nonentropoic structural pattern, and the idea of a nonentropotic functional apparatus. An object is to be regarded as a system only if it has the capacity to continue to operate as a bounded entity, distinct from an environment.

Some theorists prefer to think of a system as being open if it receives and employs any type of input from its environment. Others would prefer the view that a system is open only when its internal structure includes mechanisms that determine what inputs will enter the system and what environmental factors will be excluded. This is interpreted to mean that the system must include a means for determining which environmental inputs will be accepted, as well as when and in what quantity they will be permitted into the system. This latter point implies that in some crude sense, open systems must be capable of responding to and processing information as an automatic feature of their internal order (Maturana and Varela, 1980; Varela, 1979).

The point here is not so much to explore the ideas of open and closed systems as to point out that the idea of a boundary separating a system from its environment is essential if we are to apply the idea of system to an empirical phenomenon. This also means that even in the case of closed systems, the idea of the environment and therefore the nonsystem is essential.

What constitutes the nature of the boundary for a system is of course a matter of cognitive construction. Boundaries are cognitive elements necessary to the conceptualization of systems as a mental construction if, for no other reason than because the idea of system includes the idea of structure, and structure always includes the idea of boundary. Depending on the phenomenological target, different forms of boundaries may be conceptualized. Organisms regarded as systems may be thought of as being bounded in skins or membranes, whereas the boundaries of clocks may be thought of in terms of the physical limits of their metal parts. Even so, in the long run, the boundaries of a system can be said to be established by the conceptualization of the system's structure and how it operates to maintain the relationships among the system's parts as they operate or function in a pattern of motion, behavior, or "animation." Boundaries are reached conceptually when the established connections or relationships among the parts that operate together in forming the whole are thought of as ceasing and when elements are conceptually encountered that are thought of as varying either in an unrelated, or irrelevant, even random manner around a more stable and enduring set of operating relationships among elements.

In short, things outside the system are conceptualized as varying or changing while the internal operation of the system goes on without incorporating them as elements inside its relationship system. Boundaries are therefore a function or aspect of the conceptualization of a system's structure in terms of parts and relationships. A system cannot "have" structure without boundaries, and it cannot have boundaries without structure; the two ideas are inseparable. Furthermore, structural entropy amounts to the dissolution of the system's boundaries, and therefore its structure, while functional entropy amounts to the destruction of a system's operational process, so that it is forced into a static state, where its future leads inevitably to structural entropy.

It is apparent from this discussion that another idea included as a defining characteristic of a system is the idea that systems are always viewed as objects that operate, behave, or function. They are never static in the sense of being motionless, inert, dead, or in a state of functional entropy. In systems, things are happening; energy or pseudoenergy is being expended. The parts are interacting and impacting upon each other, even if the interaction is in the form of energy relations that are balanced or in equilibrium, as in the case of a building in which balanced forces and stresses preserve a pattern of stability in relation to an environment. The central cognitive value of the idea of system is its capacity as a cognitive apparatus to deal in a logical manner with dynamic structural relationships as they pertain to machines or organisms and social systems. This, of course, includes the notion that natural objects such as molecules or solar systems may be thought of as "natural machines."

It appears that the parts or elements of a system must not only be thought of as acting or operating in relation to each other, but also their operation must be systematic or structured and ordered, so that there is a pattern to the activity going on inside the system that is preserved by its structure. There are many implications of this idea that have important meaning for when we apply the concept *system* to an assemblage of elements perceived by an observer as coexisting in a common environment. The most important involve what we mean by the terms *part* and *relationship* when they are applied to the idea of system.

4.6   Parts and Relationships as Elements of Systems

The terms *part* and *relationship* are inseparable, because the idea of a part cannot be defined without reference to the relationship of the unit being discussed to other parts that form a bounded whole. After all, an object is only a "part" if it is taken as a unit that is embedded in a larger assemblage to which it is in some way attached. Conversely, *relationship* refers to the manner in which parts are joined or assembled and interact with each other in the mechanism of the whole and cannot be defined if there are not at least two separate parts.

The word *part* as used here implies a unit that is one among two or more that, taken in relationship to each other, form a bounded whole. Parts or units are themselves bounded and separable from each other but exist in the context of a larger structure from which they take on meaning as parts. The term *part* also implies some role or function, interpretable as "form of activity," or "pattern of operation" that characterizes the behavior of the part in relationship to other parts in forming the whole. It may be theoretically possible for all of the parts of a system to be identical in form and function, but in the case of most phenomena discussed as systems, the parts are thought of as being differentiated in terms of their defining characteristics, their behavior or operation, and their relationships to other parts and therefore their functional placement in the mechanism of the system.

To be a part of a system, a unit must be both separate from and related to other units enclosed within a boundary, and all of these parts must be capable of responding to or reacting to each other. Two objects that are merely located in the same space, that is, contained within conceptually arbitrary boundaries but not thought of as being attached to each other, or which are not conceived of as interacting in some specifiable fashion that is more than instantaneous, cannot be said to be "related" structurally. Without this insistence on structural relatedness, a conception of a system as an entity in which interaction occurs and emergent phenomena are explained in terms of structured interaction would not be sensible. This appears to mean that all the parts of a system must be related to each other in such a manner that their total pattern of interaction constitutes the behavior of the system as a whole. Elements that cannot interact with other parts of the system, or which can be removed or excluded without affecting the pattern of operation of the system, or which behave randomly with respect to units within the system, are regarded as being outside its boundaries.

All of this would appear to mean that it is only sensible to apply the concept *system* to phenomena that can be reasonably thought of as consisting of a bounded set of separate parts or units that are related to each other in such a manner as to produce a pattern of internal activity that is organized and therefore nonrandom and chaotic. This, of course, assumes that randomness and chaos are not systematic and that the concept structure or organization cannot be used to describe either. By definition, there are no random or chaotic structures or organizations, because randomness and chaos lie outside the cognitive apparatus called *structure*, and structure is the mental grounding against which the idea of system is constructed as a generalized cognitive tool. Complete randomness is nonorganization or nonstructure. On the basis of the assumption that systems are structured, it therefore follows that there can be no random or chaotic systems.

Recently, a literature has developed in physics and other fields of science on so-called chaos theory. This literature suggests not only that order grows out of chaos but also that what has often been taken as a chaotic phenomenon is actually ordered in some fashion not yet fully understood. As part of this thinking, mathematical models have been fashioned to demonstrate these points (Jantsch, 1980).

In using the term *chaos* in this book, we have reference to an abstract, cognitively constructed, theoretical concept, and we are not referring to any empirical reality. Our idea of chaos is constructed as the antithesis of order. It is the conceptual grounding against which the idea of order takes on its meaning. Under this meaning, if what is called chaos is said to contain order, the term *chaos* as well as the term *order* lose their meaning. To preserve the concepts *order* and *structure,* and to include chaos as a special type of order, would necessitate the invention of a new term and concept that takes on the meaning of "the opposite, or negation of order." Therefore, despite the current chaos literature, we will persist in using the term to refer to total disorder until some new term emerges from the debate over chaos to serve the cognitive function of grounding the idea of order.

This reasoning leads back to the case of hot gases enclosed within a boundary, for example, within a jar in a laboratory or within a soap bubble, both of which, along with clouds and water currents, are discussed as examples of "ordered chaos" in this literature (Gleick, 1987). Because the behavior of individual gas molecules in a cloud is more or less random, and because the individual molecules are not related to each other by a systematic structure but only by instantaneous encounters that themselves occur randomly, we cannot gain anything by thinking of a cloud of gas as a system apart from that which we would gain from the idea of multidimensional random interaction by itself. In short, the internal logic of the cognitive apparatus that is represented by the term *system* cannot supply anything that is useful in dealing with such a phenomenon.

Another important point is that the boundary of a gas cloud contained in a soap bubble or laboratory jar is not imposed by the structure of the relationship system that constitutes the cloud as a whole but, in the case of a laboratory jar, is imposed artificially and has nothing to do with the nature of the relationships among the molecules as molecules, except that it confines the space in which their behavior is random. Without the jar or the film of soap in a soap bubble, the relationships among the parts of the "cloud" would instantly dissolve the interaction among particles, which would move apart randomly and disintegrate into "structural entropy." What we are dealing with in this case is a nonsystem. We are dealing with chaos enclosed within a jar or, as will be claimed later, we are dealing with a complex set of relationships among the members of a population of separate systems forming a kind of ecological field.

It is important to realize that chaos and randomness *do not imply* a lack of interaction among separate systems, nor do they imply a lack of energy and energy transfers among systems, nor even a lack of *rules* or *laws* that may be used to deal with the consequences of chance encounters, once they have occurred, or even methods of calculating the probability of encounters and exchanges among separate systems. Chaos and randomness merely imply a lack of systematic structure in the sense of a persistent, repetitive pattern or structure as it pertains among the units or elements being considered as part of a larger set.

In an article dealing with systems, Karl Popper (1972) used the case of a soap bubble as an example of a system and as a means of introducing *chance* or *loose linkage* as a form of relationships among parts. We would argue, however, that the various gas molecules contained in a soap bubble, which themselves can be thought of individually as *molecular systems*, cannot be properly thought of as the parts of a larger system since, by definition, they behave independently of each other except insofar as they encounter and impact upon each other randomly. The idea of loose linkage, when carried to its logical extreme, amounts to the idea of nonlinkage. As an idea, it provides a means of preserving the empiricist program of conceptualizing all of reality as a gigantic multidimensional, multilevel system in which every phenomenon takes its place as part of an extremely complex *natural machine.*

When relationships among phenomena become indeterminate, and when it is necessary to think in terms of lower and lower probability interactions and exchanges, the idea of loose linkage and *contingent probabilistic interaction* preserves the preconception of the natural phenomenological world as a system.

But the cost is the loss of cognitive power for the idea of system. The cognitive apparatus that organizes the concept *system* is based on a deterministic or causal logic through which the behavior of the parts of a system are predictable from the mechanism contained within the structure of the system as an apparatus. If so-called probabilistic, random, contingent relationships are allowed to enter the idea of system, then the advantage of deterministic logic is undermined, and chaos is imported into systems, creating structural and operational entropy as a conceptual result. When a systems model is built by cognitive action, and when it seems necessary to conceptualize relationships among the parts of a system in terms of randomness or "loose linkage," this should be taken as a sign that we are attempting to force our conceptualization to accept a contradiction. It would be better to look conceptually for a way of modeling two or more systems that, as separate bounded entities, are nevertheless capable of interacting, if and when contingent factors produce encounters between and among them.

By such a method, it is possible to preserve and defend the cognitive value of the idea of systems, and at the same time, to begin to deal with an *ecology of systems.* This requires that we respect the idea of a boundary as an integral part of the cognitive apparatus that constructs system as an artificial image of phenomenological targets. *The fact that probability theory, the theory of thermodynamics, or even "quantum" theory may be employed to "explain" essentially random phenomena does not automatically mean that such phenomena must be thought of as members of the class of relationships to which the term* system *is usefully applied.*

Popper uses the cases of a soap bubble and a swarm of gnats to justify the contention that systems may be comprised of parts that interact more or less randomly and nevertheless exist in the same world with other "systems" such as clocks, which are highly ordered and structured, and therefore deterministic. This is necessary to set up his argument that there is freedom associated with human reason, which in effect makes the interaction among people, or more properly the behavior of people, less than determined or, perhaps more appropriately, less than systematic.

At the same time, his argument justifies scientists who often deal with clocklike mechanisms using a deterministic logic, but who wish also to think of themselves as a free and creative force in nature, to do so, since it appears by Popper's argument that the same natural world can contain "randomly organized systems" (clouds and social systems) and highly deterministic systems (clocks, atoms, social systems, etc.). In presenting this view, however, Popper is arguing about physical determinism and attempting to resolve the ideological consequences of the conflict between the probabilistic nature of quantum theory and the deterministic nature of Newtonian mechanics or Einsteinian relativity. To make intellectual peace between these points of view and to avoid thinking of the world of man as being at least, in part, deterministic, he proposes that we can have a sort of "probabilistic determinism." This form of explanation grows out of a view that there is a hierarchy of systems that has arisen out of physical evolution, such that higher order systems, once they have formed out of chance physical encounters and organized themselves level by level into systems, naturally incorporate more and more determinism and less and less chance. Even so, this view maintains that since the universe has not "fully evolved," there is always left over at least a modicum, if not a plethora, of random indeterminacy in the relationship among deterministic systems, and this randomness and indeterminacy is a form of linkage that preserves the unity of the entire natural world.

The implication is that the world of human social behavior, because it is still in the process of evolving, is characterized by a goodly measure of randomness or "freedom from determination." This manner of thinking is reinforced by the unrelated notion that ultimately intelligence or the mind, and by inference, social systems, incorporate a high degree of indeterminism and therefore randomness, because the evolution of symbolic systems that has taken place is not yet complete. The lack of a completely evolved deterministic world of social behavior leaves human actors free from "physical determinism." It is as if freedom, in the human sense of freedom of will, is simultaneously an emergent property of symbolic systems and of the incomplete evolution of human societies toward structural determinism and of the survival of chaos within human affairs, which is a consequence of this incomplete evolution.

At the same time that this argument is made in favor of more randomness and indeterminism, which is taken as the same thing as freedom and independence of behavior, Popper is forced also to recognize that there is some order in human affairs, and thus a degree of nonrandomness. To him, this is made possible by the *looseness of the linkage* both between the parts of behavior systems and the behavioral level of systematic structure, the biological level, and the purely physical level between which emergent properties, themselves arising out of structures originally springing from randomness, insulate one level of reality from the levels below it.

All of this amounts to saying that Popper would allow a certain degree of randomness in the relationships among the parts of a system, but never complete and total randomness or chaos. This is why it is necessary for him to introduce the film of soap in the bubble, which is maintained as a bubble by the pressure of the gases inside in relation to those outside and by molecular relationships among soapy water molecules. It is also why the ability of gnats to sense their separation from the swarm is posited as a means of keeping the swarm intact as an entity. There is at least the order imposed by boundaries implicit here, and also there are the thermodynamic consequences of random, instantaneous encounters among the separate units that constitute the contents of a soap bubble at any given instant.

Popper's discussion, in all fairness, was not intended to define what a system is, but to discuss the basis for a belief in the freedom of human action, especially human thought. He uses the term *system* as if it is understood as a primitive concept. There is therefore no explicit statement of what a nonsystem would be like, but it appears clear that his only criterion for establishing a system is one of interactive causation within a boundary, even if the interaction is more or less random and unstructured.

In this book, as shall be seen later when we are dealing with ecological fields, we do not mean to imply that probabilistic reasoning cannot produce useful information, nor that such information cannot be called "knowledge." Instead, we are sticking to a constructivist agenda that claims that all "knowledge" is relative to the conceptual–theoretical apparatus that constructed it.

Systems reasoning as a cognitive apparatus leads to a particular type of information, and that type of information, is based on a *deterministic logic* in which the structure of the *systemic machine* becomes the basis of explanation and understanding. In contrast, *ecological reasoning*, that is, reasoning about the interaction among systems, which employs a probabilistic logic, yields a different kind of information. This type of information is also relative to the cognitive machine that produced it. It, too, can be quite useful. Its basis, however, is entirely different from systemic reasoning.

This book will argue that there is a fundamental difference between objects comprised of (1) an assemblage of independent elements whose behavior in relationship to one another can have no deterministic causal explanation because there is a total lack of structure connecting them and constraining their interaction so that only *probabilistic statements concerning the behavior of component elements in a random assemblage can ever be made*, and (2) an assemblage of elements that are related to each other structurally in such a way that the structure itself imposes order on their behavior, making deterministic or causal statements possible. The first is defined as a nonsystem and the second as a system.

Neither open nor closed systems can be cognitively modeled using randomness or chaos as a structural pattern. All systems are thought of as being structured and as containing interconnected parts that respond to each other according to the mechanism of the whole. Closed systems, in the traditional sense of closure, cannot relate actively either to each other or to their external, nonsystem environment. They operate passively according to a fixed pattern that does not vary, except for the effects of entropy. The parts of both "open" and "closed" systems are nevertheless constrained by their placement in the whole, and their behavior is *never random*. This point of view leads to the conclusion that Popper's "clouds" are not examples of loosely linked closed systems but, instead, they are examples of nonsystems or, more properly, of the interaction among systems in an ecological field. His "clocks," on the other hand, may legitimately be regarded as closed systems.

Besides all of this, there is, as Popper rightly points out, a difference between physical determinism and social determinism. No sociologist would ever claim that social behavior, and therefore social systems, are explainable on the basis of a reductionism to physical causation, or for that matter, biological causation. For sociologists, randomness, chance, causation, determinism, and indeterminism in social affairs can only be defined and approached theoretically in terms appropriate to social phenomena. Physical or biological conceptions are not only inappropriate but downright misleading when applied in this context. However, it must be recognized that the inability to explain complex human behavior systems using physical determinism does not "prove" that social determination is impossible or that a strict application of the idea of system in the sense of a bounded deterministic mechanism is inappropriate for social behavior. To utilize the concept *system* at the social level, and to realize its cognitive benefits, it is necessary for social scientists to construct models in which the mechanisms are social rather than physical in nature. Popper's defense of human freedom on the basis of the lack of physical determinism at the social level is simply inappropriate and therefore unconvincing and epistemologically deceptive, a boost to the human ego, but nevertheless a self-deception made necessary by ideological biases and by an empiricist program that has set out to discover the systematic nature of all "natural phenomena."

4.7 The Utility of Systems Theory

The value of systems theory must, like all theories, rest upon the clarity and internal consistency of its conceptual scheme, the internal logic that assembles that scheme into a theoretical (cognitive) apparatus, and the usefulness of the apparatus in solving problems. It is the theoretical argument concerning causal explanation implicit in systems theory, operating as a paradigm for normal research, that promises to make it a powerful tool when it is applied to the problem of understanding social phenomena. To preserve the usefulness of systems theory, however, we must be aware of our assumptions and of the deductions made on the basis of them. It is actually the logical argument concerning causal explanation embedded in systems theory that leads its users to propose characteristic systematic hypotheses. Such hypotheses relate the principles of ordering present in systems theory to social phenomena and, by so doing, lead social systems theorists to view social phenomena as being understandable or predictable on the basis of a form of causal reasoning based on structuralism. What makes systems theory worthwhile to social scientists is the fact that once we assume a social object such as a group or an organization is a system, and cognitively model it as such, we are entitled by the logic of systems theory to deduce or predict certain types of regularities.

If, however, we use systems theory to cover both randomness and order by weakening the assumptions and rules of our cognitive apparatus, it will make it impossible for us to predict or explain anything using systems theory as a cognitive tool. By including both randomness and order, the cognitive apparatus called *system* will incorporate a logical contradiction. This contradiction arises out of the fundamental definitions of order and chaos and the implications of each for how we are entitled to think about prediction and explanation. After all, chaos in the cognitive sense is the very essence of the unpredictable and the inexplicable. It is the negation of regularity, structure, and order, and there is nothing to explain because order itself is inevitably the ultimate object of explanation. Because there is an absence of regularity and of stability in chaos, there can be no generalizations except one that asserts its total absence.

If, however, we reserve the notion of *system* for application only to phenomena that are regarded as displaying a dynamic operating "structural order," the propositions of systems theory can be purged of logical inconsistencies and applied straightforwardly to phenomena we choose to think of as possessing the requisite defining characteristics. This will allow us to reserve the use of the idea of "true randomness" for application to the relationships *between and among systems, but not to those within them.* By true randomness, we mean apparent chance variability that is not a result of (1) measurement error, (2) ignorance of and failure to specify the variables or elements of a system properly and completely, or (3) the disturbance of the phenomena being studied by the random and uncontrolled effects of the observational technology employed to gather data.

It is almost irresistible to fall into the language of empiricism in a discussion of systems theory because this is the tradition out of which it developed.

However, it must be made clear that this book regards the idea of systems to be a mentally constructed apparatus that imposes an ordering on empirical observations from within itself. It furnishes the mind with a particular kind of tool that produces a particular type of mental representation of reality. It forces the empirical world to conform to its own logic. But in so doing, through cognitive action, it provides the means by which predictions can be made concerning phenomena made real by the theory itself. These predictions may prove useful if they solve problems of human adaptation. It must be remembered that a theory does not have to be true in the sense of absolute empirical truth to be useful. Neither does it have to be the only useful key to adaptation.

4.8   Summary: The Essential Chareacteristics of a System

In systems, exact particular units or parts occupy a place in an overall structure and operate as parts in the sense of part discussed earlier. In communities, or soap bubbles, or ecological fields, the units making up the overall assemblage move from one place in the population to another, interact randomly, and prosper or perish, depending on their individual histories within an environmental context. Their behavior is not constrained by their placement in the overall mechanism of a systemic structure upon which they are dependent for their operation and survival as parts. They are independent of each other in the sense that they may survive as systems separately from any other particular external unit, even though they depend in the categorical sense on an environment that contains a population of such systems. In the case of living organisms in an ecological field, each individual is dependent on the population of the community for its survival as a system, but this is not the same as being totally dependent on particular individual members of that population in the sense that a particular lion's liver is dependent on that particular lion's heart and lungs for survival. Any gazelle will do for dinner, preferably the one that is by chance closest and easier to catch.

There is a fundamental difference between entities thought of as being comprised of parts that interact randomly and move from one location to another in a collection of units and other entities in which the parts interact in a repetitive, persistent pattern, where the parts continue to occupy the same location in the structure or are replaced by similar parts at that same location. It is not just a matter of open and closed systems. After all, clocks and soap bubbles (clouds) are both described by Popper as closed systems. But we are saying here that clocks are systems and clouds are not, because we can easily cognitively model clocks so that we see them as having the qualities necessary for us to use the logic of systems theory as a basis for explanation. This means that they can be thought of as having a structure that, rather than being random, is patterned. This permits us to develop theories as to how one part constrains the behavior of another and also how the overall structure constrains the interaction among any subset of parts. In contrast, clouds are not easily modeled in terms of these qualities. In their case, we are forced by our own logic to fall back on conceptions of randomness and probability if we hope even to predict the behavior of the whole assemblage, much less explain the behavior of its individual unit in a causal fashion.

4.9 The Use of Systems Theory in This Book

In this book we will consider the proposition that some human societies should be thought of as being more like clocks and others more like clouds. Or to put it in the language used earlier, that some societies are more like ecological communities or ecological fields and others more like systems. Taking this view will require the creation of a language through which social structure can be more precisely specified because whether we regard a society as a system or a community will depend upon the way we model the structure of the exact society under study.

The reason for this long discussion of systems is to provide the groundwork for considering the possibility that some societies may appropriately be thought of as systems and others may not. In this discussion, we will first consider the question of what kind of systems theory is most appropriate for dealing with social behavior. The next step will be to define ecological fields and then to start at the microlevel, creating structural models for small social units such as groups and, as we do so, to consider the appropriateness of thinking of them as systems. Step-by-step we will then consider larger and more complex social units such as organizations and communities. Finally, we will talk about whole societies and intersocietal networks, thus following the atomistic program discussed earlier in building a cognitive apparatus that generates structural models.

At each level of scale, we will consider the question of the usefulness of systems theory as a guide to modeling the social unit under consideration. For example, we will ask ourselves, "Is it useful to regard organizations, communities, and societies as systems, or do we need a new way of thinking about these larger, more complex entities?" The answer to these questions will prove complex since, in the long run, this book will conclude that it depends upon the state of integration and interdependency that we conceptualize as prevailing within such entities and between them and their environments. Some types of social units may be fruitfully regarded as systems and others may not.

All of this means that we will regard the use of systems theory in a hypothetical sense. Whether we think of a group, organization, or society as a system depends upon our ability to demonstrate through cognitive action that it can be modeled in terms of the qualities necessary to make systems reasoning fruitful.

The intention is to make the use of systems theory dependent on empirical observation that is guided and controlled by a clear, cognitive apparatus rather than upon theoretical fiat that rests upon the beginning empiricist assumption that everything in nature is a part of one gigantic, multilayered system that exists to be discovered and described by an empirical methodology.

We will proceed therefore by asking whether a given type of object can be usefully regarded as a system, and basing our argument on accessible, cognitively constructed empirical evidence. Since there are no data used in this book in the sense of deliberately collected observations, this enterprise will proceed in the form of a "thought experiment" in which information available to us all on the basis of everyday experience will be set against the theoretical apparatus as it is constructed and used to illustrate the basis of conclusions drawn concerning the systematic nature of various types of social units.

Because we will consider the possibility of modeling societies by thinking of them as interacting populations of autonomous systems, we will be forced to define a new conceptual foundation for thinking about societies. This new approach will introduce an ecological perspective into the discussion. Therefore, in one sense, it can be said that this book is aimed toward creating a new form of social ecology. This ecology will be a theoretical one and not a form of environmental sociology. Its objective will be to form a cognitive apparatus that incorporates systems theory within a framework that also has a place for dealing effectively with the relationships among systems in an ecological field.

5

Self-Referential Behavior Systems

5.1 *Introduction*

According to the foregoing discussion, the concept *system* yields a cognitively constructed image of a bounded object that consists of an organized set of active parts that function together according to a "built-in" pattern of operation. Each system, from this perspective, is set apart from other objects by a boundary that is conceptualized as enclosing its parts. This allows an observer to think of a system's parts as functioning together according to the total system's internal mechanism.

Two types of systems have usually been identified and defined on the basis of the way their relationship to their environment is conceptualized. It has been traditional to refer to these two theoretical types as open and closed systems. This classification, however, is misleading because it refers not so much to how systems themselves are conceptualized as it does to how systems are thought of as behaving with respect to events and conditions occurring outside their own boundaries. Because this seems to be true, the distinction between open and closed systems actually ignores the basic theoretical ingredients of the cognitive apparatus that defines the concept *system* as a type of cognitively constructed object of observation and focuses on a conceptualization of the relationships between such objects and phenomena thought of as being outside their boundaries.

Actually, in the most important theoretical sense, *all* systems must be thought of as being "closed," because all are conceptualized as operating according to their own internal mechanisms. This statement means that no matter how we think of a system's relationship to its environment, and no matter how we think of how its internal functioning changes in response to environmental influences, in order to remain consistent with the core meaning of the concept, we must think of a system's relationship to its environment and its response to external events as being controlled by its own internal organization (Maturana and Varela, 1987; Piaget, 1967; Luhmann, 1986). Some systems, of course, may be thought of as responding to their environments by making changes in their internal functioning, operation, or

behavior, and others may not. To think of them as responding to environmental conditions, however, we must also say that the mechanisms that govern perception of the environment and responses to it are themselves part of
the system's internal order and therefore inside its boundaries.

The environment does not select or determine the response of a system
to external events, but the system itself governs its own behavior. The environment simply presents the system with the possibility of using alternative
response patterns that are themselves generated within the system by its
own internal ordering mechanism. Although the environment may be thought
of by an observer as triggering a change in functioning within the system,
the mechanisms that allow the system to "perceive" its environment, as well
as to choose a potential response patterns to environmental events or conditions, are, by definition, generated inside the system itself.

Conceptually, it is necessary to assume that the environment of a system
only exists for the system, insofar as the system itself contains the internal
mechanisms necessary to "sense" or "monitor" external phenomena and to
convert such "sensory data" into information interpretable by the system itself. Thus, a system capable of responding to an environment by its own internal action "creates" the environment it responds to by its own internal
organization and action. By creating its own environment, we mean that a
system's sensory apparatus, its information-processing capacity, and its cognitive contents define the environment for it. Anything outside the system
that cannot be sensed and converted into information usable by the system
itself is irrelevant to the system's behavior. As far as the functioning of the
system is concerned, it does not exist. The fact that some condition or phenomenon may exist perceptually for an observer of a system is of no importance as far as explaining the system's behavior is concerned unless the
system itself is able to "perceive" it. The observer must be thought of as a
separate system from the system observed, and as being governed by an entirely independent sensory capacity and cognitive apparatus. An observer
with a complex cognitive apparatus of his or her own may perceive many
phenomena that seem to surround a system and form its environment, but
only those phenomena "sensed" by the system itself have the capacity to
trigger changes in system behavior *as a system*. Some phenomena, unsensed
by the system, may be viewed by an observer as affecting the system, and
thereby affecting the system's behavior, but they must be thought of as producing an impact upon the system and not a response by it (Varela, 1979).

For the typical home heating system, the environment consists entirely
of the temperature of the air near its thermostat. It has the capacity to "sense"
room temperature, and it has mechanisms built into its structure that respond to changes that either elevate the temperature above its thermostatic
setting or lower it. How it responds to changes in temperature, however, is
built into the system itself and has nothing to do with phenomena outside its

boundaries. Any other environmental condition that may "exist" for an observer through the operation of the observer's perceptual and cognitive apparatus does not produce a change in the behavior of the system that can be defined as an *active response* on the part of the system itself.

At this point, it is important to recognize the difference between "responding to" and "being affected by" the environment. Systems may be thought of as being passively affected by phenomena outside their boundaries, and this may be recognized by an observer who is sensitized by a cognitive apparatus to seeing such effects. For example, if the house containing a heating system is destroyed by a tornado, the heating system, like all other parts of the house, will be perceived by an observer as being affected. Its thermostat may be broken, its burners and blowers destroyed, and it will cease to function as a system.

But home heating systems themselves do not "recognize" tornadoes, or any of their physical consequences except changes in temperature. (Actually, only temperature changes that exceed the tolerance limits of the thermostatic setting are recognizable to it.) Because the system does not "recognize these effects," it does not respond actively to them, even though to an observer it is affected by them.

The theoretical significance of the previous discussion is profound. The most important conclusion that follows is that *all systems* must be thought of as being *self-contained* or *self-governed*. This also means that in order to take advantage of the logic contained within the cognitive apparatus that defines the notion "system," we must assume that all systems are *"automatons"*; that is, we must assume that their behavior is *self-referential* (Maturana and Varela, 1987). If we do not take this view, we violate the assumption that the behavior of the parts of a system is a consequence of the nature of these parts and of their placement in relation to each other in the structure of the whole. When this assumption is violated, the utility of the cognitive apparatus called *system* is sacrificed and the concept *system* and the concept *environment* can no longer be distinguished because to think of a system as being open to control by environmental forces essentially means that it is seen as being unbounded, except by a boundary that encloses some larger system.

We are not aided by a compromise that claims that systems may be "partially open," at the same time being "mostly closed," if to be partially open means that a system is "controlled" by phenomena outside itself. As we have seen, when we try to specify the mechanisms that control the system's behavior, we are forced to think of them as being internal to the system's structure.

If an object of conceptualization must be thought of as being controlled from outside itself, it must be assumed that the object cannot be thought of as a system but instead, at best, must be conceptualized as being a *part of a larger system*.

For a system to be controlled from outside itself, it would be necessary for an external observer, another system, to be completely familiar with that system's internal order and also possess a means of controlling the information it receives from its environment. But we have said earlier that no observer can ever be sure that the model he or she generates of an object in the environment truly reflects an empirical reality. This would seem to limit the possibility of external control to those cases in which the observer actually physically "manufactured" the system being observed and did so in such a way as to produce a product (system) that corresponds in detail to the model used by the observer as a "blueprint" for construction. Even so, we will argue that in such a case, where the observer controls the system he or she observes, we are dealing with a larger system made of two interrelated subsystems, the observer and his creation. Furthermore, when an observer is in the process of "controlling" a system in his or her environment, we can easily argue that the observer's controlling behavior is controlled by the system being controlled, because his or her behavior will have to fit the mechanism of that system, and it is the nature of this mechanism that ultimately determines the observer's controlling actions.

This discussion, however, does not necessarily lead to the conclusion that everything may be seen as being part of a single, universal system, because, as shall be recalled, the idea of boundary, and therefore of an environment outside the boundary, is an essential ingredient of the idea of system. If, by infinite regress, we come to the conclusion that everything is part of a single, universal system, we lose the capacity to define boundaries and, with it, the capacity to define the systemic mechanism.

5.2   Active and Passive Systems

To deal with these considerations, it is best to abandon the classification "open and closed systems" and to substitute for it the classification "active and passive systems." Active systems should be conceptualized as having the "built-in" capacity to change their behavior in response to self-generated "perceptions" of "self-defined" environments, whereas passive systems lack this capacity.

For sociologists interested in social structure, the concept *active system* is an appropriate tool for dealing with social phenomena such as individual actors, groups, and organizations, because they are usually interested in explaining the behavior of these systems in relationship to objects in their environments. Active systems, by definition, have the characteristics that have been referred to earlier as being attributes of social behavior. Such objects (active systems such as actors, groups, and organizations) seem to be best understood as having the capacity to change behavior according to perceived environmental conditions. The behavioral "episodes" produced by a given system on different occasions constitute the repertoire of possible responses generated by that system as it responds to a self-defined environment.

In this book, social systems, which are themselves a theoretically constructed type of system, will be treated as bounded, self-referential systems. Such systems will be conceptualized so as to think of them as adapting to their self-constructed environments in synchronic time by generating from within themselves a response pattern that fits a set of self-defined environmental conditions or events according to their own internally defined definitions of "fitting." In the sense of fitting used by von Glasersfeld (1987), such response patterns seem *to the system itself* to "unlock" a door between the system and its environment, allowing the system to solve an immediate adaptation problem. But it must always be remembered that the problem and its so-called solution are both defined by the system itself through its own internal organization, and they are not defined for it from outside, especially by an observer.

5.3   Morphogenic and Morphostatic Systems

A further distinction must be made with respect to systems before it is feasible to apply the cognitive apparatus that constitutes the idea of systems to social phenomena. This distinction brings diachronic time into the picture by differentiating between morphogenic and morphostatic systems (Buckley, 1967). There are two senses in which we can think of systems as "adapting" to their self-defined environments. The first is that just discussed. Systems may respond to events outside themselves by "fitting" their behavior into an immediately occurring set of events or environmental conditions by selecting, from within themselves, a response which they, themselves, define as fitting into a self-defined set of circumstances. This is *synchronic* adaptation. An automobile manufacturer increases the production of a particular model car in response to market demand, which it monitors through its own internal accounting system. A runner's heartbeat and respiratory rate increase in response to the stress of exercise, which is monitored through neurological and chemical mechanisms built into the organism. An automobile driver pushes on the brake pedal in response to a red light, interpreted by internally defined meanings of environmental events. Through such selective responses, these systems adapt to conditions external to themselves which they, themselves, define on the basis of built-in structural mechanisms as significant to their survival or functioning as systems.

The question arises, however, "How did these built-in features of the system arise to begin with?" In short, "What was the genesis of the system's structure?" Such questions necessitate the formulation of a view of diachronic systemic adaptation. For *systems theory* to be of maximum utility, especially in sociology, it is essential that it contain an explicit conceptualization of how some types of systems adapt by altering their own structure, and thereby their own repertoire of internally controlled behavior patterns and their own definitions of their environments.

The need is for an "evolutionary" view of systems if we are to apply the cognitive apparatus of systems theory to certain types of phenomena. For example, by use of a cognitive apparatus that carefully controls the way we conceptualize the structure of human groups and organizations, we can generate structural models of the same objects of observation over time. Even though these models are generated by use of a cognitive apparatus that operates to create and interpret data and are therefore relativistic images of a constructed reality, models constructed at different time intervals using the same cognitive apparatus to gather data on the same object can be compared. In so doing, as observers, we may find that structural changes have occurred over a time period. For example, we discover that a given organization has "evolved" a more complex, differentiated structure, containing new parts and new relationship patterns. The question is, "How can we employ systems theory to help us understand how these changes were generated?"

There is a very serious problem presented by such a case because we have assumed that a system's behavior is in large part determined by its structure. From this assumption, it would appear that systems cannot change themselves, because they are "self-contained" and therefore closed. If they define their own environment, and if they contain their own repertoire of responses, then how can innovations be produced from within the system itself? Because they define their own environment, how can changes be produced by the relationship of a system to its self-defined environment? Obviously, from the earlier discussion we can say that a system can be passively changed by an external impact. But such impacts, by definition, can only disrupt or destroy the system. Unless they can produce some alteration in the system's mechanism that allows the system, even though changed, to persist as a system, we cannot deal with morphogenesis.

In the long run, the only possible way out of this paradox is to introduce into the idea of system the possibility of internal parts or internal mechanisms that are themselves such that they are capable of converting externally produced effects into new information and then of accumulating information and converting it into self-alteration. Thus, there is the possibility that some systems are so constructed that they are capable of *learning* and therefore evolving on the basis of their interaction with their environment.

Such a solution would remain consistent with the assumption of boundedness, self-referentiality, and closure because the mechanisms that produce change or systemic learning are "built into" the system rather than existing in its environment. Even so, to be workable, such an approach would necessarily demand a broader evolutionary or diachronic perspective. We would have to say that some systems are capable, because of their internal organization, of "learning" from self-defined, self-controlled experience, but at the same time, we would have to admit the idea that such "learning from experience" might just as easily produce changes that result in a system failing to adapt and therefore falling into functional and structural entropy as succeeding and continuing to function and to preserve structural integrity.

At this point, it is important to remind ourselves that we are engaged in the cognitive enterprise of constructing a theoretical apparatus that yields a useful image of social phenomena lest we fall into the empiricist trap of attempting to give a true and exact account of an empirical world given by nature. To offer a useful cognitive system for sociology does not demand an answer to such questions as, "How did the human sensory apparatus come into being?" "How did human intelligence develop out of evolutionary changes of a biological sort, or for that matter, how did life itself develop out of inanimate objects?"

All of these questions might seem vital to an empiricist as a foundation for the assumption that human systems are capable of accumulating information and of processing such information in a manner that amounts to learning but that is registered or recorded as change in the structure or organization of a system. From a constructivist perspective, however, all that is needed for the purposes at hand is a clear statement of how the phenomena of learning and information processing fits into the cognitive apparatus we employ to deal with morphogenesis.

It might be comforting, however, to state that the term *learning* in the case of systems can be thought of as the capacity to convert external impacts into internal alterations in structure, in such a way as to allow the system to persist or reproduce itself. From this perspective, even certain physical, not to mention biological systems, may be thought of as being capable of morphogenic adaptation or change (see Maturana and Varela 1987; Varela, 1979).

5.4   Self-Referential Sociocultural Systems

This book is based on the assumption that social systems may be thought of as morphogenic, self-referential systems. Before entering into a more detailed discussion of morphogenesis, it will be useful to offer examples of self-referential social systems, so that the idea of self-referentiality can be established before considerations of morphogenesis further complicate the picture. To make these examples meaningful, it will be helpful to introduce them by reviewing some of the ideas that have already been discussed with respect to human behavior as a phenomenological target and to relate these ideas to the concept *culture*.

5.4.1   Culture and Behavior

The cognitive system for modeling social structure being developed in this book rests on the assumption that social systems are "behavior systems." They are systems comprised of complex webs of social relationships that express themselves in the actions and interactions of human actors. Such behavior systems, in the generic sense, are the mechanisms used by the human species to adapt to its environment and to draw the resources necessary to sustain the life of the individual from it so as to ensure the continuation of a human population. It is assumed that, like all animals, humans sustain life by performing behavior toward an environment that supplies the necessary resources to satisfy their various needs and wants. This adaptive behavior in the case of the human species, in contrast to nonsocial species, is usually performed in social units whereby a population of individuals acting in relation to each other, and jointly in relation to an environment, establish stable, normalized patterns of interaction that allow the population to survive and reproduce itself.

Such "normalized" or "institutionalized" behavior patterns express themselves as repeated episodes of action and interaction. These patterned episodes are observable in the sense that, with the proper cognitive apparatus as a guide to observation, an observer can witness behaviors performed by real actors in particular real environments in relationship to other actors as they work upon or react to each other and to their physical and social surroundings. Furthermore, persistent observation conducted according to a set of cognitive rules demonstrates that similar sets of actions occur over and over again, both temporally and spatially within the same population. That is to say, the same sets of actions may be repeated time after time by the same group of actors, or the same actions may be replicated during a given time period by many different groups of actors that are parts of the same population. These qualities of repetitiveness and replication are indicators of stability in the behavior systems employed by a population of actors and point to the necessity to conceptualize the underlying mechanisms that make it possible for patterns to persist and repeat or replicate themselves over time and through space as recurring episodes. To "see pattern" in human action, however, it is necessary for the observer to be guided by a cognitive apparatus that defines *pattern* and provides a linguistic code by which to record and interpret it. To "see" the mechanism that preserves a pattern the observer must introduce new concepts into the conceptual apparatus. This is the point at which the familiar concept *culture* enters the picture.

5.4.2   Behavior Patterns as a Concept

The words *behavior pattern* imply two things. First, they imply that there are several smaller, identifiable behavioral elements that occur as a set or a sequence and together make up the whole behavior pattern. Second, the idea of pattern implies the notion of repetitiveness and replication; that is, it implies that the same set or sequence of actions is performed on successive occasions in separate behavioral episodes, or that it is observed to be characteristic of several separate sets of actors who are part of the same population.

The idea that a behavior pattern consists of a set, sequence, or configuration of behavioral elements immediately suggests the notion of structure, especially when it is coupled with the notion of repetitiveness. In this case, repetitiveness becomes another word for regularity, stability, and order. In the case of behavior patterns, a configuration or set of behaviors persists through time and is spread through space in the sense that it repeats or reproduces itself over and over again in different episodes of human action.

Unlike architectural elements that persist continuously through time in a stable relationship to one another to form a building, however, behavioral patterns express themselves intermittently as separate episodes divided by time intervals during which they do not occur as overt observable actions. Although the pattern of behavior persists through time, it expresses itself as overt action only intermittently.

This fact presents a conceptual problem to the social sciences that is central to the study of animal, and especially human, social behavior systems. In the case of a building, the structure, in a sense, is continuously present in the actual, observable, transpiring arrangement of elements that constitutes the building. True enough, structure can only be approached intellectually by "stripping away" surface appearances and answering the question, "What underlying configuration of elements and forces maintains the stable pattern we see as the building?" This underlying structure, however, is not conceptualized as if it "flashes on and off," so that at one moment the building is there to be observed and at the next moment it is not, and then it reappears, and so on. When the cognitive apparatus that defines structure is applied to most physical phenomena, the object to which it is applied is thought of as being nonepisodic.

In the case of human social systems, however, the behavior patterns that constitute the phenomenological target of structural analysis are thought of as being intermittent. They do flash on and off. Work groups assemble, perform patterned behavior, and then disperse, only to reassemble and repeat similar actions at a later time. Families as behavior systems convene and disperse. Indeed, all of social life is episodic, yet for the most part, repetitive, patterned, and persistent. This means that we must be conceptually prepared to take into account the fact that the whole behavior system comprising any social unit is never active in the form of actually transpiring behavior at any given moment. In fact, it takes a relatively large number of episodes for all of the patterned repetitive behavior patterns that make up the total repertoire of behavior patterns employed by any given population or subpopulation to occur as actual behavior.

The fact that patterns do recur, however, points inevitably to the need to posit a "storage mechanism" through which the stable and repetitive pattern is preserved during periods of inactivity. Because we have said that repetition and stability may be defined as the same thing, and because we have said that structure is a stable arrangement of interrelated elements, then the storage mechanism must be regarded as the repository of social structure. That is to say, social structure must be sought, not in the overt behavior we see performed by human actors in relationship to each other in "real life" situations, but in the system that stores, generates, and regenerates the patterns we observe when we apply an organized cognitive strategy to the interpretation of sense impressions.

5.4.3   Culture as the Storage Mechanism for Social Structure

Social scientists have, from the beginning, recognized that culture constitutes the storage mechanism for human behavior patterns. Nevertheless, there is considerable variability in what is meant by *culture* and even more in how different social scientists think about culture in relationship to social structure and also of the relationship of social structure to social behavior. It will therefore be necessary to examine what we mean when we say that culture stores human behavior patterns and therefore may be regarded as the proper place to look when we seek to describe the social structure of a society.

It may be useful to look very briefly at all animal behavior systems as a background against which to discuss culture because it can be said, with a good deal of justification, that culture can be thought of as the human substitute for instinct. All animals perform patterned, repetitive behavior. This means that the episodic character of human behavior applies universally in the animal kingdom, at least in the case of vertebrates. The problem of how patterned behavior is stored in such a way that it is available for repetition therefore applies across the board.

In the case of many animals, the problem of explaining behavior patterns has been solved by positing the existence of biologically inherited behavior patterns called *instincts*, or of an inherited capacity to use a process called *imprinting* in connection with genetically transmitted patterns. In these cases, the storage mechanisms for behavior patterns are thought of as being built into the organism as genetic programs for action. However, in the case of some species, particularly human beings, where behavior patterns vary widely among separate populations that have the same genetic inheritance and among individuals in the same population, it is assumed that the storage mechanism depends almost entirely upon learning and not on genetic transmission. The conceptual apparatus used to represent such cases includes the assumption that the organism is provided with a nervous system and the mental capacity to accept, interpret, and store information that permits it to develop patterns of behavior. Such patterns become repetitive when they provide a relatively successful and stable relationship between the animal and its environment. In the case of both instincts and learned behavior patterns, we can think of the pattern in storage as a set of rules that governs the way the animal perceives the environment and responds to it. The individual animal is thought of as a "biological system" that controls its relationship to its environment by changing its behavior in response to perceived environmental events and conditions. Thus, a human actor is defined as a self-referential system containing the sets of rules that govern its own behavior.

It is important at this point to realize that the behavior performed by an animal in response to an instinct is not the same thing as the instinct itself (Bateson, 1972a). When an opossum feigns death in response to a perceived threat, the behavior of death feigning is not the instinct itself but a product of that instinctive pattern in interaction with an environmental event. The instinct itself is the stored set of biologically inherited rules that generate this behavior. It can be regarded as a genetically encoded information system that is organized into a set of rules that produce specific aspects of the animal's overt behavior under specific conditions. If we understand the structure of the set of rules and how this structure interacts with self-generated information concerning the environment, we will understand how the regularity in the pattern of behavior, displayed as repetitive episodes, comes about and is maintained. To do so, of course, we must use a cognitive system to generate a mental image of the behavior and of the rules that govern it, as well as a means of telling when and how the rules were biologically inherited.

In the case of learned behavior patterns that take the form of culture, the problem is the same. Structure (or pattern) must be sought in the rules for behavior that are stored in the form of learned information or culture, and not in the actual behavior that is given form and stability by the rules. Social structure, in other words, is the structure found in the system of rules that constitutes the culture of a population of human actors. *Social structure is cultural structure,* or, more properly perhaps, structure stored in the form of culture. The set of rules in storage in the form of cultural "norms" in the case of social behavior systems consists of rules that not only establish the types of acts to be performed and their arrangement into sets and sequences, but also the rules that govern who will perform these actions in relationship to which other actors and which social and nonsocial objects. They establish an organized social network of human actors and distribute patterns of behavior among the structural locations occupied by actors in that network in a way that supports the joint adaptation of the members of a human population to each other and to their self-defined environment.

The question immediately arises, "Is it useful to regard the total culture of a society as a system, and if so, what kind of system model should we employ to represent it?" Also there is the question, "Are the structure of the cultural system and the structure of the social system to be regarded as the same phenomenon or as different phenomena?" These are complex questions in need of considerable exploration.

5.4.4   Culture as an Informational System or Set of Systems

First, let us settle on the view that culture consists entirely of information. This means that we will think of it as consisting of mentally stored "ideas" that have been obtained through the experience of a population of organisms in an environment, or perhaps through the inner workings of the information-storage and processing mechanisms of the organisms constituting that population. Culture is therefore defined as an entirely "ideational," "mental," or cognitive phenomenon. It can be thought of as sets of learned rules made on the basis of the interplay of organisms in an environment over time that constitute mental generalizations stored in the form of cognitive systems. These rules that, for convenience, can be called cultural norms, operate as guidelines for the organization of the population into groups and organizations (i.e., social systems) and for the behavior of the organisms that constitute a population. They function to render the relationship between the population of organisms employing the rules and their environment predictable in terms of their survival as living and, therefore, acting biological systems. Because it provides a set of cultural rules for organizing the population into social units and distributes behavior patterns among such units according to a division of labor, culture functions to structure social behavior. Culture, in other words, contains the cognitive plan for social structure and, by so doing, renders the relationships among individual members of a population predictable.

As a totality, the culture of a society can be thought of as the complete collection of sets of stored information (cognitive systems) contained within the memories of an organized population of human beings. This large, complex collection of "rules of behavior" may be organized into subsets and subsubsets that apply to specific types of individuals who occupy positions in relationship to each other in the structure of society.

Culture constitutes a whole in much the same sense that a language such as English constitutes a totality. It can be considered a totality, even though no single individual knows every word in the vocabulary, and even though many do not know all of the rules contained within its grammar. As a totality, the various elements constitute a distinct and separate pattern from other languages. In the same sense, "a culture" as a collective whole represents a complex, organized pattern of interrelated sets of behavioral rules that are organized into cognitive systems or into sets of separate cognitive systems.

Before it is possible to make this statement more explicit, it will be necessary to introduce a number of other ideas. In particular, it will be necessary to define what we mean by *cultural structure*. It is this structure that justifies thinking about culture as a "collective" entity comprised of information stored as cognitive systems in individual minds, but at the same time articulated according to a set of rules into a complex whole. To accomplish this, it will prove helpful to introduce some new ideas concerning how a culture is constructed out of related sets of behavioral rules.

Let us assume that the total culture of a society consists of a set of what Pelanda (1989) calls "self-referential cultural systems." Such systems, like all parts of culture, are comprised of information and constitute "systems" of rules. Each system provides a set of rules for adapting to a particular environmental problem or to a particular problem related to the organization of a human population. Each therefore represents a "solution" to a set of adaptation problems faced by a human population in organizing itself and adapting to a set of environmental conditions.

It will be helpful to illustrate the idea of a self-referential sociocultural system by using games as examples. A given game (or sport) such as American football can be seen as a complex behavior pattern that exists as a persistent pattern that expresses itself over and over in particular contests (episodes) played on particular fields by particular teams. The pattern itself is stored as a set of interconnected rules and as the information necessary to employ them. These rules define the game in the sense that they specify how the game is to be played and how the various actions required to play it are organized into sets and sequences of actions performed by actors assigned to various positions in the structure of football teams. The rules, in other words, specify what constitutes the game as a performance. They make it possible for actors to learn how to play the game, or for that matter, allow spectators who also know the rules to interpret the behavior being performed on the playing field.

Each different game (sport), for example, baseball, basketball, cricket, soccer, ice hockey, tennis, bowling, and so forth, represents a separate type of self-referential system whose internal rules define separate and recognizably distinct behavioral performances. Each self-referential system is "stored" as a bounded set of rules in which each element is defined in terms of the others in such a way that they are cross-referenced with each other. It is in the sense that all of the rules of football are cross-referenced and interrelated to form a bounded organized whole that is totally separate from the rules of other games that we are justified in calling separate games (sports) "self-referential systems."

They are self-referential in the sense that each rule in the total set takes on its meaning and significance from its placement in the total set and can only be regarded as meaningful insofar as it relates to that set as a bounded whole. This is like saying the individual rules of football are only meaningful in the context of the total "system of rules." Furthermore, football rules have no place or meaning in the set of rules constituting baseball and make no sense if inserted into that context.

These rules define the meaning of the environment in which the game is played, the football field and stadium, and of such things as the lines drawn on the playing field and the meaning attributed to them. They also cover the types of uniforms worn by players and officials, the type of ball used, and other material aspects of the game.

Self-referential cultural systems generate bounded, closed, self-referential social behavior systems in the sense that they organize and constrain the behavior of the actors executing the rules in such a way that, in the case of a game such as football, each player's behavior is tied to the behavior of the other players in a pattern of interdependent coaction defined from within the set of rules itself. These rules also define the relationship of players to the physical environment in which the game is played (the playing field) and to the material objects used in playing the game. This means that when executed as behavior, football rules give coherence, structure, or organization to a self-referential, social behavior system and to its relationship to its environment.

More will be made of this example later, but the point to be made at present is that the total culture of society may be thought of, figuratively at least, as a complex set of separate games. There is the "game of family life." There is the game of "church" or "grocery store" or "public school" or "automobile factory," and so forth. Each is established and maintained by a set of "self-referential rules" that constitute a bounded cognitive system that defines how to carry out a set of behaviors that are related to the solution of some adaptive behavioral problem. Each separate, self-referential system has its own internal order, and each has boundaries that separate it from other "games" that have other rules and other meanings.

Self-referential social systems, like all systems, are bounded, but unlike other systems, they are comprised of a "set of cultural rules" that have developed out of the interaction of a population of human beings in an environment over an interval of time. Social systems are "stored" as cognitive systems comprised of cultural rules that a population has learned by its experience in interacting with its environment as it has attempted to solve problems related to its survival or to the satisfaction of its cognitively generated needs and aspirations.

The rules themselves evolve out of the interaction between members of the population and their environments in such a way as to provide a "solution," however tentative and precarious, to an adaptation problem. They continue to evolve and change until they provide a set of interrelated, cross-referenced rules that supply a predictable solution to the problem they emerged from as members of the population interacted with their environment. Once the set of rules provides a workable solution to this problem, assuming the environment to be stable, the self-referential system will itself stabilize and for all practical purposes become a fixed system, in the sense that it no longer is subject to change until it is disrupted by a change in the conditions to which it has become adapted.

5.4.5 Morphogenic, Self-Referential Behavior Systems

The culturally transmitted sets of rules that govern various specialized aspects of social behavior form self-referential cognitive systems in the sense that the rules they contain, themselves, define what constitutes the information obtained from the environment that is relevant to dealing with a particular behavioral problem. Such systems also contain the rules that define how information is to be interpreted, as well as how the information will be processed mentally and responded to in terms of overt or covert behavior. Each internal part of each culturally encoded system of rules makes sense only in terms of other parts of the same system of rules. Furthermore, each system of rules constituting a bounded, self-referential cognitive system evolves separately from other such systems of rules in their environment in such a way as to move toward closure as a bounded, self-contained system. Closure is reached when the set of rules constituting a self-referential system is able to predict its relationship to its environment (perceived as symbolically interpreted information) more or less perfectly.

5.4.6 Closure and Self-Referential Systems

At this point, it is necessary to reconsider the idea of closure as it applies to systems. Previously, I have argued that all systems, in one sense, are closed because they contain within themselves the mechanisms that define their own environments and their responses to them. At the same time, however, we have recognized that it is necessary to formulate a conception of a type of system that is capable of morphogenesis if we are ever to come to grips with the problem of how systems are formed to begin with and how they change. To justify such a conception, it is necessary to conceptualize how a system that governs its own environmental relationships from within itself can be capable of changing itself internally. To solve this problem, it is necessary to introduce a revision of the idea of closure that takes into account a self governed, internally controlled process by which certain types of systems have the built-in capacity to adapt structurally as well as behaviorally.

Earlier, the point was made that some systems contain within themselves the capacity to take in "sense impressions," "stimuli," and "impulses" from their environment. Such inputs, although generated by the system itself through use of its sensory apparatus and through its own internal organization that assigns meaning to sense data, also reflect (in a cognitively constructed fashion) selected aspects of the environment from which sense impressions are taken. In this very special sense, some systems are "open" to the input of information originating as observed environmental phenomena.

In order to understand how morphogenesis is possible, it is necessary at the very least to think of closed systems as being able to recognize that the behavior they produce sometimes fails to produce the expected results. In order to deal with morphogenesis, it is necessary to think of systems that are able to generate information on the basis of stimuli taken in from their environment as being able to interpret that information in terms of its meaning for the success or failure of the system to achieve its ends through the behavior it performs. On this basis, we can posit the possibility of information that supplies positive and negative feedback to the system, even though we assume that feedback is controlled from within the system itself.

It is possible, on the basis of this conception of information input, to think of a type of system that is capable of storing and accumulating information generated by its own apparatus as it interacts with a self-defined environment. To do so, it is necessary to posit the existence of a mechanism or set of mechanisms that are internal to the structure of the system and function to generate meaning from within itself and supply the system with (1) feedback from its own behavior and (2) a memory through which to store information. If we can add to the idea of an internal memory the idea that some systems may contain a mechanism for processing such accumulated information in such a way as to "learn" from it by drawing conclusions or making generalizations, certain forms of structural change may be explained from within the logic of systems theory. Change in structure in this case will be seen as the equivalent of learning from experience and storing the results of learning in the form of structural change.

To take advantage of this approach in the case of human behavior systems, it is necessary to assume that the human organism at birth constitutes a biological system already equipped by its genetic structure to learn from interaction with its environment, even though, at first, that environment is perceived as chaotic and unstructured (Piaget, 1967; Maturana and Varela, 1987). The necessity to assume this genetically transmitted capacity to learn is forced on us by the paradox that occurs if we assume that organisms must learn to learn. Obviously, without the prior capacity to learn, there would be no basis for learning to learn. This paradox is comparable to thinking of a computer as a machine that must "teach itself" to accept information without having inside itself a machine language and an operating system capable of organizing its operation in such a way as to "teach itself."

To solve this paradox in the case of human behavior systems, it is necessary to posit the existence of a biologically based "set of rules" that operate as automatic biological mechanisms governing the operation of the nervous system, the brain, and the sensory organs in such a way as to result in (1) the generation of information, (2) the accumulation or storage of information once generated, and (3) the transformation of information into rules that affect the behavior of the organism as it relates to the source of information in its environment.

5.5 The Biological Program for Morphogenesis

It is not the objective of this book to solve the extremely important problem of creating a fully developed cognitive image of this set of inborn rules. This, of course, is the task of cognitive psychology. Nevertheless, it will be helpful to speculate concerning the probable nature of these rules, which themselves constitute a cognitively constructed image of the biological mechanisms embedded in the organic structure of learning organisms. Such speculation is intended to illustrate the possibility that we can usefully think of the human organism as having, over time, evolved as a biosystem in such a way as to incorporate within itself the mechanisms that make morphogenesis at the social level possible. By engaging in this speculation, we are not positing an empirical reality but creating a cognitively constructed basis for forming mental images of morphogenic systems called *learning organisms*.

To begin with, it is useful to assume that at birth the human infant encounters an environment through the senses that is chaotic as far as the mental apparatus of the infant is concerned. The problem is to think of a set of rules that can be thought of as constructing an environment that has meaning to the organism and can be seen as governing the relationship of the organism to its environment in terms of its own mental operation and its own behavior. Such mechanisms would have the effect of constructing artificial "cultural images" of an environment that is structured rather than chaotic, because order is "forced" upon it by the evolving cognitive capacity of the organism. By engaging in this speculative endeavor, we are attempting to hint at the kind of biological program an observer might posit in order to perceive the learning process.

In *The Structure of Social Systems*, the suggestion was made that the mind operates according to a "primitive program" that contains a set of primitive, inborn rules that govern information processing and ultimately produce normative (cultural) patterns that control perception, cognition, and overt action (Bates and Harvey, 1975, pp. 235–262). It will be helpful here to consider a modified version of these rules as an example of the type of "precognitive" mechanisms that produce learning and therefore the formation and accumulation of culture, as well as the socialization of the organism into preexisting cultural patterns, and also allow morphogenesis as the organism continues to learn. As stated in this present book, these rules represent speculative assumptions based on consideration of what must be true if we assume that human organisms use their behavior as a means of adapting to their self-constructed environment.

As a basis for considering these rules, it is useful to assume that the organism at birth does not contain information concerning the environment outside itself. Furthermore, it is necessary to assume that, at first, sensory impressions have no "meaning" in the cognitive sense of meaning and therefore do not, in themselves, constitute information. Information, in contrast to sensory impressions, amounts to the encoded meaning attached to sensory impressions. On this basis, we must conclude that the newborn organism must build up meaning out of interaction between its environment and its mental apparatus using sensory data that is, at first, meaningless to the organism. The building up of the capacity to assign meaning and, therefore, to convert sensory impressions into information, which is accumulated *as information*, must be thought of as stemming from a "primitive program for learning" and from the biologically transmitted rules that constitute that program. An organism could not be taught to attribute meaning unless it were prepared in advance to be taught, and to be taught means to be able to attribute meaning. An organism unable to attribute meaning would be unable to learn and, therefore, to be taught.

"Meaning" as a concept is itself a rather complex cognitive system consisting of many interrelated conceptual elements. Because meaning as a concept is so closely related to the concept *information*, and because both are critical to understanding morphogenesis, it is important for us to specify what we mean by meaning and also how we are going to "explain" its origin within the cognitive apparatus we are developing to deal with morphogenesis. We are attempting to build a self-contained, bounded cognitive apparatus that constructs images of the structure of social objects that contain within themselves the capacity to evolve structurally or to transform themselves from within. It is essential that this theoretical apparatus include a closed, self-contained system for "explaining itself." The task of revealing the basis of meaning, however, must be postponed until we have considered all of the necessary rules for "information" processing needed to form the foundation for explaining how meaning develops and how, on the basis of it, morphogenesis takes place. This is necessary because the explanation itself is embedded as an integral part of the rules and cannot be presented until the complete system of rules is known. Tentatively the rules for learning that constitute an inborn program may be stated as follows:

1. The Temporal Rule   The primitive (unsocialized) mental apparatus of a learning organism must contain a "rule" that allows the organism to record sequences of events occurring in its environment, or between its own behavior and its environment, if it is to be able to learn and reproduce sequences of action. Let us assume a unit of information (or sensory data) called a "bit."

Let us further use the letters of the alphabet to represent particular bits of information. Using these terms, the temporal rule could be stated as follows:

When bits of information (i.e., sensory impressions) are received in a temporal sequence (permutation) such as A, B, C, store them in your memory in such a way that this order is preserved and can be recalled.

Such a rule is necessary if the organism is to be able to adapt its behavior to transpiring events and conditions occurring in its environment, or between itself and its environment. For example, a human actor would be unable to learn behavioral processes or to relate to sequences of events without the capacity to record information in temporal order. Language itself, which incorporates word order and, for that matter, words that themselves consist of phonemes occurring in a permutation, could not be recalled or reproduced. Without such a rule, the environment, as well as the behavior of the organism in relation to it, would appear chaotic with respect to time, and each temporal sequence would appear to the observing organism as a unique, one-time occurrence. On this basis, we must assume that organisms capable of learning must be biologically programmed to record sensory impressions in temporal sequences. Because behavior itself is sequential and patterned, this capacity is vital to the construction of learned programs for behavior.

2. The Configuration or Spatial Rule The unsocialized mind must also contain the inborn capacity to record and remember spatial patterns; otherwise, it would be impossible for the organism to recognize phenomena in its environment vital to its survival. This spatial rule could be renamed the "combination rule" in contrast to the "permutation rule" that relates to time. It requires the mental apparatus of the organism to record configurations of sensory impressions in such a way as to reproduce a mental image of an object of observation. It might also be called the Gestalt rule, because it relates to a recording of a configuration of sensory impressions made up of many discrete bits of information. It could be stated as follows:

When several bits of information such as A, B, C are received simultaneously, store them together in such a way as to record their spatial relationship to each other as a combination, or spatial set.

Such a rule is required if the organism is to learn how to recognize objects in its environment that produce complex sensory inputs into the organism. A human actor could not learn to recognize its mother's face, or its own, for that matter, unless this capacity were built into its mental apparatus. The learning of language would also be impossible unless sounds and objects occurring together could be recorded and remembered. Similarly, the ability to read the written word requires it to be associated with a sound and/or a sensory impression.

3. The Comparison or Association Rule   Learning requires the organism to accumulate information that eventually allows it to predict its environment by ordering its own image of that environment. By ordering it, we mean that the organism must "see" pattern and regularity in it if it is to be able to shape its own behavior to fit its environment. If the environment remains chaotic as far as the organism's perception of it is concerned, there is no way for the organism to develop behavior patterns that are themselves nonchaotic. Without the capacity to predict the consequences of its own behavior, or of environmental events for its own well-being, the probability of survival of the organism is virtually zero. The inborn program for mental development contained within the organism must therefore contain some mechanism that allows the mind to organize itself, but to do so in such a way that it creates stable images of its environment that allow it to adapt its behavior in such a way as to fit within the survival limits imposed by external conditions. On this basis, we are warranted in assuming a rule that results in the accumulation of information in such a way that it allows prediction of the environment. Because prediction is useful only when it is coupled with the capacity to recognize a set of environmental conditions or events, the comparison rule rests on the ability to match or compare already recorded information stored in the memory with incoming information freshly arising in the environment. This rule could be stated as follows:

> *When permutations or combinations of information are received, search the memory for similar, already recorded permutations or combinations and store the new information in association with the old, so that they are recorded together.*

This rule says, in effect, that when phenomena are encountered that are alike in sensory characteristics to objects or events previously encountered, they should be placed in the memory so that they are thought of as being similar occurrences of the same phenomenon. This rule is necessary if for no other reason than to allow the organism to recognize objects encountered in the past. It results in the building of a kind of mentally constructed classification scheme for phenomena and makes it possible, among other things, to develop a linguistic code, because such codes use symbols to represent categories of objects and events. It also seems apparent that learning rests on repetition, and for repetition to produce cognitive results, it requires a comparison rule through which repetitions are recognized as similar phenomena. Actually, we could say that the permutation and combination rules furnish the capacity of the brain to build structural models of phenomena in the environment, thereby constructing artificial mental images of things outside the mind while the third, or comparison, rule furnishes the capacity to classify and thereby recognize external phenomena and represent them by artificial symbols. In the long run, the mind is built up around the two mental strategies of structural modeling and classification, which, operating together, organize it (see Bates and Peacock 1989; Watson, Bates, Garbin, and Peacock, 1989).

4. *The Attention Rule*   We must assume that the organism never takes in all sensory impressions available from the environment in which it operates as a living organism. Instead, the "mind" and sensory apparatus of the organism operate to screen sensory impressions, admitting only a small proportion of all the "data" available in the so-called "real world." The question is, "How can we conceptualize a rule or set of rules that would function as a mechanism to select those stimuli to be admitted to the part of the brain or 'mind,' where they can be transformed into information and recorded as memory, assuming also the existence of those rules already stated earlier?" If we reason that the behavior of any animal organism is the means by which the organism obtains the inputs it needs to survive and function from its environment, and also is the means by which it adapts itself to environmental conditions that affect its survival and its "quality of life," then we may ask, "How must the process of perception be directed so as to be compatible with this perspective?"

It seems reasonable to assume that perception must be guided in such a way as to meet the needs of the organism for resources originating in the environment, and also to meet its need for protection from life-threatening or other aversive environmental consequences. On this basis, we may assume that there is a biologically built-in "rule" that leads the organism to focus its senses upon stimuli in its environment that are (1) related to its motivational state and its need for environmental resources, (2) to the completion of the behavioral episode the organism is engaged in relative to obtaining inputs from environment, and (3) to the protection of the organism from environmental events or conditions that can harm the organism or cause pain, or which threaten its life or its access to the resources it is seeking in its environment. In other words, for a species to survive and reproduce itself, its members must be programmed in such a way as to focus their sensory organs on environmental phenomena that are significant to their survival and well-being or enable them to achieve goals that satisfy their organically derived motivations. In the case of human beings, we must think of the mind, which is built-up out of experience as intervening in this process of perception by assigning meaning to sensory experience. In this case, *meaning* refers to the significance assigned to sensory impressions in terms of their relationship to the survival and well-being of the organism.

Of course, we must assume that, at first, the organism will have no basis for screening sensory impressions according to an attention rule, unless there are already biologically transmitted patterns of perception (instincts) present in the organism at birth, as seems to be the case in some species. Nevertheless, even in organisms that lack instincts, if the organism contains the temporal, spatial, and comparison rules discussed earlier, and also contains biological mechanisms that produce internal sensations such as hunger and pain, as well as pleasurable sensations produced by the senses in interaction with the environment, and these sensations are placed in the context of sensory impression of environmental events and conditions, such sensations will come to be associated with the motivational state of the organism and with the sensations of pain and pleasure produced by contact with the environment. By the process of repetition, and according to the temporal, spatial, and comparison rules, the mind will build up a learned or "cultural" basis for selecting sensory impressions that are significant in terms of the satisfaction of its needs and wants, and with the avoidance of negative consequences. By this process, the organism will learn to attribute "meaning" to selected aspects of its environment and to attend to those sensory impressions that have meaning in terms of its own survival and well-being, and eventually to its culturally derived value system.

Culturally acquired values and motives that are normally acquired through the capacity to use symbols and to communicate through language furnish a socially rather than biologically acquired basis for attributing meaning. Both language, and the cultural content obtained through it, are built up on the basis of a primitive program that, at first, builds up a system of meaning based on inherited organic characteristics. The acquisition of culture and, along with it, language, is based on the fact that in the case of human infants, the environment is controlled by other human beings who have already built up a cultural system in their minds. The newborn infant is presented with temporal sequences and spatial sets of stimuli repeatedly by others who control the flow of stimulation and thereby the potential for acquiring information. Not only is this true, but other human beings also "force" the infant to pay attention to stimuli they define as significant by using sanctions that work upon the senses of the infant in such a way as to reward and punish or to overcome the threshold of perceptual attention. Also, it must be recognized that the social world of the newborn human being is structured by social and cultural systems that, because they are structured, present the human actor with sensory stimuli that are ordered and repetitive.

Even so, the success of the adult world or of "society" in socializing the newborn human organism depends upon the existence within the organism of the biological mechanisms that make socialization not only possible but, in a sense, also inevitable in "normal" individuals. It is these mechanisms I am speculating about in this discussion. My argument is that the mechanisms that produce learning, and therefore the accumulation of information in the mind of the individual, may be characterized as a set of rules constituting an inborn program having the consequence of building up the "mind" of the organism, the mind being defined as the learned content of the organ called the "brain." This content is organized according to the spatial, temporal, and comparison rules once it enters the mental apparatus from the senses but is selected according to a fourth rule called the attention rule, which could be stated as follows:

Pay attention to objects or events in your environment that have meaning in terms of the goals you are seeking or are related to the behavior you are engaged in, or threaten your survival or well-being, or are likely to cause pain or discomfort. Associate these objects or events in your memory with the consequences they have had in terms of the above previous types of meaning according to the temporal, spatial, and comparison rules.

According to this reasoning, organisms will learn to attribute meaning to environmental events by processes akin to operant conditioning, as described by B. F. Skinner (1971). But once language is acquired and the rudiments of culture have been built upon the basis of such a process, artificial values and norms will divert the process of learning away from simple operant conditioning into more cognitively dominated processes that will now control the attention rule and provide an artificial basis for perceiving sequences of events, configurations of stimuli, and bases for comparison. Culture and its associated symbol systems will, in other words, supply a secondary basis for assigning meaning and for furnishing motivation, as well as for defining the environment in terms of resources and threatening conditions and events. Even so, we must assume that beneath culture lies an organic substratum of biological predisposition, through which the operation of the mind (defined as an acquired set of cognitive systems) is governed by a set of biologically based mechanisms that can conceivably be thought of as a "program for learning."

5. The Probability or Expectation Rule For the previous rules to provide the organism with an adaptive mechanism that shapes behavior in a direction favorable to the survival of the species, it is necessary to add a rule that allows the organism to predict its environment's response to its own behavior and also to predict the consequences of environmental events for the organism. Information can only be useful to the survival of the organism if it can be used as a basis for selecting behavior that results in the satisfaction of its needs or in protecting it from the harmful consequences of its own behavior, or from threatening environmental conditions. The organism must be able to anticipate the consequences of its own action. It must also be able to predict the consequence of environmental events (such as the behavior of other organisms) for its own survival and well-being. To do this, it must not only build up a record of experience that reproduces sequences and configurations and allows it to recognize previously encountered phenomena by use of comparison, but also it must use this stored information to predict its relationship to the world it perceives by controlling its own behavior. To take this need into account, we must therefore introduce a fifth rule, which can be called the probability rule. It can be stated as follows:

> *When you store a sequence such as the permutation A, B, C, on a tempo-*
> *ral set such as the combination X, Y, Z, and according to the comparison*
> *rule you again encounter the first member of the permutation (e.g., A) or*
> *any member of the combination XYZ (e.g., X), then expect the other mem-*
> *bers of the permutation (B,C) to follow, or other members of the combi-*
> *nation (YZ) also to be present. Each time a permutation or combination*
> *is encountered and is added to the memory according to the comparison*
> *rule, raise your estimation of the probability (expectation) that other*
> *members of the permutation or combination will also be encountered.*

The result of following such a rule is that the repetition of perceptual episodes builds up a basis for the organism predicting its environment. If information on the behavior of the organism itself is placed as one member of a permutation or combination, then the organism will come to predict the consequences of its own behavior for events it perceives as taking place in its self-defined environment. By this inborn rule, it will build up a set of "artificial" rules that are themselves based on the organism's self-perceived relationship to its environment as it has experienced itself and its environment through time. These rules become a secondary basis for experiencing the environment and the self in relation to it. In fact, they become "cultural systems" built up in the form of artificial norms, values, and beliefs that form the set of cognitive systems that supply the architecture of the mind (for a discussion of that architecture, see *The Structure of Social Systems*, Chapter 16, Bates and Harvey, 1975).

The mind, in contrast to the brain, is artificial in the sense that it is formed from experience that itself is constructed out of previous experience as information accumulates in the organism and is organized at first according to a primitive organic program, and later by the "artifacts of the mind" this experience in interaction with the primitive organic program constructs. The mind is a self-generating, self-constructing system or set of systems that is based on the organic capacity and predisposition of the organism to construct an information file organized according to a biologically based plan, and through which it constructs and continually reconstructs itself and its environment.

6. *The Feedback Rule*   Although it is implicit in the other five rules, it might be wise to insert an additional feedback rule into the set of biologically programmed instructions that produce adaptive behavior and morphogenic change in self-referential behavior systems just so we will recognize it. Such a rule instructs the system to pay attention to the effects of its own behavior on its environment. When the system acts, it observes the effects of its action

in terms of how it furthers its progress toward its self-defined objective, or on how it produces a response requiring further action. Positive feedback reinforces the stored pattern that produced the behavior, and negative feedback undermines it. Irrelevant environmental responses observed by the system have a neutral effect. Exploratory behavior having an unexpected positive effect becomes the foundation for forming a new pattern or changing an old pattern. Negative feedback tends to extinguish the exploratory behavior that produced it.

The feedback rule working along and in cross-reference with the other five rules would produce morphogenic change in the system's cognitive apparatus and yield behavior change on future occasions. This rule could be stated as follows:

Pay attention to the effects of your behavior on your environment and the response of other systems in the environment to your behavior by placing your action in the temporal and spatial sequences and sets produced by rules one and two.

Thus the morphogenesis of mind, that is, the origin, growth, and transformation of the mind is a process contained within a bounded, self-referential system called the organism. In the previous discussion, we have constructed an exploratory conception of a bounded, closed system called the organism that creates within itself an artificial system called the "mind." This mental "system" changes from within itself, according to its own internal structure, but does so by using sensory impressions of a self-defined environment as the resource it employs in its own structural evolution.

This discussion is not intended to provide an empirically based account of the organism as a closed system. It does not claim to correspond to an independent reality called "the human organism" that has been discovered or even glimpsed vaguely through empirical observation. Instead, it constructs a cognitive apparatus consisting of a set of assumptions and of conclusions drawn from those assumptions that provides a theoretical basis for creating and organizing information in a manner that is consistent with the assumptions and corollaries of the theory of closed self-referential systems. It is meant to provide a defense for the notion that a closed, self-referential system can also be thought of as being capable of "self-structuring" or of self-generated "structural adaptation."

It becomes necessary now to move beyond the individual level of analysis to the level of the social system. We must now formulate a basis for defending the notion that such social units as groups and organizations, which consist of the behavior of more than a single individual, and therefore involve the operation of more than a single mind, can be thought of in such a way as to conform to the various assumptions and corollaries embedded in the idea of "self-referential systems."

6

Self-Referential Social Systems

6.1   Introduction

Self-referential sociocultural systems that are dependent on learning for supplying the rules that pattern behavior consist entirely of symbolically encoded information. They are therefore intangible and ideational in character. They are systems in the sense that they are bounded, internally structured entities, comprised of elements that are cross-referenced, interconnected, and internally integrated in such a way that one element gives meaning to the others. When the cultural system is activated, the various elements comprising the structure of the system interact in the sense that they are expressed in the cobehavior of the actors practicing the rules. They are systems in the same sense that a language such as English may be regarded as a system. A language contains a vocabulary in which words take on meaning only in relation to each other and in terms of their use according to a set of phonetic, syntactical, and grammatical rules. This vocabulary and its associated rules of grammar and syntax, in interaction with their environment, generates the enormous variety of meaningful utterances observed as actual overt speech. Because linguistic rules form an integrated set of bounded, interrelated rules, a language, itself, may be regarded as a self-referential system.

All self-referential sociocultural systems can be thought of as consisting of an organized set of cognitive rules that define an organized repertoire of meaningful actions and a kind of "behavioral grammar" for assembling this repertoire into meaningful behavioral episodes involving the coaction of human actors. One type of cognitive rule defines what constitutes relevant information as far as the functioning of the system is concerned. Another type governs how the information will be interpreted and processed in order to select an appropriate response. They also contain a set of response patterns that are interpretable as a set of rules for the response of the organism or the group to its environment, stored as cognitive systems or as parts of such systems. Finally, they contain rules that assign roles to individual actors and prescribe who shall be the persons toward whom roles will be performed. Such sociocultural systems, as cognitive systems, store potential behavioral responses as a repertoire, or figuratively, a "vocabulary" of action, and organize them by using rules of social organization into a kind of behavioral "grammar." This organization makes sequences or sets of actions meaningful to the person performing them, as well as to the other actors involved in a behavioral episode. As already noted, a game such as American football can be modeled as a self-referential social system. From this point of view, football, as a game, consists of a set of rules that determine what constitutes football as an athletic event. These rules define the kinds of information that are relevant to players of the game, as well as the way to interpret the information and respond to it in actually playing the game. More to the point of a discussion of social systems, the rules define what positions and roles players occupy and play and how they are expected to relate to each other in terms of a joint performance. These rules are totally self-referential in that they make no sense except in terms of each other and in terms of the total set of rules that define the game. They have evolved separately as a system of rules from the rules of other games such as basketball and baseball. The rules of these other games are irrelevant as far as football is concerned.

What the rules do furnish is a cognitive apparatus that makes it possible for the players to understand and predict the behavior of various players and their relationship to the environment in which the game is played, within limits that make the whole performance meaningful or comprehensible and therefore interpretable and under the control of the participating actors. When we say the rules render things predictable and under control, we do not mean this in a machinelike sense of either term. Instead, we mean "sufficiently predictable" to prevent the behavior of actors participating in a common episode from degenerating into more or less random, idiosyncratic, unorganized performances by individual actors. We also mean that the players, although they may not predict the next move by the opposite team, are prepared by the rules forming the cognitive apparatus that defines football to interpret what happens and to respond to it with an appropriate response that is understood by the players to have meaning within the rules of the game. These rules define their own environment and through cognitive action create a reality to which the players respond individually and jointly.

Because the rules form a set of interacting cognitive elements, if one rule is changed, then the whole process of the game is affected in greater or lesser degree, and adjustments in the self-referential set must occur to reestablish predictability within the limits acceptable to the players. For example, if it became necessary to move the ball 15 yards, rather than 10, to make a first down, then the rules for playing the roles of quarterback and tailback, as well as all other players, would have to change in order to take this new rule into account, so that the game as an organized behavioral system could continue.

In a sense, the systematic aspect of self-referential social systems is found in the orderliness and interconnectedness of their internal structure. It is this internal organization that imposes order on the behavior generated by the system in different episodic occurrences of behavior. Because this is true, the social structure of football as a type of game is to be found in the structure of its system of rules and not in the actual behavior of players in any given game. These rules may be inferred by an observer who is equipped with the proper cognitive tools on which to base inferences from observation of many particular games played at different times and, of course, by examining verbal statements concerning rules made by coaches, players, and football officials. It should be understood, however, that many of the rules constituting the self-referential cognitive system called football may be so taken for granted and unconsciously practiced that they can never be found in rule books or elicited from verbal reports but must be inferred from theoretically controlled observation. It is also important to realize that each team, as well as each player and spectator, will develop their own particular version of the rules, and this will result in each team and each player developing their own particular style of play or style of observing a game in progress. In other words, the self-referential system called football contains not only the rules in the rule book but also the formal and informal norms that are part of the "culture" of each particular team and player. Actually, each team must be regarded as a separate, self-referential social system, and the game as a generic sport must be regarded as a category of such systems or, more specifically, as a "social form." Moreover, actual contests on particular days must be regarded as examples of the interaction among separate, self-referential systems in a common environment, and therefore as events occurring as part of the operation of an ecological field!

This discussion leads to the conclusion that the structure of social behavior systems should be sought in the "structure" of the self-referential, cognitively organized, cultural systems that stand behind observable, overt social behavior and preserve the order or stability that is observed to persist and recur in that behavior. It also suggests that this system is morphogenic in the sense that its structure is constantly in the process of being built up, torn down, or revised by a natural process common to all members of the species. That process, as suggested in the last chapter, is learning.

The structure of self-referential social systems represents what has been learned and recorded in the form of an organized cognitive system of rules (i.e., norms, values, beliefs, and practices) that converts that learning into a form that makes it cognitively usable and therefore adaptive for a human population or for individual members of that population. It is the assumption that such systems are oriented by their internal makeup toward making the relationships of their users to their environments predictable that leads eventually to the conclusion that behavior will inevitably move in the direction of becoming patterned and repetitive, and therefore structured, and that this structure must be sought in what is learned and how it is ordered as a cognitive apparatus.

It is important at this point to call attention to the fact that the orientation of such systems toward achieving predictability and eventually closure does not imply that they will, in fact, achieve this state of affairs. In fact, such systems may succeed only relatively in achieving predictability and closure, or they may move away from this state of affairs, and indeed, completely break down and disappear. The achievement of predictability and closure depends also on the environment and, of course, in social systems, upon the capacity of human actors to develop personal cognitive tools that permit the sociocultural system to operate and survive. As a consequence, we must assume that for social systems to approach high levels of predictability in their relationships to their environments, that environment itself must remain stable and cannot be radically altered by the system's response to it. The survival of a self-referential system and its relative success in achieving adaptation to its environment depends also on its capacity to resolve internal contradictions and to accommodate individual differences in actors thought of as separate, self-referential personality systems.

Even with these things in mind, it will be useful to assume that there is a natural, built-in tendency for human behavior systems to be oriented toward achieving predictable, and therefore adaptive, relationships to their environments, because this assumption furnishes a starting point for studying the process of structural formation and change. This assumption is based on the idea that human behavior is goal directed, in the sense that it is oriented toward drawing the resources needed to satisfy human needs and wants from the environment and toward adaptation to aversive conditions. Needs and wants are likely to be satisfied on a continuing basis, and threatening conditions are managed when behavior patterns are developed that routinely succeed in solving adaptation problems. A self-referential system moves toward structural stability by seeking to achieve predictability and closure, and away from it, and therefore toward restructuring as the level of predictability of its relationship to its environment decreases to the level at which the behavior system itself is threatened with instability and collapse.

More will be said on this topic later, but now it is time to remind ourselves of our constructivist philosophical foundation. The previous discussion is meant to illustrate how we will construct an image of social phenomena, such as the game of football, if we apply the logic of self-referential systems theory. We are *not* asserting that such phenomena are in reality, by their very nature, self-referential systems and that we can demonstrate the truth of this statement through observation. Instead, we are saying that if we use the cognitive apparatus supplied by self-referential systems theory, we will create an image in our minds of social phenomena, such as games or, for that matter, social groups and organizations, that allows us to use self-referential systems theory as a basis for "explanation" and "prediction." Such a cognitive apparatus will prove useful if it is sufficiently explicit and sufficiently integrated to yield predictions that can be understood as stemming from its internal order. If it does accomplish this, then we will find it useful in ordering our perceptions of part of our environment.

6.2   Culture and Society as Sets of Self-Referential Systems

It is now time to discuss the issue of whether our cognitive apparatus should always regard the total culture of a society as a single, self-referential system or, instead, as something less integrated and systematic. To do so, it will be necessary to recognize again that self-referential systems constitute more or less closed integrated sets of rules for behavior that, because they are bounded, evolve separately from other systems of rules. They are, in other words, bounded. As a matter of fact, they are constantly seeking closure.

If this is part of our definition of self-referentiality, then the question concerning culture becomes one of whether we should regard the total culture of a society as a single, complex, more or less integrated set of rules that is evolving toward closure as a bounded unit separately from other cultures. The word *closure* is meant to refer to closure with respect to new information and to learning and, therefore, morphogenesis based on it. As already pointed out, all systems are closed in the sense of being bounded, but some are able to accept and interpret information and change their internal order on the basis of it. When a system achieves closure in the second sense used, we mean that because of its ability to predict perfectly, it no longer encounters new information because its internal order furnishes it with an adequate repertoire of responses to assure its continued functioning.

There is an alternative to the view that total cultures may be treated as single systems that seems intuitively more representative of the situation that pertains, at least, to modern industrial societies. The culture found in a particular society, for example, in complex urban–industrial societies, may instead, be regarded as a large, complex set or population of separately evolving self-referential systems, each representing a solution to a different adaptive problem faced by a population of human actors. For convenience, we can think metaphorically of these separate systems as different sorts of adaptive games. We have said earlier that football, baseball, basketball, cricket, rugby, lacrosse, tennis, ice hockey, and so forth, all may be viewed as *separate self-referential systems*. Because it contains many types of games that are evolving separately, "sports culture" cannot be regarded as a single, integrated self-referential system. Instead, sports culture is a name given to a *category of self-referential systems*, each member of which is undergoing a separate evolution, but each of which is like the others in that they all represent games or sports. The evolution of each game, though separate, is taking place in an environment (ecological field) in which the other games are also evolving and therefore is affected by what is happening with respect to other systems. In a sense, football and basketball are in competition for public attention; therefore, the evolution of each is affected by the evolution of the other. But as games, they have not evolved a joint set of rules that render their relationships to each other a part of a common, self-referential system adapting to a common environment as a bounded integrated whole.

The culture of a complex industrial society may be modeled in a manner similar to this. Each kinship or family unit may be thought of as a separate, self-referential system from each factory, school, church, and commercial establishment, and governmental agency. Indeed, steel mills, computer companies, agribusinesses, and governmental bureaus, all of which may be modeled as complex organizations, may also be viewed as separate, self-referential systems in that each can be thought of as representing a separate adaptive game played by separate "teams" of actors, so to speak.

If these separate games have not as yet evolved an overarching structural "architecture" in the form of a common set of rules that permit them to adapt *jointly* to a common environment, then they cannot be thought of as one large, bounded, self-referential system. Instead, they must be thought of as separate systems that are evolving separately, but in relationship to each other's morphogenic processes. *They must be seen, instead, as a set of separate systems in interaction in a kind of ecological field.*

For example, the many economic and political organizations in American society are structurally separate and as much in competition or conflict with each other as they are integrated into a rule-guided system of coaction. They might, therefore, more fruitfully be regarded as many separate, self-referential systems that do not, together, form a larger system but interact in a common environment, thus forming elements in an ecological field. If this is reasonable, then at least some societies should not themselves be modeled as total self-referential systems, since they lack an overarching integrated, self-referential set of rules that renders the whole society's relationships to its overall environment predictable and under control of a single integrated set of rules (i.e., a control system in the cybernetic sense).

Most modern societies may be better represented as lacking an integrated overall cultural system, but instead, as depending upon many interacting but separate self-referential cultural systems that apply to specific adaptive problems faced by specific sets of actors forming an overall population. In such societies, particular families may be regarded as systems, and a specific bureaucratic organization such as General Motors may be regarded as a system, but it may not be useful to think of them as having a system of cognitively stored rules that integrates both. A specific society such as our own may be thought of as not having reached this level of integration, or perhaps as having done so at some time in the past, but as having lost that integration as its parts have differentiated and evolved separately in a changing environment.

In modern industrial societies, social differentiation may be viewed as having produced a large number of separately evolving self-referential systems that furnish a population of people with many separate adaptive patterns applicable to distinctly separate environments and environmental conditions.

Because predictability is increased and adaptation improved when higher order integration is achieved, these separate systems may be thought of as being in the process of evolving toward a higher level of integration but as not having reached this point as yet, if, indeed, they ever will. On the other hand, some societies may be thought to have reached a high level of integration in the past but, as they have continued to change, having shattered apart in terms of a former higher order integration and perhaps being still in the process of disintegration.

Neither culture in terms of total culture, nor society in terms of a total society can therefore automatically and universally, by definition, be regarded as unitary self-referential systems. They may, at times, be best represented as consisting of a population or set of such systems evolving separately toward closure and together toward some future state of integration. We cannot assume that societies and their various parts have been discovered to be systems on the basis of empirical observation. We must remain aware of the fact that it is our cognitive apparatus or our theoretical system that creates our image of a society, and that we are free to create alternative images of society, depending on the cognitive apparatus we develop.

The view of society presented in this book implies a conception of a dialectical interaction between forces moving many separate self-referential social systems toward separation and closure as separate bounded entities on the one hand, and forces moving them on the other hand, toward openness and integration at a higher level of integration with other systems. One set of forces tends to keep the many self-referential systems making up a society separate and bounded, and the other set moves them toward coalescence or merger into a single system. In between these tendencies (that are built into the nature of such systems) lies the environment, which may be stable or unstable, and which may be affected by the behavior of self-referential systems and feedback unpredicted influences upon their movements toward closure and integration, thereby destabilizing them.

Self-referential social systems are also assumed to be affected by the population of specific human actors whose individual members are evolving separately as actors, containing individual populations of self-referential cognitive systems, and who are members of different sets of separately evolving self-referential social systems that themselves may be moving in conflicting directions with respect to one another.

Thinking of culture and society as populations of self-referential systems evolving toward closure and toward integration as they simultaneously attempt to move toward adaptation to their specific environments has the advantage of opening up a discussion of evolution and change in the cases of culture and social structure, both at the micro- and macrolevel of analysis, and offering a theoretical foundation for the study of morphogenesis as a natural process. This cannot be easily claimed by the competing view that total societies and their associated cultures are systems by definition or by empirical discovery! The alternative suggested here is to think of them as emerging systems in the process of formation and reformation, not necessarily integrated and complete, but perhaps oriented toward achieving integration and completion.

6.3   The System Concept

This whole discussion revolves around the way we define the concept of *system*, and especially around self-referentiality as it applies in the case of social behavior. It also requires that we clarify what is meant by such words as *closed* and *open*, as well as *morphogenic* and *morphostatic*, when they are applied to social systems. This is especially true because much of what has been said about self-referential systems contradicts the usual understanding of these terms as they are applied to society, for example, as by Walter Buckley (1967).

I will begin by saying, as in the preceding chapters, that any system must be regarded as a bounded entity containing several (often many) separate parts or elements that are interrelated or interconnected in such a way as to be interdependent and to affect each other and thereby to relate to their environment as a more or less bounded, integrated whole. The key elements in this definition are boundary, interconnectedness, integration, interaction of parts, and unitary response to an environment. All of these imply the "systematic" nature of systems in the sense that there is an internal order or "logic" to the way the parts are put together in forming the whole and to how they operate in relationship to each other and, as a whole, in relation to their environment. This internal order constitutes the mechanisms of the system. As stated earlier, the parts of a system may not, by definition, be randomly related but must be joined structurally to each other in such a manner that they are constrained in their behavior by their placement in a structural pattern.

The central point in the idea of system implies an object with a certain type of structure, specifically one in which the parts act or operate in relation to one another as a whole and are not free to behave independently but, because of their linkage or relationship to each other, are constrained within relatively narrow limits by their placement in the structure of the whole. This means that each part of a system is dependent on the specific other parts to which it is linked, attached, or related in such a way that its operation is as part of a whole, and not as a separate independent unit. This statement amounts to saying that the parts of a self-referential system are not, themselves, self-referential because they are not self-controlled.

The idea of boundary is used to isolate the interconnected set of parts or units that are dependent for their operation on a common structural mechanism from other objects that are not constrained by the same mechanism. As noted in earlier chapters, there have been many phenomena to which the term *system* has been applied, varying from natural physical systems such as the solar system, to man-made objects such as clocks and machines, and finally, to biological and social behavioral systems. Each application carries with it a particular way of thinking about the issue of how to define a system, but most imply some form of orderly arrangement of parts that interact with each other in a nonrandom pattern in forming a bounded "structural whole."

6.4 Societies and Open and Closed Systems

It has long been assumed that human societies can be regarded as open systems, dependent for their survival as systems on inputs from their environments and, at the same time, capable of responding to that environment differentially, depending upon environmental conditions. In contrast to a closed system, an open system is ordinarily defined as being one capable of obtaining inputs from its environment as a result of its own behavior, whereas closed systems cannot do so. Open systems, according to the traditional view, act toward and upon their environments by taking in inputs as a result of their own action and according to their own control mechanisms. They are, in short, active rather than passive in at least one aspect of their relationship to their environment. According to this view, a wind up clock is a closed system, because it cannot take in energy as a part of its own functioning. It is passive and closed with respect to the resources necessary to keep it operating and depends upon external intervention to receive energy.

On the other hand, a home heating system equipped with a thermostat is an open system, because it can regulate or control its intake of energy in terms of its thermostatic perception of its environment. Obviously, all animals qualify as open organic systems because they are capable of obtaining and controlling the input of various needed resources from their environments. So, it appears, are social groups and organizations. We shall suspend judgment on societies with respect to this issue.

As pointed out earlier, a problem immediately arises in dealing with the issue of openness. There are two ways to define the concept. One way ignores the nature of the inputs and the degree of openness and the locus of control over internal operation. The other examines the nature of the input and the degree of closure implied by this nature and locates control within the system itself. From the first point of view, any system is open that can take in inputs from its environment and utilize these inputs to sustain its functioning as a system. The second perspective centers attention on information as the critical input. It is reasoned that for a system to take in any form of input on its own accord, it is necessary for that system to be able to generate and interpret information. It is assumed that what constitutes information is determined by the internal structure of the system generating and using the information and on the relationship of that internal structure to its environment. In other words, according to this view, open systems are systems capable of generating, processing, and reacting to information.

The emphasis is on the word *generation*, which implies that the system itself creates or "manufactures" information as a normal feature of its operation. Information arises from within the system as it converts environmental stimulation or input into meaning relevant to its own internal functioning. With respect to a home heating system, the thermostat operates as a "sensory mechanism" that generates and interprets information concerning the temperature of its environment. The thermostat is connected to the rest of the system by a set of switches and valves and servomotors that respond to signals by acting in such a way that energy inputs are taken in and utilized.

Not only do open systems take in such inputs as energy and raw materials, but they also regulate their internal functioning by use of information they generate from sensory impressions or stimuli they take in from their environments. Thus, open systems are capable of generating and processing information and of changing their functioning on the basis of it. Because of this, they also must contain mechanisms that monitor their environments in one way or another, so that they are capable of responding to conditions outside themselves. Obviously, animals are capable of these things and are open information generating systems. Because human social networks such as groups and organizations are made up of actors with the capacity to generate and process information, and because the network provides social-decision mechanisms whereby the group as a unit can respond to it, such social units may also be regarded as open systems.

Even so, it must be recognized that all systems have boundaries, and boundaries themselves imply closure of a certain sort. Also, it is apparent that no system ever senses or monitors every aspect of its environment and therefore is only "open" to a narrow range of stimuli from which to generate information by its own internal functioning. This means that systems are always only partially open in the informational sense. They are closed with respect to aspects of the environment from which they cannot generate information, or in other words, as far as most environmental conditions are concerned. These unsensed environmental conditions are taken for granted by the system or, in another sense, treated as irrelevant or nonexistent. The ordinary home heating system can only measure the temperature of its environment and convert this into information used to signal changes in its internal functioning. It cannot sense light, or humidity, or the chemical content of the air, and so forth. As far as it is concerned, these things do not exist or are ignored or taken for granted. It is therefore acted upon passively by these conditions.

What constitutes information to an open system is strictly defined by the structure of the system itself. The structural rules of a system determine and define what constitutes information and how it will be processed and responded to by the system. Because this is true, it can be argued that so-called open systems, at least from one point of view, are in reality closed, because only they define what constitutes information. The environment plays no role in determining this aspect of a system. The environment, though changing and responding to the behavior of the open system, *does not* supply it with information under the control of the environment itself. The environment must be regarded as acting upon a system as a source of stimulation, and therefore of "potential information." But information itself is a function of systemic structure and mechanism.

It is in this sense that self-referential systems are closed. They are open if the definition of *openness* is the capacity to generate and process information, but they are closed if *closure* is defined as containing within themselves the rules or mechanisms that determine what constitutes information in the first place. Before more can be made of this argument, it is necessary to consider the meaning of morphogenesis when it is applied to systems, because morphogenic processes could conceivably be considered the source of change in what is defined as *information* by a system, and also in how systems process and respond to information. If this were to turn out to be the case, then "true openness" may only occur in systems that are morphogenic.

6.5 Morphogenesis in Systems

Morphogenesis, of course, refers to the process of generating structure or to structural change and development. It applies in the case of systems that are capable not only of *responding* to their environments but of *adapting* to them by altering their own internal organization. Morphogenesis arises out of the information processes through which a system is able to respond to its environment, perceived as information, by changing its structure to arrive at a new adaptation to perceived environmental conditions. It therefore depends upon the openness of the system in terms of generating, accumulating, and interpreting information.

In the case of morphogenesis, a system is not only able to generate, process, and respond to self-defined information, but also to store or accumulate it in a form that amounts to "learning from its experience." It can convert information into what amounts to "new rules" for structuring its own behavior. What is "learned" is recorded as morphological change. The parts of the system and their relationship to each other are altered in response to accumulated experience so that the system is, in a sense, more adapted to the environment as far as the information it receives from it is concerned. It is in this sense that we say that a self-referential system is oriented toward "routinizing" or "normalizing" its relationship to its environment in such a way as to be able to predict its relationship to that environment, and therefore to increase the probability of its own survival.

In other words (in the long run, although not always in the short run) systems that survive over relatively long periods move in the direction of changes that improve the adaptation of the system to its environment. But it must always be recalled that the environment, as far as the system is concerned, consists only of a narrow range of information and that what constitutes information to begin with is governed by the rules of the system itself. These characteristics place limits on morphogenesis. Systems can only be morphogenic within the limits set by their own internal structure. Any given system, therefore, can only adapt within the range permitted by its own rules, and these rules affect and are affected by the range of information it can generate. This does not mean that it cannot develop new rules, but it appears to mean that systems are unlikely to change what they define as information to include types of information ruled out by their own information-generating and -processing capacity. They are therefore unlikely to change their degree and type of "openness" without external intervention in the form of something other than self-generated, self-controlled, self-interpreted information.

Nothing said previously should be interpreted to mean that only positive morphogenic changes can occur. New forms of systemic behavior may arise out of information processes that may prove maladaptive and lead to the destruction of a system. This can easily occur, because a system can only adapt actively to the environment it "creates" through its own information-generation and -processing capacity. An "adaptive" change to self-defined environmental conditions can expose a system to destruction by conditions it does not perceive or misperceives. Because systems never monitor the entire environment, they are always vulnerable to conditions outside the range of their information-generating capacity.

This discussion opens up the need to consider long-range evolution as a morphogenic process in order to deal with sources of structural change other than those generated by automatic morphogenic processes that are akin to learning. In the case of organisms, morphogenesis occurs in response to physical exercise, because one can build larger muscles, greater lung power, and can acquire calluses and bunions. These change the structure of the organism to a degree, but only within the limits imposed by the structure of the body as a system to begin with. But, as we know, types of organisms thought of as species evolve, and as they do, other types of structural changes occur. This type is recorded in the genetics of the organism, which the first type is not. We also know that some species of organisms fail and become extinct in some cases, because they are so well adapted to an environment that itself changes and disappears.

Genetic changes in a species, which result in structural changes of a hereditary sort *do not arise* from the morphogenic qualities of a single organism. Instead, they arise out of interventions called *mutations*, which are not under the control of the organism as a morphogenic system. Such changes are a result of external factors to which the system can only respond passively. Mutations, once they have arisen, are selected for survival or extinction by a process that occurs in an ecological field. This larger, longer evolutionary process of morphogenesis applies to a gene pool and not to an individual member of a species, and it has nothing to do with morphogenesis as it applies to the individual except insofar as it limits it.

In social affairs, it is necessary to face these two types of structural change. Social groups are morphogenic systems in the sense that they are able, within limits set by their own self-referential systems of rules, to adapt to environmental conditions by altering their internal cultural structures. At the same time, innovations not produced by this sort of morphogenic process can occur and bring into being new forms of self-referential systems side by side with those that are changing by internal morphogenesis. When a mutation occurs in the case of organisms, it first occurs in the genes of a particular organism, which in turn "reproduces" an organism with this new trait in the same population with organisms without the trait. It does not change the structure of an already existing organism. The structure of an existing organism is regulated by its own already existent internal rules that limit how it may adapt. The mutant organism is one constructed according to a new set of rules.

In the case of social units, morphogenesis in an existing unit is limited by its own internal rules, at least as far as adaptive structural change is concerned. It can only go as far as those internal rules permit it to go. But more radical change may arise from other processes occurring in the larger ecological field, where innovations are introduced in newly formed systems whose structure does not impose the same constraints. This is like saying that factories as forms of economic production systems did not, and probably could not, evolve out of morphogenic changes in guild shops. Instead, they arose as a kind of "social mutation" or innovation side by side with guild shops out of processes occurring in the larger ecological field.

There are, according to this discussion, two levels or types of morphogenic processes that must be taken into account. The first is concerned with adaptive structural change at the level of the individual social unit, for example, in the case of a particular family or business establishment. The other is at the level of the larger network comprised of many separate, often specialized, competing and conflicting units that serve a single population. It is not reasonable to assume that all structural change comes about by a process whereby existing units are transformed by internal morphogenic processes into new species of social units. Medieval guilds were not gradually or suddenly transformed into factories as the industrial revolution took place, so that factories may be regarded as guilds having undergone morphogenesis. Neither are modern labor unions transformed guilds. As a matter of fact, guilds opposed factorylike production and, unlike unions, included master craftsmen, the owners of a shop, and their associated journeymen and apprentices in the same organization.

The point is that morphogenesis at the societal level involves a totally different process than morphogenesis at the level of the individual unit. At the macrolevel, it is necessary to consider the introduction into the social network of new units with novel internal structures to account for the transition, for example, from feudalism to capitalism. It is furthermore necessary to explain how such innovations occur and how they are selected for survival and proliferation before we will be able to account for long-range diachronic change in societal organization. This is beyond the scope of this chapter.

The point made here is that with respect to any self-referential system, the internal rules of the system place limits on morphogenesis. These limits are in large part an outgrowth of the system's determination of what constitutes information. It is apparent that if there were not limits on morphogenesis, which must be interpreted to mean limits on the capacity to adapt, systems could go on forever adapting and changing, therefore never failing and ceasing to exist. The fact that systems fail and are destroyed or dismantled itself is testimony to the limits of morphogenesis. In the case of self-referential social systems, the internal rules of system structure limit the capacity of the system to adapt, and if environmental change exceeds this capacity, then the system fails. Guilds could not adapt to the demand for mass production and at the same time remain guilds as defined by their own internal rules. They could not compete with factories as trade expanded and as national and international markets formed. As a consequence, they failed. In Marxian terms, they contained the seeds of their own destruction, those seeds being in the form of their own internal structure and the restraints it placed on their adaptive capacity.

The conclusion to be drawn from this discussion concerning the nature of self-referential systems is as follows: They may be considered both open and morphogenic if we consider openness to mean being capable of generating and responding to information, and morphogenic to mean being capable within limits set by their internal structure of generating a limited range of structural adaptation. They may be thought of as closed, however, if we consider the limits of adaptability to be a function of their own internal order.

6.6 Summary

Self-referential social systems, because they are assumed to exist to provide solutions to behavioral adaptation problems for the people who "practice them," are oriented toward rendering their relationship to their environment predictable and therefore routine and normal. The assumption that this orientation guides systems is based on the postulates concerning the learning processes discussed in the previous chapter, where learning was viewed as the basis for forming the rules that constitute the structure of the system in the first place. Learning implies the formation of rules that store behavior patterns. These rules are like mental generalizations that allow the organism containing the rules to recognize, and therefore generate, information from the environment, and to predict on the basis of it what will happen if the organism emits a certain behavior. Learned rules have the characteristic of routinizing or normalizing response patterns based on experience. We are assuming that the nature of learning as a process is such that it automatically, as part of the process itself, orients the system doing the learning toward the formation of rules that render its relationship to its environment predictable and comprehensible.

These statements should not be interpreted to mean that self-referential systems are "motivated" to achieve predictability in their interaction with their environments. The word *orientation* was deliberately selected to avoid this implication. Instead, it means that the built-in rules for learning that are part of the structure of learning organisms are "hardwired" into the perceptual and neurological apparatus of learning organisms and simply work that way. At the level of the social unit, we are assuming that there are similar, as yet not well understood natural principles that control the joint learning that takes place in social networks as the culture of the network evolves as a product of "colearning."

When we say that self-referential systems move toward closure, we mean that they operate in such a way as to evolve a set of rules that predict their transactions with their environment within limits that permit the survival of the system of rules as a bounded, self-reproducing entity. When this is achieved, it has the effect of providing the self-referential system with no information-processing problems. In reality, if all predictions by a set of rules were interpreted by it as being correct or useful, we could say that the system has no basis for adding to its store of information as it interacts with its environment. Instead, each transaction merely reinforces or reproduces a rule that is already present and replicates the information it is based on. If this is the case, the system, by definition, ceases to learn, and because its structure records what it learns, it would cease to change structurally. In other words, it would become a perfectly closed system of rules.

6.7   Prologue to Ecological Fields

In the next chapter, I will go deeper into the application of the concept self-referential system to society. I shall also begin to examine how to conceptualize the internal structure of self-referential systems. In future chapters, the relationships among independent, self-referential social systems will be explored and the conception of an ecological field will be discussed in detail.

Ecological Fields

7.1 Introduction

The objective of this chapter is to lay a foundation for conceptualizing a form of social ecology that places human systems in the context of a larger ecological field. This will be done by explicitly taking into account *closed* or *self-referential systems* theory and extending the logic of that approach by considering how we must think about the relationship among such systems when they inhabit a common environment. This exploratory effort in cognitive construction will challenge the common view that human societies are best understood when we model them as systems rather than as ecological fields. It will also, to a lesser extent, revise and thereby challenge the conceptualization held by ecologists that biotic communities should be thought of as systems, or more properly, ecosystems.

The viewpoint to be presented here will explicitly reject the idea that either human societies or biotic communities are best conceptualized as systems. Instead, they will be regarded as "nonsystems." Nevertheless they will be conceptualized as objects of study that can be cognitively modeled using a structural approach that builds an image of the relationships *among*, rather than *within* systems.

As background to this discussion, it will be useful to keep in mind that ecologists since the 1950s have employed the concept *ecosystem* as a basic cognitive tool used in modeling biological communities and their relationships to their nonbiotic environment. In an excellent article entitled "The Ecosystem Concept: A Search for Order," Frank B. Golley (1991) traces the development of the concept *ecosystem* and relates it to the social climate in which the concept developed. The article points out, among other things, that the concept *ecosystem* developed out of the study of ponds and lakes as biotic communities and emphasizes the energy transfers among species within a bounded environment. These energy transfers along "food chains" and their relationship to population phenomena and to the maintenance of stable population distributions were and remain the basis for thinking of bounded biological communities as systems. Actually, the concept *ecosystem* emerged before systems theory itself had fully developed and has continued to develop alongside systems theory.

For the most part, ecology, in its application of the concept *ecosystem*, has sidestepped the problem of how organisms interact as behaving or acting individuals forming a social network and has focused on the consequences of interaction in terms of energy transfers, resource utilization, and population dynamics (Odum, 1953; Ehrlich, Ehrlich, and Holdren, 1977). This has been done largely without conscious and critical evaluation of the appropriateness of systems theory to ecology or to how systems theory, when applied in a holistic manner to biotic communities, might limit our capacity to deal with the social behavior of animals, and particularly of human beings, in an ecological context.

In particular, it leaves ambiguous, to say the least, how societies and the various social groupings that comprise them fit into an ecological order. In sociology, a great deal of attention has been paid to the relationship of human systems to their environment and to how environmental or ecological factors affect the social organization of human communities (Hawley, 1968). These efforts have themselves been limited by the absence of a fully developed means of dealing with social organization or social structure. The consequence has been an uncritical acceptance of systems theory as the basis for sociological ecology. The objective of this chapter will be to examine the appropriateness of systems theory to biological and social ecology by focusing not on energy transfers as such, but on the behavior of organisms that stands behind and produces such "ecological relationships." The position to be taken in the end will not be so far from that implied by Golley (1991) in the final paragraph of his article.

> The central idea (in the concept ecosystem) . . . is the organized network of interacting systems which produce sustainable, stable, and harmonious living systems, in which human well-being is enhanced and non-human nature is understood to be an essential and valued element in the web of relationships. (p. 138).

7.2   Key Elements in Systems Theory Relevant to Conceptualizing Ecological Relationships

Notwithstanding discussions in previous chapters, let it be granted that there are many interpretations of the concept *system* and that there is no valid empirical basis for claiming one usage is clearly superior to another. Let it also be granted that each perspective, when employed as a guide to thought and as a means of ordering an image of a so-called empirical world, yields a different "reality" relative to itself. In the pages to follow, it will not be productive to quibble further over the "best interpretation" of the word system, nor will it be fruitful to engage in the scholastic exercise of meticulously documenting the source of every nuance of interpretation employed in discussing it.

The objective here will be to employ a particular meaning of the concept *system* as the basis for creating a new type of social ecology. The task of developing a new social ecology will be difficult enough without the additional burden of diverting our train of thought into a search for historical origins, a search that will lead into a morass of varying interpretations of the ideas under discussion, thus obscuring the logic of the cognitive system being development. It will be best to mark a clear cognitive path by means of specially created guideposts that have admittedly been shaped out of materials provided, in part, by others.

Even so, it is only fair, as well as useful, to indicate the general historical roots of the ideas to be developed. They lie in so-called "closed" or "self-referential" systems theory, particularly as that theory has been employed by such scholars as Maturana and Varela (1980), Nicholas Luhman (1986), and Carlo Pelanda (1989). For an excellent discussion of autopoetic systems theory, see *Self-Producing Systems* (Minges, 1995). The thoughts being set down here have grown most immediately out of the interaction between myself and Carlo Pelanda, and out of interaction with our colleagues in the INTER-LAB network, especially those in the theoretical systemics program in Italy. They also owe a great deal to Walter Peacock and Daniel Rodeheaver, and especially to Davide Nicholini, with whom I spent several hours a week for nearly a year talking about these matters.

The building of the cognitive system presented here starts from the proposition developed in earlier chapters that, by definition, all systems are closed and self-referential. They are bounded and therefore separated from their environments and act with respect to things external to themselves as automatons. There is also the assumption that as far as an active system is concerned, the environment it responds to is generated from within itself by systemic mechanisms. A self-referential system's environment, in the cognitive sense, is a creation of the system itself, and there is no independent environment that exists as a factual reality outside of the boundaries of the system as far as the system's behavior is concerned, other than that which the system itself generates from within its own mechanisms.

Only by positing the existence of an independent observer, who generates a conception of a system and of an environment independent of the system by use of the observer's own cognitive apparatus, can an environment that was not generated by the system itself be identified. This, however, does not contradict the notion that for a self-referential system, the only environment that exists as far as its actions are concerned is that which the system generates from within itself. This does mean, however, that an observer may, through cognitive action, generate a conceptualization that sees a system as being passively affected by things outside itself that the system, itself, cannot "perceive" or to which it cannot respond on its own terms.

What makes us say that systems are self-referential and closed is the assumption that *their behavior as systems* is generated from within by internal mechanisms that define an environment relevant to their own behavior. To see self-referentiality in this sense, it is necessary to distinguish between an active response on the part of a system, in the form of a systemic behavior, and an effect or impact upon a system. Again, an observer must intervene to make this distinction possible. An active response is one perceived by an observer as being generated by the internal operation of a system that is perceived as containing many possible alternative behavior patterns, only one of which is emitted as a response to a particular perception of the environment. In contrast, an impact is seen by an observer as being delivered from outside the system and as eliciting no response on the part of the system, although it can affect the system's capacity to respond actively on future occasions. Such an impact is seen and recognized only by an observer who is equipped by a cognitive apparatus to construct such a view, but it is not perceived by the system itself.

All of this is said to establish the meaning of closedness and self-referentiality, and to give a brief foundation for the statement that all self-referential systems are closed as far as they will be considered in this discussion. The point is that the capacity of a system to generate information concerning an environment is not sufficient to support a claim of openness because the information generated is produced from within the system itself by its own mechanisms.

The fact that an observer can see an environment other than that to which the system responds, using a cognitive apparatus of his own, does not establish openness as far as self-referential systems are concerned. That the system appears to an observer to take in information (which is also perceived by the observer through the observer's own cognitive operation) does not mean that the system is being penetrated by its environment and making it a part of itself. Such a view is a consequence of the mind of an observer who is observing a system that, itself, is observing an environment shifting the objects of reference and the cognitive apparatuses used to generate them.

One other idea needs exploration before the main task of this discussion can be furthered. It is useful to distinguish between active and passive systems, even when it is assumed that all systems are closed. Active systems are configurations of interacting parts or elements capable of acting with reference to self-generated information that defines their environment. Thus, they are capable of generating their own information or facts and of selectively responding or acting with reference to these facts. A passive system is one that cannot generate information concerning its environment and therefore is incapable of generating responses to environmental events or conditions. As far as the passive system, itself, is concerned, there is no environment.

Both passive and active systems may be passively impacted upon by an environment, but to see this, an observer must be placed into the cognitive picture to define the impact and to differentiate it from a response. In creating an ecology of systems capable of generating images of an evolutionary sort, it will be necessary to develop a cognitive apparatus through which an observer can see passive impacts as a possible source of the negative selection or destruction of systems. By recognizing the possibility and broad outlines of a built-in capacity to learn and the possibility of negative selection by passively accepted impacts, such a cognitive apparatus may make it possible to conceptualize morphogenesis.

From an evolutionary perspective, it will be useful to assume that systems are selected for survival or extinction on the basis of their relative capacity to generate active, adaptive responses to environmental conditions or events. To do this on a more than random basis, it can be argued that the system must generate information concerning its environment that protects it, within limits, from impacts stemming from the environment that could destroy it. Passive impacts are those for which a system has no active defense and may therefore represent a source of systemic destruction or a source of morphogenesis.

7.3 A Broad Outline of an Ecological Perspective

In order to build a cognitive apparatus that can generate ecological models appropriate to the study of human systems, it will be necessary to define a whole language for a new field called *sociopolitical ecology*. Part of this language can be borrowed from existing usage and redefined to suit the present task, but part must be invented. At the very least, the task calls for the bringing together of many conceptualizations usually not thought of as being related. We will begin the task of creating such a language, by presenting a very general sketch of the kind of problem we refer to in order to identify the general arena of interest.

7.3.1 An Ecological Field

First, let us define the notion of an ecological field by presenting a crude idea of the content and organization of such an object. Accordingly, it can be said that an *ecological field* is a space within which a population of systems is located, and in which the members of the population interact. Because systems are defined as being "closed" and bounded, each system in the field operates as a system on the basis of its own self-referential order and therefore is an autonomous actor with respect to things outside itself. It defines the field for itself and acts with respect to the field on its own by defining its own "environment" and by generating its own responses to it. The environment as far as each system is concerned is defined as that which the system itself "perceives" outside itself.

Thus, for each system, only part of the field, as perceived by an observer equipped with a cognitive apparatus capable of seeing separate systems interact, constitutes the environment. The various systems inhabiting the field perceive different environments even though, for the observer of the field, the "environment" of all of the systems taken together may appear to be the whole field. We must remember that there is the possibility of elements, conditions, or systems existing in the field that neither the observer nor the systems inhabiting the field has the capacity to perceive!

Nevertheless, an ecological field may be said by an observer to be "organized" if the observer is able to conceptualize a "division of labor" among the systems inhabiting the field, such that types of systems constituting subpopulations occupy niches in a web of interdependencies. This amounts to saying that some types of systems in the field are themselves so constructed that they are dependent upon specific other types for the resources they need for their own internal operation and for their own survival as functioning systems. Also, they may be interdependent in the sense that specific types of systems are vulnerable to disruption by the behavior of other systems that can negatively affect their internal operation or survival.

From several other perspectives, it can be said that a field is organized if an observer uses a framework capable of incorporating concepts that can construct an image of such organization into a constructed image of the field. First, the size of the populations of various types of systems at any given time can be thought of as a feature of the field's organization. Some types of systems may be prevalent and others scarce, and when this is added to the idea of a "division of labor" among species of systems, it becomes a feature that has meaning for the interaction that takes place among particular systems in the field. Second, there is the possibility of conceptualizing the distribution of systems in space relative to one another such that some particular systems are closer to each other than others. This geographical or spatial distribution has implications for how systems in the field behave in relationship to each other and with respect to the field itself.

It can now be said that an ecological field is a defined space populated by systems differentiated according to the niches they occupy in the field and particular locations they occupy with respect to one another, understanding that species of systems differ in their prevalence within the field.

In order to complete the picture, it is necessary to take into account the characteristics of the space or territory within which the field exists and within which the individual systems making it up are spatially distributed and operate. Because we are really talking about biological or social systems as the systems populating the field, and perhaps about the self-governing machines or nonbiotic systems they have created, we need to include a substratum of nonsystems in the form of physical resources and conditions that form the characteristics of the territory within which systems operate and interact. Included in this aspect of the field would be the mineral resources and the topological features of the earth, along with air and water resources and climatic conditions. It is also assumed that these physical features would be spatially distributed unequally in relationship to each other and in relationship to the systems inhabiting the field.

For my purposes, it will be sufficient to say that an ecological field includes a geographic area and its physical features, along with the biological and social systems that inhabit it. It is a populated space with its own physical characteristics and its own organization. In other words, it is a territory inhabited by a set of systems, differentiated into species according to a biotic and/or social "division of labor."

7.4 Structural Differences between Systems and Ecological Fields

In order to develop a clearly defined ecological perspective that has a known and well-defined metatheoretical foundation, it will be necessary to make a clear distinction between the structural characteristics of a system and those of an ecological field. This is necessary because a structural approach underlies the notion of systems as distinct, self-referential entities, and because ecological fields are, by definition, comprised of populations of independent systems organized according to a division of labor. Such a division of labor establishes specialized niches in a "food chain" and has the effect of bounding the autonomy of self-referential systems. For this reason, the distinction between an ecological field and a system depends upon a structural logic. Accordingly, the next few pages will be devoted to a discussion of *system structure* as compared to *ecological structure*, or to the structure of ecological fields.

In this discussion, the term *structure* or *organization* will be interpreted to mean a set of parts, elements, or units arranged in accordance with a set of relationships to form a coherent configuration or pattern that persists through an interval of time, during which the set of parts or units and their relationship to each other remains stable. It is helpful to think in terms of synchronic and diachronic time intervals when discussing the structure of systems and their relations to each other, because this makes it possible to deal with both fixed and changing structural patterns and think in terms of operating structures. In a synchronic interval of time, a systemic structure consists of a pattern of parts and relationships that does not change, although the parts operate and the system may act toward its environment. During the synchronic interval, the structure, and therefore the pattern of operation, by definition, remains as it was at the starting point, without alteration in the parts making it up, their characteristics as parts, their "functions" or behavior patterns with respect to each other, and their patterns of interaction and/or input–output relationships. In diachronic time, several synchronic time intervals are included, and a structure can change without at the same time dissolving into its environment. In diachronic time, morphogenesis or structural transformation may take place without the structure of an object becoming "unstructured" or falling apart and becoming indistinguishable from its environment.

This statement makes the idea of "boundary" essential to the idea "structure." In addition, it is apparent that a notion of "integrity" is required to conceptualize structure, especially if we wish to entertain the notion of morphogenesis or structural change. If a thing can be thought of as being structured and, at the same time, as changing in structure, then the idea of structure cannot mean that a bounded pattern of parts and relationships must remain fixed and unaltered through time. In order to think of structural change, we must be able to think of the object as maintaining its identity, and therefore its separation from its environment *as it changes*. Changes must fit into and be an element of a bounded pattern that continues through a diachronic interval such that changes do not destroy our capacity as observers to conceptualize continuously the way the object is structured even though, to do so, we must allow relationships among parts to be altered, "new parts" to be added, and "old parts" altered in their characteristics.

To do this requires the use of a stable set of cognitive elements to model structure at each synchronic time interval; that is, as suggested earlier, the following subelements of the idea of structure must be applied consistently through time by use of a stable language to enable us to track the structure through time:

1. Ideas standing for the parts, units, or elements of structure that are incorporated into the cognitive system that constructs a mental model of structure, including ideas defining the characteristics of these parts or elements.
2. Concepts standing for the relationships among parts used to construct a conception of a structural configuration.
3. An idea of boundary or limit that can be used to define the separation of a structure from things outside it and therefore to identify which are the parts and relationships to be included inside the boundaries.
4. A spatial grounding against which to conceptualize the separation of parts or units and their relationships to each other, and against which to define boundaries.
5. A temporal grounding against which to conceptualize the operation of parts in relationship to each other in synchronic time, and to recognize morphogenesis or change in diachronic time.
6. An idea that defines the integrity or integration of the structure as opposed to nonstructure or nonpattern. The object must be seen as con-

tinuously hanging together as a pattern distinct from its environment even as it changes.

I will argue that systems are objects seen through cognitive construction as having a particular kind of structure. This means that when we think of an object or thing as "being" a system, we order our conception of it by use of a structural strategy that models it in terms of certain structural characteristics. This does not mean that we discover, by observation, that some entities in nature are, in fact, systems, but that we construct certain objects or entities in our minds by modeling them according to the rules of a cognitive apparatus that generates a certain kind of conceptual order. Having done this, we use this representation to make statements about such objects, some of which may predict its behavior, and some of which may be used to explain how that behavior is produced. Such statements may prove useful if we wish to control the object we model, or if we wish to control our relationship to it.

Self-referential systems, according to the cognitive system being generated in these pages, are objects or things an observer sees through cognitive action as displaying certain structural attributes. First, they have dynamic structures. Their parts behave, act, move, exert force, produce outputs, interact with each other, impact upon each other, or otherwise act with respect to each other. Systems are *not* inert, dead, still, unmoving, "static" objects but are objects that are, by definition, "dynamic."

The cognitive utility of the concept system lies in its use in dealing with the behavior of objects perceived as being comprised of interacting parts that together, as a functioning whole, display a stable pattern of activity. The cognitive apparatus that generates a "systems model" in the mind of an observer is used to allow the observer to comprehend the "mechanism" that produces the behavior of the object. The idea of system is not, therefore, useful in dealing with inoperative, nonacting objects comprised of inert or static parts.

This definition of the concept system (which uses the idea of structure as a key element) leaves room for conceptualizing objects that are not internally active or do not act toward an environment and therefore cannot be thought of as systems. It is obvious that we can think of an object as "being structured" but, at the same time, as being a nonsystem. It should furthermore be apparent that the concept structure leaves the possibility of conceptualizing relationship patterns among objects, for example among systems, or between systems and nonsystems, even when the entire structure including all of these objects and relationships fails to meet the criteria of systemic structures.

To differentiate system structure from nonsystem structure, it is necessary to go a step further than we have gone so far and to focus on the problem of how we establish a system's boundaries conceptually. The method chosen for this discussion is to focus on the characteristics of the relationships among the parts of a system as opposed to the relationship of a system to objects in its environment.

7.4.1   Bonding and Contingency

The conceptual difference between systems and ecological fields lies in the cognitive rules employed in the construction of an image of their structures. Systems are always comprised of a set of specific, acting parts joined to each other in a relationship pattern to form a bounded whole. Ecological fields are comprised of many separate active systems that may also be conceptualized as being, in some way, related to each other. In ecological fields, however, the units that constitute the parts of structure are whole systems, whereas in the case of systems, the units are fragments or parts of whole systems. Thus, both ecological fields and systems have structures comprised of units or elements that interact in terms of a relationship pattern. The patterns, however, are quite different. To see this difference, a clear distinction between the form of the relationships among parts that are characteristic of a system as distinct from the relationships among systems (the parts) in an ecological field is required.

The approach to be employed here makes a distinction between bonded or unit-specific relationships and contingent or categorical relationships. Inside the boundaries of a system, a specific set of parts are joined to each other in an internal "division of labor" that makes them interdependent in a *unit-specific* sense. Particular, exact parts occupy particular locations in a systemic mechanism where each part occupies a location in a "division of labor." The mechanism of the system is such that each part has no alternative inside the systemic mechanism but to interact with other specific units that are parts of the same bounded division of labor. They are, in other words, *bonded* to each other.

The word *bonding* is not meant to imply a kind of "gluing together" as much as to imply a stable interdependency among particular units in the functional sense. One exact part of a system depends upon other particular exact parts in order to perform its own function or role within the larger mechanism. For example, in an organism, a particular heart is linked to and depends upon a particular pair of lungs and particular other organs in the same body. The biological system called the *organism* operates as a total bounded entity in an environment it defines for itself through its own mechanism. That mechanism is constituted out of an assemblage of particular interdependent, interacting organs, unique unto themselves. Similarly, a social system is constructed out of particular exact units. The sociology department at the University of Georgia is dependent upon the same university dean's office, business office, library, and registrar for its functioning as part of a systemic mechanism which, as a whole, adapts according to its own definition of an environment, functioning internally as a set of unit-specific relationships.

The point of *bonding* is that a system is always comprised of a particular exact set of parts that operate through time in relation to each other as parts of a particular systemic mechanism within a single, specific operating whole.

Around the boundaries of a system, outside the system's internal mechanism, the units interacting with the system change or vary with the passage of time. At one time system X is observed interacting with another system Y in order to obtain a particular resource from its self-defined environment. At a later time, it is seen interacting with Z in order to perform the same function. As time progresses, it interacts with many different external units in order to accomplish the same end. Which external object it interacts with is *contingent* upon the internal state of the system and the state of its perception of the external ecological field in which it is located.

A *contingent relationship*, as defined here, is one that is not generated by a single systemic mechanism in which particular, exact parts are constrained within a single systemic mechanism but one in which there is no overall systemic mechanism controlling interaction among separate units. Each unit involved in the interaction contains its own separately operating internal mechanism.

In an ecological field, encounters among systems occur on the basis of the separate, independent operation of many bounded, self-referential systemic mechanisms operating separately in a common field, where many different types or species of bounded self-referential systems are themselves specialized in terms of their placement in *categorical* niches in a *nonsystemic division of labor*. In this case, the division of labor is ecological.

The separate systems populating an ecological field are *not* in systemic, unit-specific interdependence with each other but in categorical, ecological interdependence. In the case of an ecological division of labor, whole systems are used as the unit of analysis, but the interdependence among systems characteristic of ecological fields is between and among species or categories of systems, not specific exact members of a population of similar units. In an ecological field, each self-referential system is structurally autonomous with respect to any particular other system. There are no *bonds* between particular systems such that they are part of a common mechanism requiring those exact systems to interact to the exclusion of interaction with other systems in the same category. Instead, systems of a particular type "A" are dependent on systems of types "B" and "C" for particular inputs or resources, and are not dependent on other systems in the same field, such as "X" and "Y." For system A1, (a particular system from species A) any particular member of species B may satisfy the need for a particular resource.

Let us use an oversimplified example to illustrate the point under discussion. Assume that lions (System type "L") are so constructed as self-referential biological systems that they only eat zebras (Class Z). So lions as a species of biological systems are dependent on zebras, another species of system. But a particular lion, L1 (a separate biological system), may satisfy its need for food by eating any zebra from Z1 to Zn. Which zebra L1 will eat depends upon (1) L1's construction of its environment, including its perception of zebras and zebra behavior; (2) Z1 to Zn's location in the field relative to L1's construction of its environment; and (3) the construction of their environments by Z1 to Zn, including their construction of the behavior of L1, (4) the behavior of other lions, and (5) many other factors.

Thus, we say that the occurrence of interaction between L1 and Z1 is *contingent* upon the operation of many independent systems in an environment organized spatially and temporally into a field of contingencies. A contingent relationship is one that is generated by categorical rather than unit-specific interdependence, and by the fact that categories of systems are comprised of individual systems, each of which is a separate, autonomous, self-referential system in itself. The category comprised of many similar systems is itself a "nonsystem" because it lacks the unit-specific bonding of the members of the category to one another in a self-referential systemic mechanism.

The categories (species) lions and zebras are not systems. Instead, each individual lion and each individual zebra is regarded as a separate biological system, acting as such with respect to other systems. In this example, I have deliberately ignored the possibility that lions might hunt in prides and zebras go in herds, so as to avoid, for the moment, the complexities introduced by social systems. I am, however, aware of these complexities and will deal with them later.

Contingency is a *product of autonomy* constrained by *categorical interdependence*. Such interdependence is generated by an ecological division of labor and by other structural features of the field. Each lion acts as a separate system, as does each zebra, but the actions of the individual lion are constrained by the fact that lions are so constructed as systems that their internal order constructs an environment in which zebras are recognized as food. This constraint, however, comes from within the self-referential biological order of the individual lion's organism, and allows the individual lion the "autonomy" of selecting which exact zebra to pursue. On the zebra's side of the equation, the same is true. Zebras are internally ordered in such a way (whether by instinct or by learning) as to recognize lions as a threat, and thereby to flee from them when they perceive a threat of attack. This behavior is also autonomous, and this makes the behavior of lions and zebras *contingent* upon each other's self-constructed actions. *Contingency, in this case, is a type of bounded indeterminacy.*

With respect to bonded relationships within a system, the same units interact within a mechanism that controls their interaction and renders their relationship stable and determinate. Knowledge of the mechanism makes prediction of the behavior of the parts possible on a "deterministic" basis. Assuming complete understanding of the mechanism, an observer would be able to make "lawlike" statements that would yield "perfect prediction," assuming no errors in cognitively modeling the system in question. In a contingent field occupied by many populations of different species of systems in multidimensional, categorical interdependency, predictions cannot be based on knowledge of a controlling mechanism because none is present. In this case, prediction must always be contingent and probabilistic. The observer is forced by the nature of his or her cognitive models to use a probability approach, and this approach can never yield "lawlike" precision at the level of the relationships among specific systems.

These considerations lead to the conclusion that a different form of "explanation" is needed to deal with the ecological phenomena characteristic of an ecological field than is needed for use in dealing with the operations inside the boundaries of a system. In the next section, a foundation for arriving at such an explanatory approach will be laid. To do this, I must return to a self-conscious discussion of how an observer constructs a reality that he or she first models and then attempts to explain. This will take us into a world of mirrors in which the mind looks into itself only to find its own reflection as its ultimate reality.

7.5   Levels of Abstraction and Types of "Reality"

We will begin with a Kantian foundation and attempt to move beyond that back into an ecology of mind reminiscent of Bateson, von Glasersfeld, and von Foerster, with a touch of Korzybski thrown in along the way (Kant, 1943; Bateson, 1972b; von Glaserfeld, 1987; von Foerster, 1981; Korzybski, 1941). The attempt will be to isolate what will be called "levels of abstraction" with respect to the concepts the mind forms as it deals with sensory stimulation and constructs models to represent its environment.

My contention is that, even with a constructivist agenda, it is possible to distinguish differences in the degree to which conceptualizations, meant to represent things outside the mind, are removed from the world they are intended to represent. At the outset, it is assumed that the mind deals only with abstractions or with mental constructs formed according to a cognitive code of one sort or another. Nevertheless, it is possible to compound abstractions by deriving more abstract conceptions from other abstractions, thus piling one layer of mental construction upon another (Korzybski, 1941).

Levels of abstraction are defined in terms of the hierarchy of cognitive operations the mind uses to create and use concepts, and the cognitive images they yield when applied in the cognitive action that organizes sensory data. Each time a new cognitive operation is performed, using the fruits of a previous cognitive action as the substance it works upon, the level of abstraction is raised by one step upward on a "ladder of abstraction."

The terminology employed by Kant will supply a useful beginning point for a discussion of such levels of abstraction. In order to separate ultimate reality, that is, things as they are, independent of an observer, from things as cognitively perceived by an observer, Kant used the terms *noumena*, and *phenomena*. The following definitions will be used for these terms here (Kant, 1943):

Noumenon—a thing as it is; an object in its natural full state of being in a so-called "real world" uninterpreted by an observer.

Phenomenon—a thing as perceived by an observer, a mental image that stands for a thing in the mind of an observer. A cognitive construct organized according to a cognitive code. A mentally constructed reality taken by an observer to be a representation of a noumenon.

If I use the numbers 0, 1, 2, 3 . . . to represent levels of abstraction, then *noumena* are defined as being at the "zero" level of abstraction because they are nonmental in character and therefore not abstract, being objects or things as they "really are" in nature. *Phenomena* are thought of as being at the first level of abstraction, because they are regarded as cognitively constructed, abstract images of objects that are encountered through the senses. The first level of abstraction is reached when an observer takes in sensory stimulation and converts these sensations into information by use of a cognitive action. This cognitive action encodes and organizes sensory "data" according to a preexisting set of cognitive rules and preexisting patterns of mental operation, and gives meaning to such "data," thus converting sensations into information.

Information is distinguished from sensory data in this statement, as follows: Sensory data are raw, sensory stimuli transmitted to the brain as neural impulses. Information is sensory data after being cognitively processed and converted into a form the mind recognizes as being meaningful. When the observer's "eyes," already controlled by a set of cognitive systems that direct or control the process of observation, take in light rays from a round, red object and convert them into neural energy, transmitting this energy to the brain that is already "programmed" to organize such stimulation according to a cognitive code, the observer's mind registers the cognitively organized image as an apple. This cognitive action of organizing neural stimulation derived from the operation of the senses creates a first-level abstraction, a mental image of a *particular* apple.

When this occurs, a cognitive process has intervened between a noumenon, an apple as it is in "nature," and the observer's mental contact with the noumenon. The observer as a thinking, knowing subject knows only the cognitively coded image and is separated from "true reality" by one step up the ladder of abstraction.

In reasoning about this environment and in relating to it in terms of action, the mind of the observer (which is the locus of cognitive action) works only upon phenomena, and never upon noumena. Because the mind is a kind of cognitive machine, it always operates above the zero level of abstraction. This is the same thing as saying the mind is a generator and user of abstractions. But since it generates its own abstractions, it can never know whether its own observations correspond to the nonabstract world of noumena. Furthermore, because the senses, as organic operations, are sensitive only to a certain restricted range of stimulation, and stimulation itself converts "real-world" noumena into neural energy according to a biological code, the observer cannot be in contact with any noumenon as it really is in nature.

Even so, at the first level of abstraction, the observer, guided by a cognitive apparatus, uses the senses as the source of stimulation that initiates a process of cognitive action. For this reason, we can say that he or she is only one step away from the world outside the mind, even though that world remains unknown until it is converted into neural energy, and then into an abstract form by cognitive action. At this level of abstraction, the observer is dealing with particular things, *individual* objects and events, that are indirectly experienced through the senses and assigned a *particular identity* as individual objects in the mind of an observer.

7.5.1   Metaphenomena

Once the mind has generated information, internationalizing it as abstract cognitive material, it can perform additional cognitive operations on this information. These actions have the effect of further raising the level of abstraction of the ideas the mind itself has generated by generating secondary mental constructions. If the mind takes phenomena rather than noumena as its "raw material" and constructs a generalized conception on the basis of conceptions referring to many separate specific phenomena, then it generates a *metaphenomenon*. For example, assume that there are thousands upon thousands of noumena (individual things) that the mind has converted by cognitive action into phenomena (concepts referring to individual things), and then the mind creates a class term (or uses an already formed class term) to apply to all of them as if they were cognitively substitutable, one for the other, being members of the same class. This class or categorical concept would constitute a second-order abstraction, which we called a metaphenomenon. Table 7.1 may be used to represent the ideas being presented. The example of apples can be used for this purpose.

There is a problem in understanding the difference between the cognitive experience of a phenomenon and a metaphenomenon stemming from the nature of language, the code used to create and refer to abstractions. The word *apple*, like all words, is a categorical term referring to a class or category of phenomena. In the act of perception, an observer usually uses a linguistic code as the basis for converting sensory impressions into cognitive materials

TABLE 7.1
Levels of Abstraction

1. Noumena	Real individual apples as they are
2. Phenomena	Mental conception of Apple 1, Apple 2, Apple 3, Apple 4–Apple *N* (concept of particular, separate, individual objects, without thinking of them as belonging to a class of similar objects)
3. Metaphenomena	Apples as a type of object (all of the phenomena encoded as individual objects converted by cognitive action into a categorical concept)

usable by the mind, which itself is organized by the structure of the code (Korzybski, 1958). Therefore, Table 7.1, and the discussion of it, seems to say that the first cognitive step above the zero level of abstraction is the step of identifying a noumena (an apple) in terms of a linguistic code, that is, as a member of the class of fruit called apples. This would be like saying that in order to recognize an individual apple as a distinct object, we would have to associate sensory data with a categorical abstraction, thus jumping to the second level of abstraction without ever passing through the first. Here, however, the claim is that prior to categorization, the mind must organize a mental image that cognitively "models" a phenomenon, thus furnishing it with a surrogate for a noumenon, a particular object of observation, and only then can it fit that cognitive image into a class. Perception of individual objects is therefore prior to classification. First, the mind must "see" configuration and individuality, and then it can give a categorical meaning to the configuration. We are first aware of individual "objects," or "things," and then of classes of similar things.

Another difficulty arises when the mind operates in the opposite direction. I start with the idea apple and then search my environment for an object falling into that class. The problem is that the mind of the mature observer is already filled with cognitive systems that define class terms and the language used to refer to them. As Bateson (1972b) pointed out, there is a whole "ecology of mind" that operates to organize perception and cognition. When an observer, with a mind already filled with cognitive systems, a set of which define fruit, and therefore "apple," confronts an environment that presents the mind with sensory stimuli it is prepared to interpret as "apple," the observer "sees" both an individual apple and apples as members of a class called apples, or perhaps fruit or food. Nevertheless, we will claim that the word *phenomenon* refers only to individual objects with separate identities, and only after comparing such objects (a cognitive operation) and "seeing similarity" among them (another cognitive operation) can we say that several cases fall into the same category.

At the phenomenological level, concepts refer to objects thought of as occupying specific locations in time and space, and being capable of operating or being operated upon. Included also would be processes or behaviors executed by objects, along with their interaction with each other. The key to understanding the idea "phenomenon" is that they are thought of as being *observable*. Here, *observable* implies the use of an apparatus through which observation takes place, be the apparatus the biological senses of an observer or an artificial apparatus used as a substitute for the senses. In all cases, it implies the use of a cognitive system that converts sensory data into information.

Cognitive conceptions of categories or classes of things are at a higher level of abstraction than conceptions of individual objects, and therefore metaphenomena are at a higher level of abstraction than phenomena. This is illustrated in Table 7.2, showing the cognitive actions performed to reach each level of abstraction.

It is apparent that the reasoning followed here could be pressed further to show that second-order metaphenomena are also possible and that they are a step higher in abstraction than first-order metaphenomena. For example, once the metaphenomenological designations apples, oranges, and bananas have been formed, it is possible to form the notion "fruit," which requires that the classes apples, oranges, and bananas be compared and considered similar along some dimension or dimensions, this being an additional cognitive action. Thus, there could also be third, fourth and nth level metaphenomena. This idea, however, is beyond what is needed for this discussion of ecology that, by now, must seem lost in the haze of an abstract philosophical discussion.

TABLE 7.2
Cognitive Operations and Levels of Abstraction

Level of abstraction	Type of "reality"	Example
0. Zero level of abstraction	Nomenon	Apple #1 as is
Cognitive Action 1	Organizing a mental image of a particular object, Apple #1.	
1. First level of abstraction	Phenomenon	That particular apple as it is perceived in the mind of an observer
Cognitive Action 2	Seeing similarity in a number of separate objects and assigning a common name and concept to all of them.	
2. Second level of abstraction	Metaphenomenon	The class, apples

7.5.2   Self-Referential Systems and Ecological Fields: Phenomena or Metaphenomena?

Let us make a cognitive leap back into the discussion of systems and ecological fields by making a definitive statement couched in the terms just
discussed. First, consider whether to regard systems as phenomena or
metaphenomena. From the previous discussion, it should be apparent that
conceptualizations referring to particular systems cannot be regarded as
noumena, because to "see" a system, it is necessary for the mind to organize
its image of an object that is identified cognitively as a system using a particular language and a particular logic. The mind, therefore, constructs a mental
model of an object that conforms to an a priori cognitive apparatus. Once
constructed, even though on the basis of sensory data, the mental construct
must be called a phenomenon. The mind sees the phenomenon "system" but
not the noumenon from which sensory data are taken in order to construct
an image of the system.

Particular systems, as dealt with in the mind, are therefore phenomena
when we think of them as particular cases with an identity unique unto
themselves. My image of Harvard University, organized in such a way that I
think of Harvard as a system, refers to a phenomenon. My mentally constructed image of my own body as an organic system is a phenomenological
image. All independent, bounded, self-referential systems perceived by the
mind as individual objects are phenomena.

According to this definition, the category universities, even with the
proviso that I think of *all* universities as systems, constitutes a metaphenomenon. The same applies to such categories as lions, zebras, and human beings
thought of as classes or species of organic systems. These terms refer to categories of phenomena (mentally constructed images of objects) that are considered similar in that they are thought of by means of a cognitive apparatus
as particular types of systems.

This being true by definition, then, it becomes apparent that when we
consider ecological fields and wish to pass beyond the statement that such
fields are comprised of many separate, particular systems, we are forced to
raise the level of abstraction of our ideas above the phenomenological level
to include the metaphenomenological level. We might risk saying at this
point that the structure of ecological fields is "comprised of" or "conceptualized as" very high-order metaphenomena by use of a set of cognitive operations that raise the level of abstraction of the concepts used to generate the
idea of such a structure.

There are many problems with this statement that must be addressed
before its implications are clear, but it will serve as a beginning point. For the
mind to remain consistent with the notion of system as defined earlier, and
at the same time to generate the idea of an ecological field that contains sys-

tems as a conceptual element, it is necessary to introduce a new set of cognitive operations into the cognitive apparatus that generate what we have called metaphenomena.

I might oversimplify the argument by saying that "systems" as conceptualized here lie at the phenomenological level (first level of abstraction), but ecological fields lie at the metaphenomenological level (second or higher level of abstraction). This means that the difference between the two constructs is not merely one of scale or size, one being at the micro- and the other at the macrolevel, but a difference that involves the cognitive processes utilized in formulating the constructs and using them as a basis for explanation.

This difference can be seen most easily by considering two of the ideas presented earlier in the discussion of ecological fields: (1) the idea of populations of systems, and (2) the idea of "categorical interdependence." To comprehend the significance of this discussion, it will be necessary at the same time to consider what is meant by "causal explanation," or perhaps what is meant by the statement that the behavior of one object impacts upon or affects another.

7.5.3 Populations of Systems as Metaphenomena

Let me begin by considering populations of systems. I have said that an ecological field contains populations of systems, differentiated according to a division of labor into niches. In terms of the present discussion of phenomena and metaphenomena, it is clear that the idea of a "population of systems" is at the metaphenomenological level, because it requires us to think of many separate objects called *systems*, all of which fall into the same category. If we return to the discussion of lions and zebras, the category lions and the idea of a population of lions both require the mind to go beyond constructing a mental surrogate for particular lions as organic systems. We must now compare individual organisms using cognitive criteria for judging them similar and then place them mentally in the same category. The idea of a population of lions also requires a means of "counting" or thinking of the size of the category. When these two operations are performed, we have taken a step or two away from the phenomenological level and have "invented" a conception at the metaphenomenological level. Individual lions conceptualized as separate organic systems are constructed in the mind at the phenomenological level. They are the objects taken as the material upon which the mind works in constructing a new level of abstraction.

At the phenomenological level we can easily think of an individual lion as biting us, or eating a zebra, because it is conceptualized at the first level of abstraction and is thought of as representing a noumena capable of biting. We cannot, however, as easily think of the category lions as either biting or eating, because it is a second-level abstraction made up of first-level abstractions.

Only individual lions (phenomena) have teeth that can bite, and only individual lions may eat. As a matter of fact, biting and eating are part of the constructed image of the system called *lion*.

This is not a matter of empirical fact but one of conceptualization. Categories and populations are mental constructs created by using other abstractions as their raw material. Mental constructions neither bite nor eat! Similarly, it must be admitted that a phenomenological image of a lion can neither bite nor eat, but it can be said that the phenomenological model of a lion may include biting and eating as part of the abstract construction that is meant to serve as a surrogate for a biting–eating object. But including such a conception for a category, as if the category itself has teeth, strains the imagination of even the most naive empiricist and certainly violates the logic of the cognitive procedures used to create and use categories.

Nevertheless, we can still argue that the size of the zebra population "affects" or "limits" the chances that a particular lion will bite or eat on the basis that the "supply" of zebras is important for understanding the *probability* that individual lions will have the opportunity to exercise their capacity to engage in such behavior. On this basis we cannot say that the metaphenomenon called "zebra population" has no relevance for the operation of the individual organic system of a particular lion (that serves here as a metaphor for a phenomenon).

This consideration leads to the conclusion that we must include within the cognitive apparatus, used to represent ecological fields, some means of dealing with how phenomena and metaphenomena will be conceptualized in relation to each other in an explanatory mechanism. The explanatory mechanism will, itself, be a cognitive apparatus that generates an artificial image of how ecological fields function. In that functioning, we must make room for the idea that metaphenomena may be seen as limiting or "affecting" phenomena. This is like saying that populations of systems may affect or limit the behavior of individual members of the population. To accomplish this, it will be necessary to examine the idea of explanation more closely, but before this, consider the idea of the differentiation of populations according to niches in a division of labor.

7.5.4   Division of Labor and Interdependence as Metaphenomena

Earlier I said that ecological fields are differentiated according to a division of labor within which species of systems occupy niches relative to one another. Obviously, this idea rests on the capacity to categorize systems into types or species and to conceptualize niches in a web of interdependence. This requires a set of metaphenomenological constructs that the mind uses to "see" a set of categorical relationships. Furthermore, the idea of categorical interdependence is at a higher level of abstraction than the idea of the actual interaction between systems in real time and space. To see two autonomous, self-referential systems interact in an ecological field, a particular lion and a particular zebra, for example, it is necessary for an observer to utilize a cognitive apparatus that includes the idea of system and the idea of interaction, both defined in such a manner as to generate an image of a particular case. This leads me to say that the actual interaction between two systems viewed as a particular case is conceptualized at the phenomenological level, because it refers to a particular incident from which data are obtained according to a cognitive plan. On the other hand, the idea that one species of system (lions) is dependent for food supply upon another species (zebras) in a categorical sense is at the metaphenomenological level, because it requires the combination of cases defined at the phenomenological level into a categorical generalization that not only sees all lions and all zebras as being similar or alike but also defines their relationship to each other categorically in terms of niches in a food chain.

Even so, it can be said that the behavior of individual members of one species of systems (zebras) is *constrained* by categorical interdependence with another species (lions). The division of labor, viewed as the whole relationship network among categories of systems, that defines the structure of an ecological field requires even a higher level of abstraction in which second- or third-order metaphenomena enter the constructed image. First-order metaphenomena, species, are seen as occupying niches in a division of labor or a food chain, these latter concepts constituting, at the very least, second-order metaphenomena. At this level of abstraction, we are faced with the need to make explicit how we can understand the dynamics of an ecological field that has been defined using metaphenomenological terms and itself is *not a system* but, instead, a cognitive object comprised of many separate interacting systems.

The problem is to devise a means of representing the way an ecological field works or operates, and how it evolves or changes as a field, given the assumption that we cannot think of such a field in the same way we think of systems. The crux of the matter lies in the difference between how we think of bonded and contingent relationships and how we think of explanation with respect to networks of categorical elationships.

To conceptualize bonded relationships, we remain at the phenomenological level of conceptualization, because such relationships occur between specific exact units that are parts of the same mechanism. They are indirectly "observable" through the use of a cognitive system and are thought of as being elements in a noumenon under observation. The idea of a particular bonded relationship is at the first level of abstraction, even though we may think more abstractly of all such relationships as forming a category at the metaphenomenological level. The mechanism that "governs" the operation of a system is made up entirely of such relationships. This fact entitles us to think of the behavior of particular parts of a system as being *determined* by their placement in the mechanism. The actual operation of a system consists of the behavior of its parts or elements in relation to each other inside the mechanism of the whole. We can become cognitively aware of how a system operates on the basis of knowing how it is constructed as a kind of machine or organism. In short, we can use some form of deterministic (mechanistic) logic to predict the behavior of a system's parts from knowledge of its internal order. This is true even though that knowledge is itself generated by a cognitive apparatus that organizes it.

In the case of ecological fields, we are operating at a higher level of abstraction and are dealing with metaphenomena that have only indirect observational referents. Here, the referents for our concepts are often categories or classes of phenomena conceptualized by use of a cognitive operation that removes them an additional step or two away from the observational level. The question now becomes how to conceptualize the operation of metaphenomena that are themselves mental constructs referring not to noumena that operate in time and space and are observable, but to abstract conceptions of classes of noumena constructed according to a set of cognitive rules. Can a category, *as a category*, produce an impact or an effect on anything? Can a metaphenomenon such as the population of lions that is present in a field produce any outcome that affects, influences, constrains, or impacts upon other categories, the population of zebras, for example? For that matter, can a population produce an effect on an individual member of that category or of another category?

Certainly, we cannot usefully say that categories of systems, like individual systems, can form parts of a larger systematic mechanism. Systems are not comprised of categories of parts but of particular parts. It is this very idea that allows us to use knowledge of a systemic mechanism to explain the operation of a system!

7.6   Possible Solutions to the Problem of Explanation at the Level of an Ecological Field

There are two possible paths that can lead us to answers for these questions. These paths lie at the core of ecological reasoning. First, we can assume that, in an ecological field, the behavior of individual systems in relation to other systems in the field, and in relation to the substratum that supports these systems, produces impacts on particular elements in the field. These interactions and the resultant impacts in individual cases are observable, given the proper cognitive apparatus, and lie at what I have called the *phenomenological level*. By using metaphenomenological constructs, we can see the cumulative effects of such individual-level behaviors. The aggregate effects we see will, by definition, be metaphenomena, but they will have significance for interpreting other metaphenomena as well as phenomena, because they summarize changes that alter the environments to which individual systems must adapt.

For example, the impact of the behavior of individual lions who eat individual zebras (a phenomenon) will be reflected in changes in the populations of lions and zebras (a metaphenomenon) such that in the long run, we may make statements such as the following: "As the population of lions increases, the population of zebras decreases until the zebra population falls below a given point, at which time the lion population will stabilize or begin to decrease." This statement uses metaphenomenological constructs as the basis for making a prediction, but it can prove valuable as a prediction of metaphenomena.

It is important to note, however, that such a statement says nothing about the relationship between particular systems. It is a statement about the relationship between populations of systems. On the basis of such a statement, we cannot predict which lion will eat which zebra and how a particular lion will act toward the other elements in the field in which it is located. The reason lies in the fact that the relationships between lions as organic systems and other systems in the same ecological field is one of *contingency*, rather than one of *systemic determination*. Lions as a species, according to the fiction created here, are related to zebras in a categorical, metaphenomenological division of labor, such that they are dependent on zebras as a category. Which lion and which zebra interacts is dependent upon a set of contingencies that itself is generated by the organization of the field.

These contingencies are multidimensional; nevertheless, each contingency is constrained or bounded and limited by the organization of the whole ecological field. When we deal with the interaction among systems, we are dealing with a form of *bounded indeterminacy*. Only an actuarial prediction concerning the interaction between particular systems can be made under these conditions. The question now becomes, "How can we conceptualize the mechanisms that place boundaries or limits on the contingent relationships among particular systems?"

This brings us back to the general discussion of metaphenomena. It will be our contention that metaphenomenological constructs can be seen as a means of dealing cognitively with contingency and bounded indeterminacy. By oversimplification, we might say metaphenomenological constructs function to allow us to conceive of the limits placed on the behavior of systems, which, themselves, have been conceptualized at the phenomenological level. This is like saying that metaphenomena such as the population of lions and zebras function to limit the possibilities of interaction between individual lions and zebras. Or it is like saying that the categorical interdependence between lions and zebras limits the probabilities of various forms of behavior on the part of individual lions and zebras.

By conceptualizing metaphenomena, we open the cognitive possibility of using "probability theory" as a means of making ecological predictions. This amounts in cognitive-systems-theory terms to saying that by creating a cognitive system that incorporates metaphenomenological concepts constructed on the basis of a classification strategy, we can use the cognitive apparatus of probability theory to deal with the bounded indeterminacy stemming from the contingent relationships we have conceived as prevailing among the separate, self-governing systems that inhabit an ecological field. What results is the cognitive capacity to make predictions at the categorical level. Such predictions do not rest on an understanding of an overall ecological mechanism, but instead on an "actuarial" approach to prediction.

This sort of reasoning can be illustrated by the following example that will allow me to expand upon the issue of bounded indeterminacy in an ecological field. Let us focus on the behavior of a single lion, and assume that a lion can eat nothing but zebras and that as an organism, it is prepared to recognize, pursue, and devour zebras. Let us also assume that zebras are biologically prepared to recognize lions as a threat and to flee from them when they approach. Let us assume further that each zebra is identical to each other in capacity to flee and that there are four zebras in the ecological field with the single lion and that they are located equidistant from the lion on a flat field with no obstructions. This is shown in Figure 7.1.

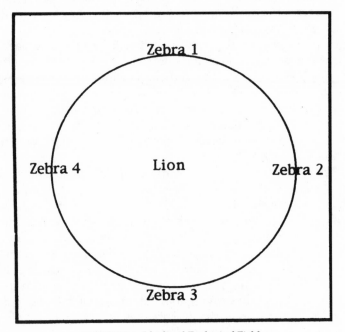

FIGURE 7.1. Idealized Ecological Field.

Obviously, under these conditions, the probability that the lion will pursue and eat a given zebra is one in four. Which zebra is pursued depends upon the lion's internal decision to attack one particular prey. But suppose the population is increased to 20 zebras, still situated equidistant from the lion. Now the probability of any given zebra being eaten is 1 in 20. Obviously, the size of the population of zebras has affected the probability that a given zebra will survive or be eaten. Thus, we are using a metaphenomenological concept (the size of the zebra population) to help us conceive of how survival contingencies are limited for individual systems.

This example can be altered, and we can now see a whole complex field of contingencies begin to operate to limit or bound the probabilities of encounters and outcomes among independently operating systems. Suppose, in the above example, one zebra moves closer to the lion than the others, so that spatial distribution is no longer equal between all members of the field, and suppose we think that distance is a factor that a lion perceives and considers in selecting its behavioral response. The probability that the lion will attack this particular zebra goes up from 1 in 10 to some higher probability, assuming a lion will attack the nearest prey. Suppose that when the lion attacks, the zebra jumps out of reach and runs away, now leaving the lion closer to the other zebras than himself. The probabilities again change. Or suppose we introduce irregularities into the "playing field," such that some zebras are protected by obstructions between them and the lion. Now the probabilities would change again. We might introduce more and more complexity into the example until our capacity to make probabilistic statements would be overwhelmed, and we would be left only with the possibility of the most general and least useful categorical statements, all based on broad metaphenomenological constructs. We might now be able to say that a zebra has a given probability of being eaten by some lion if we know how many zebras and lions there are and how many zebras are eaten by lions in a given time period, assuming that we have posited a propensity of lions to eat zebras in the first place.

Because each individual system in an ecological field is an autonomous entity capable of controlling its own behavior, and each system has a whole repertoire of behavior patterns at its disposal, the probability of predicting individual-level events involving relationships between specific systems becomes very remote indeed. Even so, we can still hold that we are not dealing with total chaos (Glick, 1988) in an ecological field, where prediction is impossible, but with multidimensional contingencies that are limited but whose relationship to each other is so complex that they must remain unknown at the level of individual systems. As a consequence, the order we perceive in ecological fields is a metaphenomenological order, a kind of *ordered chaos* or *bounded indeterminacy!*

In other words, when we are dealing with the relations between particular systems (a specific lion and zebra), we are unable to find a basis of prediction that is deterministic, because zebras and lions are autonomous systems capable of acting independently of each other, and because their behavior takes place in a field in which there are so many separate contingencies affecting their behavior that a positive, lawlike statement cannot be made at the level of individual systems. This means that we are forced to deal with the behavior of a system in relation to an ecological field at the metaphenomenological level rather than at the phenomenological level, and to make probabilistic rather than deteministic statements. At this level, we are dealing with the relations among categories of systems and with the impacts of populations of elements in the field upon each other. It furthermore means that we are using a probabilistic logic rather than a deterministic one.

There is a paradox here. Within systems, when dealing with the operation of parts in relation to each other within a systemic mechanism, we can use a deterministic logic to predict the behavior of the parts in relationship to each other with a high degree of certainty. This logic is based on the assumption that a system is like a machine in which the structure of the machine "determines" its internal operation. But when we leave the boundaries of the "systemic machine" and deal with the system's behavior toward an environment it does not itself control by means of its internal mechanism, deterministic logic fails, and we are forced to depend upon contingent statements couched in probabilistic terms. This is made necessary because the environment of a given autonomous system contains other autonomous systems whose behavior *is not predictable from inside a single systemic mechanism.*

Between or among systems, relationships must therefore be dealt with on the basis of indeterminacy or probabilistic contingency. The ecological field comprised of many separate systems is a kind of organized chaos or bounded indeterminacy, where we can think in terms of the metaphenomena that limit or bound indeterminacy by setting the conditions to which systems must adapt in order to operate and in order to survive as systems. As observers we must "see" an ecological field through the use of a cognitive apparatus that uses a logic and a conceptual framework that is entirely different than the one we use when dealing with the internal functioning of systems. The paradox is that the deterministic logic used to understand the internal functioning of systems cannot be used when we look at the relations between systems. *The very autonomy or self-referentiality built into the idea of systems that makes it possible for us to make deterministic predictions makes it impossible to think deterministically about the relations among systems!*

This would seem to lead to the conclusion that the world of ecological fields we build by cognitive action contains the paradox that highly deterministic objects called systems behave toward their environments indeterministically; thus, the very ideas that produce an image of an ordered or deterministic world at the same time generate a conception of indeterminacy. Order produces chaos! It is not simply a matter of the idea of order demanding the idea of disorder as its grounding, but the idea that autonomy and boundedness as ideas necessary to conceptualize order, lead, at another level of abstraction, to a conception of disorder because random behavior on the part of a population of separate objects will occur if each object acts independently of the others, a condition that prevails among separate, self-referential systems inhabiting a common space.

7.7   Types of Metaphenomenological Conditions in Ecological Fields

It is possible to identify several dimensions along which metaphenomena limit and affect the behavior of systems in an ecological field. As stated earlier, metaphenomena place limits on the behavior of systems by establishing a set of conditions to which systems must adapt. Because they set the conditions of adaptation, metaphenomena function to select systems for survival and are therefore keys to understanding the evolution of ecological fields. They are implicated in the survival or nonsurvival of specific types of systems and in the morphogenic change that occurs as systems adapt to conditions in their environments.

Such a statement is justified by the following reasoning. In order for an individual system to survive and reproduce itself, it must be capable of controlling its relationship to its environment by generating within itself, as part of its internal mechanism, the capacity to conduct successful transactions with its environment. By *successful*, I mean transactions that supply it with needed resources utilized to sustain itself as a system or transactions that defend the system against being injured or destroyed by events occurring outside itself.

To control its relationship with its environment, a system must develop mechanisms that provide it with a means of generating information concerning its environment, enabling it to predict the outcome of its own behavior when it interacts with other systems, or when it encounters threatening environmental conditions. Such predictions do not have to be perfect but must fall within a range that tolerates the survival of the system. A lion, for example, has to contain within itself the capacity to be successful enough in hunting zebras to be supplied with food sufficient for its survival. The lion need not be successful every time it hunts a zebra.

The survival of a species of systems furthermore depends upon a sufficient number of individual systems within the species being successful in adapting to conditions in their ecological fields to allow them to reproduce themselves, thus maintaining the population that constitutes the species as a metaphenomenological element in the ecological field.

If conditions change, so that the survival of individual members of a species is threatened in sufficient numbers, and if the species of systems does not undergo morphogenic change, the species will become extinct. On the other hand, if morphogenic change that allows them to adapt to the new conditions can be produced in a sufficient number of individual members of a species, the species, although changed, will survive. This, of course, demands a mechanism capable of producing morphogenic change and also a mechanism that reproduces such change on a generational basis.

In biological ecology, such mechanisms are thought of as being genetic and being produced by mutation. It is not surprising in light of the previous discussion that both concepts, *genetics* and *mutations*, require metaphenomenological conceptualizations to explain how the mechanisms of evolution work. Later, I will discuss human social systems and offer a conceptualization of mechanisms appropriate to such systems. The point of this rather brief and oversimplified discussion of evolution is to call attention to the role of metaphenomena in dealing with an evolutionary perspective. In conceptualizing evolution, it is necessary to pay attention to metaphenomena that, as mental constructs, conceptualize the conditions of survival for systems, and by so doing point to the mechanisms involved in species-level extinction and survival. Because survival of individual systems, as well as species of systems, is deeply affected by metaphenomena, so is the evolution of the ecological field in which they are embedded as elements.

Let me now point to two classes of metaphenomena that are important to understanding evolutionary change, as well as the behavior of the underlying phenomena upon which conceptions of metaphenomena rest. The list to be given is by no means exhaustive and is offered only to suggest some of the types of metaphenomena that must be considered in dealing with change in ecological fields.

7.7.1   Population and Spatial Distribution

As already noted, the relative sizes of various systemic populations operate as elements in ecological fields to limit the behavior of individual members of populations and also to set the condition of survival for species of systems. So, too, does the geographic distribution of these populations relative to one another. Both population size and distribution affect the contingencies and probabilities that set the conditions of adaptation for members of the field. This statement holds equally for organic systems and social systems. As I shall point out later, population factors are involved in the competition among members of a given species for survival, as well as in the conflict between species that arises out of the relationships among the niches they occupy in such things as food chains or energy-exchange networks.

7.7.2   Aggregate Resource Consumption

Closely related to population sizes and spatial distribution is the metaphenomenon *aggregate resource consumption*. Each population of systems utilizes certain elements in the environment as the raw materials processed within the system to ensure its survival. In the case of biological systems such as lions and zebras, the resources are things such as air, water, and food. In the case of human social systems, resources might include things like iron and steel, bricks and mortar, paper, and various types of machines, all of which in earlier stages of production require other resources to produce, for example, iron ore, coal and oil, water, and so forth.

It is usually the case that many different types of systems make demands on the same resources and are in competition for access to them. For example, zebras eat grass, but so do many other species, for example, antelopes and wildebeests. Similarly, many human systems use iron and steel, oil and water. This means that if we are to examine the effects of the behavior of many species of systems on an ecological field, we will have to identify categories of critical resources and may wish to examine *aggregate resource consumption* with respect to particular types of resources, because the drawdown on resources affects the behavior of individual systems, as well as the survival of species of systems. This enterprise, of course, requires the use of metaphenomenological concepts organized into a complex cognitive apparatus. For example, since many species of animals eat grass, the aggregate consumption of grass available in an ecological field is an important matter in understanding the growth or decline of populations that in a reverse manner is related to the aggregate consumption of resources. Obviously, some resources are renewable and others are not, and this makes a difference in how we think about the evolution of the field and the survival of species within it.

Metaphenomena such as the supply of grass or of petroleum or iron ore do not operate as determinants of the survival of systems in the same way as intrasystemic factors do, but they set limits on survival and create the conditions to which individual systems and species of systems must adapt. They raise or lower the probability of success in the game of survival. Through the use of metaphenomenological concepts, the observer is allowed to "see" the aggregate effects of the behavior of many individual systems on a common field and to construct a mental image of how the behavior of individual systems impacts upon the environment of all systems, thus feeding back upon their own behavior or on the behavior of similar systems.

7.7.3   Aggregate Environmental Impact of Systemic By-Products and Waste

Within any cognitive apparatus meant for use in creating images of ecological fields, it is necessary to introduce concepts that deal with the so-called "waste products" produced by systems. At the phenomenological level, biological and social systems are thought of as taking in resources from their self-defined environments and using them in their own internal functioning. They rarely, however, make use of all aspects of a given input, and there is almost always some leftover waste sent back into the environment. There are also by-products produced by systemic functioning that cross the system's boundaries and end up in its environment. For example, many species of animals breathe in air and exhale carbon dioxide. They also exhale water vapor and other chemical substances and radiate heat. Organic as well as social systems may also artificialize their environment by constructing habitats such as nests, or burrows, or houses, office buildings, and factories. They wear trails on the earth's surface, build roads and highways, bridges and dams, and so forth.

The point is that systems not only utilize resources taken from their environments but also produce waste products and make changes in the landscape to suit their own purposes. Some of these changes or impacts upon the environment may have positive effects on the functioning and survival of other systems, and some may have negative effects. What is noteworthy, however, is the fact that the aggregate effects of the behavior of individual systems, each operating according to their own internal mechanisms in adapting to conditions outside themselves, according to their own view of those conditions, change the characteristics of the ecological field in which they are located and thereby feed back upon the adaptation of individual systems as well as the species they represent, affecting both their behavior and their survival.

The examples of aggregate population effects on environmental resources and waste production are sufficient to illustrate the point I am trying to make. The aggregate effects of systemic behaviors are not produced by a controlling, overall systemic mechanism built into the structure of an ecological field such that the field itself adapts as a whole and maintains itself as an organized entity, as if it were, itself, a higher order system. Such aggregate effects are produced by the operation of individual systems, behaving according to their own self-referential order in contingent relationships with other elements in their environments. These effects are mentally comprehended by an observer only by use of concepts that lie at the level of metaphenomena. Because metaphenomena are defined at the categorical level, where the mind introduces a new cognitive operation as a means of conceptualizing a "collective" or "categorical" generalization, we cannot see them as constituting parts or elements in an organized megasystem. As already pointed out, systems contain networks of particular parts that stand in unit-specific relationships to form a mechanism that controls the functioning of its own component elements. In addition, we have noted that such elements and their relationships to each other may be observed by use of first-order abstractions that convert them into phenomenological concepts the mind may manipulate in constructing an image of an object and its functioning.

Categorical or metaphenomenological concepts do not refer to anything that can be thought of as functioning or operating as if it were a part of a machine or an organ in a biological system. Metaphenomena cannot therefore be conceived of as elements in a structural mechanism that controls the operation of a system. For this reason, it appears that ecological fields are misnamed when they are called ecosystems. Instead, they may be thought of more usefully as a totally different kind of object of observation than a system. They are objects comprised of the relationships among systems in contingent networks formed on the basis of a set of categorical rather than unit-specific relationships. Such contingent networks do not themselves form a system but an ecological field. Here, the concept *field* is used to represent an object of cognition that can be modeled and understood on the basis of categorical reasoning, employing concepts that generalize about the aggregate consequences of multidimensional contingency relations among elements in the field.

7.8   *Balance, Equilibrium, and Ecological Fields*

Ecologists and social scientists using ecological concepts are fond of employing the ideas of equilibrium or balance when talking about ecological problems. They often say, for example, that this or that human action is destroying the balance of nature or of the ecosystem. If left alone by man or by external intervention, the ecosystem will achieve a kind of balance that will have the effect of reproducing the various species in the field and maintaining the relative populations of species over a long period of time.

It is perhaps on the basis of such ideas that the belief that "natural areas" are best regarded as systems has been accepted. From this perspective, anything that can be conceptualized as achieving a form of nonentropotic equilibrium qualifies as a system. Obviously, any set of objects in a state of entropy, the ultimate equilibrium, would not constitute a system, because systems are always active and bounded.

Given these arguments concerning the well-known idea of balance, it is important to address the problem of how ecological fields operate to affect the persistence of the field itself and of its internal organization and equilibrium. It is apparent from the earlier discussion that this problem must be approached using metaphenomenological concepts and the notion of contingency as the key elements used to defend the claim that ecological fields are nonsystems but nevertheless may appear to maintain a form of stability if left undisturbed.

A beginning can be made by assuming that metaphenomena such as those discussed earlier under the heading of aggregate population and aggregate environmental impacts, taken together in a multidimensional matrix, set multidimensional limits for the behavior of systems, and therefore for their adaptation and survival at the species level. It should be apparent that each species of system, conceived as a collective metaphenomenon, and each dimension of system resource utilization and environmental impact provides a source for the conceptualization of the limiting factors, or the conditions of survival for each system in the field. At the same time, because we have recognized the interdependence of species systems at the metaphenomenological level and have introduced the idea of contingent relationships as a means of dealing with the relations among specific systems, we have provided within the cognitive apparatus that defines a field the means by which to conceptualize how a field may maintain itself, given no outside disturbance.

For example, the relative populations of systems are interdependent and cannot exceed the limits set by the contingencies of their relationship to each other. Therefore, if lions eat so many zebras that the contingencies are altered in the direction that some lions must starve, then the lion population is reduced until there is again a sufficient number of zebras to feed the population. Uncertainty of survival, an inevitable corollary of contingent relationships, produces fluctuation in the populations found in a territory around some mean. It is this fluctuation around a mean that is perceived as "balance" in an ecological field.

Fluctuation in the probability of survival success, contingent upon multidimensional metaphenomena in an ecological field, produces the tendency of populations to vary interdependently around some mean level and in so doing supplies the mechanism that produces so-called "balance." Balance is no more than the perception that this mean level of copopulations will reestablish itself if no external change is introduced into the field that alters the matrix of contingencies, or if no morphogenic change occurs within the field that alters those contingencies. The order perceived in ecological fields as balance or equilibrium is an order produced by multidimensional random variation. After all, there is an order revealed when probability theory is applied to random events, and it is this sort of order that is ecological.

Even with this sort of conception, it must be admitted that the so-called balance is itself produced by imbalance, that is, by populations of one species exceeding the limits of contingency and then being forced back into line by the failure of individual systems to survive. Such balance perceived as a set of relatively stable populations is one achieved by the negative or limiting factors that work upon the probability of systemic success in the game of survival and not a positive, controlling mechanism that guides or determines the functioning of the parts of an overall systemic mechanism.

The source of the regulation in an ecological field, if it can be called such, is the "struggle for survival" or "the competition" among systems for limited resources within the context of a set of limiting conditions. Developments that change the adaptive capacity of systems change their competitive advantage and impact upon other systems by altering the probabilities of their survival. But the very success of a species of systems in achieving short-range competitive advantage may prove, in the long run, to be its undoing, because it alters its own environment and changes the future contingencies of its own survival.

The complex, multidimensional conditions conceptualized as metaphenomena operating simultaneously through time have the effect of confining the fluctuation in the populations of systems inhabiting the same field within limits which, over long periods of time, tend to prevent catastrophic changes in the field itself. By a catastrophic change I mean one that completely reorders the division of labor in the field (or the organization of ecological niches) and results in massive species extinction, as well as in the generation of new systems with different internal orders and survival probabilities. These new types of systems result in new species being introduced into the field when they are sufficiently numerous to be recognized by an observer as occupying a common niche in a newly organized ecological field. Catastrophic change amounts to change in which the conditions of survival for most or all of the systems in the field are altered beyond their capacity to act adaptively without radical morphogenic change.

7.9   *Conclusions*

The concept *ecological field* is made necessary by the very definition of the concept *self-referential system*. Systems cannot be closed and self-referential, and at the same time be parts of a larger system. Similarly, they cannot be in control of their own behavior and of their perceptions of their environments if they are controlled by a larger mechanism. Self-referential systems are automatons. These things being true, by definition, it becomes necessary to think about the relationships among systems that interact with each other in a common space. The object that consists conceptually of a number of systems in interaction is called an *ecological field*.

In order to define the structure of an ecological field, it is necessary to invent a set of metaphenomenological concepts that allow us to think in terms of a division of labor among species of systems and of populations of systems, and of the collective outputs for their environments. To explain the consequences of metaphenomena for the field and its constituent units and categories of units, we have been forced to deal with probabilistic reasoning. Our conclusion has been that deterministic reasoning is appropriate to explaining causation within systems, but contingent probability is required to deal with the indeterminacy that is characteristic of ecological fields.

8

Social Systems in the Context of Ecological Fields

8.1   Introduction

The previous chapter presented a cognitive system through which an observer can build mental models of ecological fields. This discussion purposely avoided a detailed examination of social systems and their relationship to each other in the context of the environments they inhabit. As a matter of fact, that discussion "sidestepped" the issue of how social systems in contrast to individual organisms are viewed as elements in ecological fields and concentrated on simplified biological examples to illustrate concepts. This was done to allow ecological fields to be defined in the most general terms, without the discussion becoming mired down in details that pertain to the various forms that systems take.

This chapter will focus on human social systems and on their participation in ecological fields. The discussion will rest on the assumption that the general propositions concerning systems and the environments they inhabit, given in the previous chapter, hold true for social systems as well as for individual organisms. Furthermore, I will assume that the view presented concerning the nature and role of metaphenomena in understanding such things as stability and change in ecological fields also holds for all types of systems.

8.2   Thesis of This Chapter

The first problem to be faced involves the question of what is meant by the term *social system* and which types of phenomena the term will be used to refer to when discussing human societies. Since there is no time to engage in a long and detailed technical argument that establishes the identity of social systems on a highly technical basis from within sociological theory, I will begin this chapter by taking a shortcut and making certain assertions concerning how social systems will be treated in the arguments to be presented later. After this, a basis for making such assertions will be given by referring back to the last chapter.

Assertion 1: Human societies that utilize a market economy and employ a democratic form of government should not be thought of as systems but are more usefully regarded as sets of bounded, autonomous systems organized into an ecological network that, itself, is structured in terms of a categorical division of labor into interdependent ecological niches.

Assertion 2: The systems that form the elements of societies are (1) independent or detached social groups, such as families or small businesses; and (2) complex organizations consisting of several groups bonded together in an internal division of labor and controlled by a common authority or decision-making structure and a communication network. In such multigroup systems, the component groups act together as an organized whole in processing resources taken from the system's environment and in producing a common output or set of outputs. Examples of organizations are government agencies, manufacturing firms, retail organizations, schools, churches, and so forth.

Assertion 3: The independent groups and organizations contained within the structure of a society that has a market economy and democratic political institutions form an *ecological network* and operate as separate, self-referential systems in an *ecological field* that also contains biological systems and a substratum of physical elements and conditions.

8.2.1   Discussion of the Assertions

Human social systems, like all systems, consist of a set of parts or units bonded together in a set of unit-specific relationships to form a stable, bounded structure. In the case of independent or freestanding groups, the parts are actor-occupied positions containing differentiated roles, whereas in organizations the parts are groups with specialized functions to perform in a larger mechanism (see Bates and Harvey, 1975). The structure of social systems operates as the mechanism that organizes the behavior of the various units of structure and coordinates their behaviors in such a manner that they operate as specialized parts in a larger whole. In so doing, the parts, together, process resources and produce common outputs so that the whole system adapts to its environment as a bounded whole.

The key to identifying the boundaries of social systems is conceptually the same as that for identifying boundaries for any system. The parts or units of a social system are *bonded* to each other in *unit-specific relationships* in which exact subunits (actor-occupied positions or specialized groups) function or operate together in a persistent pattern to produce the behavior of the whole system and of its component parts. The boundaries of a social system are reached when contingent categorical relationships are encountered.

Social systems are self-referential systems and, as such, are autonomous actors whose internal operation is controlled or governed by internal mechanisms, and whose behavior with respect to an environment is also self-governing. Because the environment of a social system, although defined for the system by internal mechanisms, contains other autonomous systems capable of self-regulation and therefore capable of selectively responding on their own terms, the relationship of social systems to their environment is *contingent*. If we can think of such units of societal structure as organizations (e.g., manufacturing firms or government agencies) that are self-referential in character, and of standing in categorical rather than unit-specific relationships to other systems in their environments, we must conclude that together they form what we have earlier called an ecological network located in an ecological field rather than a higher order system called a society. Using this perspective, a society would therefore be seen as an ecological subfield and not as a system.

The ecological nature of societal-level social networks can best be illustrated by examining the structure of market-exchange networks. This is true because such networks involve interaction between independent groups and organizations (economic units) in a set of contingent rather than bonded exchange relationships. These relationships arise out of an "economic division of labor" in an ecological subfield.

In market-exchange networks, bounded, self-governing social systems seeking inputs or resources for internal processing or consumption engage in exchanges with other social systems that have products to sell or exchange. The market is structured as an ecological subfield, because categories of specialized systems occupying niches in a division of labor seek inputs or resources from their environments containing categories of other systems upon which they are functionally dependent because a specific category or categories of other systems are potential suppliers of these inputs. At the same time, each system, being self-referential, has the structural autonomy necessary to select which exchange partner out of a category of potential exchange partners it will interact with in order to conduct a specific transaction. Which other system a particular system seeking resources deals with is contingent upon its own internal agenda and upon conditions in the ecological field, as well as on its own construction of that field by use of its own cognitive resources. This field contains a population of potential exchange partners and a population of competing resource users distributed geographically relative to each other.

Various types of social units may be regarded as "species of social systems," and individual cases within a category may be seen as separate, bounded, self-referential systems in much the same way that biological organisms were treated in the previous chapter. For example, clothing manufacturing firms may be regarded as one "species" or "class" of social systems in an ecological field that also contains another category, textile mills. Let us suppose that the economic division of labor at a given moment is such that clothing manufacturers do not produce their own textiles. Under such conditions, they would be dependent in a division of labor on a set of systems (textile mills) that do produce the raw materials they use in their own internal operation. In a market economy, each clothing manufacturer as an autonomous, self-referential system would be free to choose the textile mill from which it obtains cloth. Each textile mill would also be free to choose which customer to supply with cloth. Thus, the relationships between the two species of systems is a form of categorical contingent relationship. In the case of global markets, the systems referred to might not even be in the same society, as societies have been defined traditionally.

This is somewhat, though not entirely, like the relationships between lions and zebras caricatured in the last chapter. It is different because the lion–zebra game is zero-sum when applied between two particular animals, whereas the market economy game is not. Nevertheless, the market can be seen as a specialized ecological subfield within which a changing contingent exchange network operates to transfer resources among systems that are themselves structurally separate and behaviorally independent of any specific exchange partner. Even so, they remain categorically dependent on being successful in accomplishing an exchange with some particular system in the category upon which they are dependent.

This has the theoretical meaning that the various systems comprising the elements in a market do not form a larger system. They are not incorporated into a common, controlling systemic mechanism by the formation of a set of unit-specific interrelationships. In other words, the market itself cannot be regarded as a system or a subsystem that is part of a larger system, even though it is comprised of many separate categorically independent systems. Instead, it should be thought of as a specialized ecological subfield.

When the word *system* is used in connection with the word *market* in the expression "market system," it does not refer so much to a kind of "economic organism" or "machine" as it does to an organized or established *method* or *procedure* of accomplishing the goal of distributing the outputs of the various component units comprising a society. In the same way, the term *economic system*, according to this reasoning, does not refer to a system in the sense of an organic whole, but instead to a style or method for organizing an ecological field into a division of labor and into exchange networks. Thus, the economic sector of a society, from the perspective presented here, is regarded as an ecological subfield comprised of producers and consumers of products, each individual case of which constitutes a separate, self-referential system in and of itself.

Out of the interaction among the various systems comprising a market emerge many metaphenomena, two of which are referred to by the terms *supply* and *demand*. Each of these ideas represents a metaphenomenological concept employed to deal cognitively with the cumulative effects of the behavior of individual systems, and to reveal trends and changes in the economic subfield at a categorical level. Supply and demand, for example, are concepts that refer, on the one hand, to the aggregate availability of individual products, summing up the outputs of all potential suppliers, and on the other to the aggregate readiness of many different potential buyers to purchase those products at a given price. Similarly the "market price" of a given commodity amounts to the average or median price paid for a given product by all purchasers during a given time interval. All of these concepts are part of a cognitive apparatus that creates its own artificial reality through which a user adapts cognitively to an environment that cannot be known without cognitive action.

By using other metaphenomenological concepts, it is possible to think of "aggregate resource consumption" or "aggregate waste production" for a given category of economic producers or consumers, and therefore of the impacts produced on an environment (an ecological field) by the operation of many separate systems in interaction in that field. In other words, to see the role of social systems in relationship to the evolution of an ecological field, it is necessary to create concepts appropriate for dealing with the aggregate effects of contingent relationships among many independent systems that differ in their placement in a categorical division of labor. This is much the same as the perspective that would be used to think of biological systems and their placement in, and aggregate impact upon, an ecological field.

It is not enough, however, to think only of markets as ecological subfields; it is necessary to go further and see all of the systems comprising a society in this way, even though they may not be economic enterprises. For example, families or households also qualify as self-referential systems under the criteria being used here. So do governmental agencies, religious bodies, and so forth. The point is that each social system in an ecological field operates as an independent unit in relationship to its environment, drawing resources from it and producing outputs that impact upon it, and in so doing, contributes to the production of metaphenomenological consequences.

In such a field, no single system is "in control" of the other units in the field in the sense of being able to dictate the behavior of all systems in the field. The relative power one system has over another is a function of the multidimensional contingencies that prevail in the field and the capacity of individual systems to defend themselves against threats to their survival or well-being from outside their own boundaries. Even so, some systems participating in a field may have greater impact upon the field than others, or may have the capacity to dominate other systems and reduce the range of options open to less dominant systems. At the metaphenomenological level, we could therefore think in terms of the relative dominance of species of systems. This is like saying that humans are the dominant biological species participating in the ecological field viewed as containing many populations of biological systems.

8.3   Governments in Ecological Fields

If it is granted that all social systems are independent, self-referential units organized into an ecological field, governmental units must be regarded as a category of organizations (systems) in which various individual governmental bureaucracies are themselves separate systems. Like all systems in the field, governmental units are adapting to an environment using their own self-managed behavior, and their own resources as they interact with other systems.

It has long been assumed on ideological grounds that separate sovereign nations constitute separate, bounded sociopolitical systems, and as systems, they are "governed" or "controlled" by a set of governmental institutions. Thus, the governments of nations have been seen as the "management" of a society in much the same way that the management of a business firm is viewed as the control center of a business enterprise. Although this image might be appropriate and useful for extreme cases of centrally managed societies such as Nazi Germany or the former Soviet Union, or for some ancient empires, it certainly seems to misrepresent the situation in present-day societies with market economies and democratic forms of political organization.

Given the often accepted assumption that even market-oriented democratic societies are in fact systems managed by a state apparatus, it has not been difficult to think consciously or unconsciously of the world as being somewhat like an ecological field comprised of autonomous systems called nations. From this perspective, nations interact in a global geopolitical and economic environment as separate, self-guided systems. Because nations have been thought of as autonomous sociopolitical systems, the relationships among nations have for a long time been thought of in contingent terms, and the interaction among nations has been seen as an uncontrolled process in which nations vie for resources and for advantage in a kind of global, geopolitical competition, without any global authority being actually in control.

What is being suggested here is that a similar view should be taken with respect to the individual components that go into the makeup of governments in societies that have market-exchange systems and democratic political institutions. In such social orders, governmental bureaus can be regarded as constituting a specific subset of social systems that is structured in such a way that each governmental unit or bureau has limited roles to play in a societal division of labor. As specialized systems, their powers are limited to specific jurisdictions and, within them, to specific functional domains. Governmental units in such a political economy act as self-referential systems according to their own internal ordering mechanisms and through their actions produce conditions to which other systems in the same ecological field must adapt. This includes other governmental units in the same field.

The structure of the ecological field is such that nongovernmental systems in the same field are capable of, and do act upon the basis of, their own internal ordering mechanisms. The outcome of the interaction between governmental and nongovernmental systems is contingent upon the reactions that separate, self-guided systems provoke in each other. Governmental organizations control their own actions but can only present other independent systems with a set of conditions to which they may respond in many alternative ways.

The so-called "freedom" believed, on the basis of ideological codes, to be present in such systems is an ecologically based freedom stemming from the structure inherent in an ecological field where independent, bounded autonomous systems differentiated according to a division of labor into a web of multidimensional interdependencies, operate as autonomous systems on a contingent basis as they adapt to an environment in which other systems also act in their own interests. The preference for freedom that is part of the ideological code of many cultures is expressed structurally in the autonomy of, and separation among, the members of the population of self-referential social systems that inhabit a common ecological field. Each system in such a field is so structured as to enable it to act separately from the others. Nevertheless, each is constrained by the structure of the field itself and especially by its division of labor, and by the contingencies presented to it by the actions of other systems in the field. They are also constrained by the cumulative effects of the actions of the members of the field on the field itself.

8.3.1   Government as a Set of Self-Referential Systems

Governmental bureaus, legislative and judicial bodies, at both the national and local levels in a democratic society must be regarded as separate systems acting in an ecological field containing other systems, because their own internal mechanisms are limited to control over their own behavior and do not extend to control over the internal affairs of other social systems. Governmental units may act in such a manner as to force other systems to adapt to conditions set by their behavior, for example, by passing and enforcing laws and regulations.

This, however, does not constitute control in the sense of being able to direct or determine the internal affairs or the external reactions of other systems. Governmental actions in the case of societies organized as ecological networks limit the options and set some of the conditions to which other systems must adapt. For example, a law setting the speed limit on a highway creates a set of conditions to which drivers must adapt. If drivers exceed the speed limit, there is a chance they may be caught by a highway patrolman, taken to court and fined, or perhaps, under some conditions, lose their driver's license. This presents each driver on the highway with a set of contingencies. The driver must decide how likely he or she is to be caught when speeding, how many miles over the speed limit will be tolerated by the highway patrolman, what the fine is likely to be, and how much inconvenience and embarrassment it will involve. The driver must consciously or unconsciously answer such questions as: "How important is it to me to drive faster than the speed limit?" "How dangerous is it?" How much faster do I want to drive?"

The answers to all of these questions and the behavioral response based implicitly or explicitly on them are given by the driver him- or herself and not by the government that passed the law and attempts to enforce it. The driver's action is a contingent response on the part of a self-referential system to a set of environmental conditions that include imagined potential and actual actions on the part of governmental units of various sorts. These governmental units set some of the conditions to which the driver adapts, but they do not control the driver's behavior. The fact that a law that reduces the speed limit from 65 to 55 miles per hour can be shown to have the metaphenomenological effect of reducing the average speed of drivers on highways does not prove that the government is controlling the action of individual drivers. It merely summarizes the effects of the change in contingencies produced by the change in legal driving speed.

In this example, the driver is a metaphor standing for the members of the population of nongovernmental systems that inhabit the ecological field in which governmental systems are also located. Each of the millions of drivers on the highways are separate, self-referential systems operating in a common field that contains all of the other drivers as well as pedestrians, animals that wander on the highway, highway patrolmen, the courts, legislative bodies, and millions of other systems. Governmental bodies are members of this field, with the same status as all other self-referential systems as far as the cognitive apparatus that constructs the field as a mental model is concerned.

Of course, the government may exercise the power to sanction the behavior of other systems through offering rewards and meting out punishment. It may set up an administrative apparatus to execute its will and a judicial system to mediate between these institutions and nongovernmental systems when laws are violated. Nevertheless, as far as the cognitive system being described here is concerned, these various parts of the governmental apparatus constitute separate, self-referential systems operating in a common ecological field.

Even so, in some societies, governmental bureaus may constitute the dominant species of social systems operating within the field. In such a case, the behavior of governmental units sets important conditions to which other systems are forced to adapt. In other societies, other species of systems may dominate governmental units and force governmental units to adapt to their behavior, for example, large economic enterprises or powerful religious bodies.

These statements are not based on empirical observations but on cognitive construction. They represent a way of looking at the social world and interpreting it in cognitive terms. We are constructing a "reality" that is ecological, not discovering the ecological nature of things, as they are. Our cognitive alternatives are to see a society as a system and therefore as a set of bonded parts under the control of a single, admittedly complex, mechanism or to see it as a nonsystem. If we look at it as a nonsystem, one alternative is to see it as an ecological field. When this is done, the units that go into the makeup of what has been called a society become separate, self-referential systems, differentiated in a division of labor into interdependent categories and interacting in networks of association on a contingent basis.

If this view is adopted, then we are forced to construct in our mind an image of what the functions of government are in such a field. The answer seems to be that governmental units operate to place conditions into the ecological field that are intended to limit the freedom of other self-referential systems to take certain actions with respect to each other and with respect to the field itself. These governmental actions can be seen as attempts to deal with metaphenomena in the sense that this term was defined above.

For example, a government wishes to reduce the number of highway deaths and injuries produced by automobiles. It also wants to lower the consumption of gasoline in order to lower dependence on foreign oil and to reduce air pollution. From research, it is known that the speed at which an automobile travels is related to the probability of fatal automobile accidents as well as to the rate of gasoline consumption. A decision is made to reduce the speed limit by 10 miles per hour. Predictions are that this will result in a given reduction in highway fatalities, as well as the lowering of gasoline consumption by a certain amount and a reduction in air pollution. Now, drivers on the highway have a new condition to which to adapt. Their behavior remains self-referential, however. At the same time, the highway police, the courts, gasoline producers and purveyors, oil refineries and drillers, investors in petroleum company stocks, and many other separate, independent systems must adapt to a new set of conditions in their ecological fields by estimating the contingencies associated with various options open to them in the ecological field they inhabit. The government has not "controlled" their behavior, but it has affected it.

These effects may be seen by an observer (who is equipped with the proper cognitive apparatus) as metaphenomena such as a reduction in the rate of highway deaths, a reduction in the consumption of gasoline, a reduction in oil prices, more time on average spent in traveling to and from various locations, and perhaps a change in the value of petroleum company stocks and the level of profits for gasoline producers and distributors. If an observer is not aware of the nature of this cognitive apparatus, it may appear to him or her that an action on the part of government *directly* produced a whole set of metaphenomena, when, in fact, a complex web of contingencies operating in a multidimensional field produced a set of specific events that when subjected to cognitive processing by use of metaphenomenological concepts create the appearance that government produced the factual reality of such metaphenomena.

The capacity to predict a decrease in highway deaths or a reduction in gasoline consumption is based on cognitive systems that model individual events and then convert the consequences of these events into a "quantitative reality" using metaphenomenological constructs. One such model involves the physics of high-speed collisions, coupled with the biology of human organic frailty. The other is a model that allows us to predict gasoline consumption of automobiles traveling at various speeds. Added to these is a conceptualization of human behavior systems that contains the notion that human actors will take into account the probability of being ticketed, and some will lower their driving speed. It may also contain the idea that most drivers are "law abiding" and usually conform to the law. The point is that an aggregate-level metaphenomenon is perceived by an observer by accumulating information, the cognitive basis of which lies at the phenomenological level of conceptualization.

8.4 Environmental Consequences of Societies Organized as Ecological Networks

If it is granted that modern, market-oriented industrial democracies are best conceptualized as ecological subfields in the manner outlined previously, what should be expected with respect to their relationship to and impacts upon the environments they inhabit? Under this conceptualization, societies are comprised of thousands upon thousands of self-referential behavior systems operating autonomously and simultaneously in a common field from which they draw resources and to which they return outputs, including waste products. Social systems therefore collectively have the capacity to alter the field they depend upon for existence. At the same time, each system, by its very construction as a system, determines its own behavior and is not controlled by any overarching structure that is at the disposal of any human agency.

Also, each system, in its attempts to survive and adapt, is in competition for resources with other systems similar to itself and often in conflict with systems that attempt to draw resources from it on terms favorable to themselves. This means that the short-term survival interests of each system will tend to dominate its selection of behavioral responses to its environment and lead it to give lower priorities to long-term survival problems such as protecting the environment upon which it depends.

In practical terms, this also means that human systems, such as manufacturing firms, will tend to give higher priority to remaining in business and being profitable than to solving problems such as resource depletion or air and water pollution. For example, it may prove more profitable in a competitive market for a manufacturing firm to continue to use vast quantities of oil or petroleum-based products in supporting its own operation and to continue to feed back waste products and pollutants into its environment than to convert to some other resource or to control its output of environmentally damaging materials. This would be especially true if competitors are also likely to continue these practices, thus lowering their costs of production. To be environmentally sensitive and convert to a technology less damaging might increase production costs and put the firm that does so at a competitive disadvantage, thus threatening its survival.

Each system operating on a self-referential basis is allowed by the structure of the ecological field to pursue its own interests as an individual system, and there is no megastructure that requires pursuit of the collective interest. The result is that the aggregate consequences of the individual actions of all of the systems in a common ecological field transform the field and feed back upon individual systems, perhaps destroying them in the long run. For example, each farm-family enterprise that clears land and cultivates row crops using chemical fertilizer and petroleum-burning farm equipment is responding as an autonomous system to a set of conditions in an ecological field, and the individual farmer who ignores certain of those conditions, because he is in competition with the others, is threatened with failure and may not survive. The aggregate consequences are likely, among other things, to be soil erosion, deforestation, water pollution, and the depletion of petroleum resources.

Each individual family or household that exists in an ecological field structured as an urbanized industrial democracy is required by social structure to seek employment for its members outside the household and to obtain food, clothing, and other household goods from commercial establishments scattered across a landscape organized by a division of labor. To do so, it is in each family's interest to own one or more automobiles and to consume petroleum products and, in the process, emit pollutants into the air. The aggregate effects of all households, taken together, result in major impacts on the common environment. However, given the structure of the ecological field, the household without transportation ends up suffering a reduction in what it perceives to be its quality of life.

Of course, if human systems are to survive in the long run, the metaphenomena produced by the aggregate impact of individual-system operation will inevitably force adaptive change. There is nothing built into ecological fields, however, that particularly favors the survival of human systems, and the field itself might survive only by experiencing a catastrophic reduction in the number of human behavior systems operating within it, or even by forcing them into complete extinction.

The fact that industrial democracies as well as more centrally controlled economic and political systems have survived in a world that, until now, has also contained more traditional, less industrialized and urbanized systems does not give assurance of continued survival. Instead, it testifies to the capacity of our planet to tolerate huge impacts upon the common environment without, at the same time, producing catastrophic impacts upon the human species. It also testifies to the incompleteness of the transition from traditional to modern industrial forms of social and economic organization. The industrialized world has, in all likelihood, survived and grown more environmentally intrusive because a good part of the world, until the last quarter of the 20th century, has remained underindustrialized. Now, however, the movement to modernize traditional societies has reached the farthest corners of the earth, and the tolerance limits for the survival of all human systems, at least in their present form, are closing in.

If all that has been said here can be accepted, then mankind is faced with a dilemma whose solution cannot yet be clearly specified. Until now, human sociocultural systems have developed largely without severe global environmental constraints and, to a large extent, without regard to the future of the planet as a common environment. Even though there have been examples of societies and cultures that have disappeared because of their extreme impact on their environment, space enough has remained elsewhere to foster the survival of huge human populations.

Because the planet has tolerated uncontrolled growth in human populations and unplanned technological change, the institutional patterns and the economic and political organization utilized up to the present have not been forced to develop the mechanisms or the thought patterns needed to solve environmental problems. This is probably true because until now human populations have remained below the tolerance limits of the planet, and the technologies used to support these populations have been such that they have also been within those limits. As a consequence, human systems have not developed the capacity to respond to the threat of environmental catastrophe on a global scale. In this respect, virtually all human systems remain underdeveloped and ill-equipped to face the future they themselves have created.

For the most part, human institutions assume an environment that can supply the need for resources and tolerate the impact of their behaviors and the outputs they produce without threatening the very foundation of their sociocultural order. At the same time, the dominant theme that runs through the fabric of the social world is that of human economic well-being, or perhaps more accurately, the aspiration for affluence. No comfort can be taken from the possibility of returning to the less industrialized, less technologically complex modes of adaptation of the past as a means of lowering the level of environmental impact. To do so would require a political or economic mechanism that would force a return to a lower level of production and, consequently, a lower level of consumption, both of which would require a drastic reduction in population. Besides this, given the ecological organization of present industrial societies into populations of autonomous systems, such a solution is not possible without first transforming the social order of most of the world into a systemlike form of global organization requiring a highly centralized power structure and a decisively dominant role for a global governmental structure. Besides that, a return to the simpler technologies of the past, which were less environmentally threatening, would undoubtedly require a huge reduction in human population and an accompanying reduction in the level of consumption and perhaps well-being. For the most part, past technological systems were less environmentally threatening at the global level because human populations were small, and most of the planet was left unused by human systems.

8.5   The Modern Ecological Dilemma

The dilemma facing mankind today is that evolutionary processes appear to have produced a social order in which no single social system is able to control the behavior of other systems in its environment and thereby utilize the power of its dominance to force a solution to environmental problems. At the same time, the very form that the global social order has taken, and the technological systems it uses, has produced an ever-escalating trend toward environmental degeneration, fueled in large part by the burgeoning growth of human populations and in the replication of human systems. Thus, the possibility of controlling the behavior of human systems is absent at the very time that it is most needed. Also, the very absence of control is highly valued as the foundation of human freedom and the engine of human material well-being.

Without using a strong centralized form of international government to manage human systems, an option that is not only ideologically unacceptable to most people but also probably technically impossible at the present, even at the level of a single society, we are left to search for other, more "democratic" means of solving the modern ecological dilemma. These means must involve either (1) efforts to alter the contingencies faced by autonomous human systems in a direction that will reduce the probability that the ecological field they depend upon will collapse; or (2) altering the cognitive systems that define the internal order of the self-referential systems themselves, so that they change their self-managed behavior in a direction that lowers the probability the ecological field will collapse; or (3) developing technologies that are "environmentally friendly"; or (4) completely revising the way human systems approach their relationship to their environment by accepting the view that the human species should aggressively and systematically "engineer" the ecological field so that it assures human survival, even though this could result in drastic changes in the so-called natural world. Of course, these options are not necessarily mutually exclusive, and a combination of them could be chosen as an alternative to the centralized management of human affairs in the interest of environmental preservation.

9

A Language for Constructing
Structural Models of
Social Networks within and
among Self-Referential Systems

9.1   Introduction

Thinking of modern industrial societies as ecological networks comprised of separate systems, rather than as systems in and of themselves, demands clarification of what is meant by a social network. It also calls for a specification of the conceptual apparatus to be used in dealing with network structure, and this in turn requires specification of how the networks that are found within, as opposed to among self-referential systems are constructed. These latter tasks are particularly difficult, because there is little of value in the literature of sociology to guide us. In dealing with these issues, we must also face the question of how deeply we must probe beneath the surface characteristics of social networks to define the structure embedded in them.

First, let me define a social network as an articulated set of relationships among social positions, and among the subnetworks formed by connections between these positions. The relationships forming such networks need not be fixed or bonded but may be temporary and contingent. Furthermore, the network itself may change form rapidly or slowly, but at any given moment is thought of as the pattern of connections that prevails among social units.

When dealing with network structure, it is extremely important to note that the units involved at the microlevel *are not actors, or individual human beings, but positions*. These positions represent the behavior patterns expected on the basis of a set of normative rules to occur at a particular location in social space. Positions are not mere locations in the sense of points in social space but consist sociologically of behavior patterns stored as cognitive rules. Such rules generate repeated patterns of action at those locations in relationship to other repeated patterns of action occurring at other adjacent locations (Linton, 1936; Davis, 1949; Bates, 1956; Merton, 1968; Gross, 1958).

If our cognitive objective is to model some aspect of the structure of society, we *cannot*, as has been the practice of many social scientists, use individual actors as the units of analysis for a number of rather obvious reasons. First, all actors, being biological organisms, are subject to the processes of birth, maturation, senescence, and death. As a consequence, actors enter and exit the arena of social behavior at particular times, but even so, the social structure persists. Second, within the life span of an individual actor, the actor changes the positions he or she occupies in the social structure. Third, even though actors come and go, and in the meantime move about from one position to another, most of the existing groups and organizations comprising the units of social structure persist by constantly replacing their members.

Our interest is in modeling the structure of the social network, and as we have seen, structure implies stability and persistence, which in turn implies that behavior patterns are capable of surviving changes in the actors that perform them. Also, because of the activity–latency problem, we are forced to think of structure as existing in the form of rules, and not as overt behavior; otherwise, the episodic nature of behavior will make it impossible to map the whole network or structure because the network will change instant by instant as the actual behavior occurring and the actors actually in contact change. Social structure, and the structure of social networks, must therefore be sought in latent or cognitively stored behavior patterns and not in the actual behaviors being performed during any given time interval. These patterns exist as integrated sets of rules (called *cognitive systems*) that govern where and in relation to what objects, social or otherwise, behavior will occur as overt action performed by real actors.

The term *relationship* also implies attention to positions and sets of positions, not to actors. Social relationships in the structural sense, as opposed to the interpersonal sense, are rule-guided patterns of cobehavior through which positions are joined to each other by *rules of interaction*. Because interaction is itself intermittent and episodic, during periods of inactivity it is the system of rules for interaction or cobehavior that maintains the connection between the positions comprising the elements of social structure. It follows therefore that the structure of complex relationship systems is maintained by a complex web of interrelated behavioral expectations stored in the form of cognitively operable rules that reproduce the complex structure of the whole network, even though the performance of expected behavior is episodic.

Networks defined in this manner differ in the nature of the connections that articulate their various units, as well as in the "geometry" of their internal structure and their external connections. In this chapter, an attempt will be made to defend the claim that groups, organizations, communities, and societies constitute networks with quite different sorts of structure. These differences are associated with whether each can be regarded as a self-referential system or, instead, must be considered a nonsystem occurring in the form of an ecological or contingency network. In discussing types of networks, an attempt will be made to define subclasses of network forms within each category of social unit.

9.2   Groups as Social Networks

Sociologists have so abused the term *group* as to make it almost meaningless as a technical term in a scientific vocabulary. It has been applied to everything from a family to a racial or ethnic category, even to societies and world systems. In the discussion to follow, the term *group* will be used in a very restricted sense to apply to only one form of social network. This is being done in order to make it possible to define the structure of larger entities comprised of several groups as bounded units or parts.

For these purposes, a *group* may be defined as consisting of the behavior of two or more actors who occupy social positions, each of which is connected to all of the others in the group's structure by a direct, rule-guided relationship. The key to this definition is the concept *direct relationship*, which refers to expected, rule-guided coaction or interaction between the occupants of two positions. This, in turn, rests on the assumption that social interaction involves actual action–reaction, stimulus–response exchanges between position occupants, without intervening parties being required to transfer information or other inputs and outputs between the parties involved. Interaction also implies that the actors carrying out the behavior patterns perceive each other's behavior as it is in the process of occurring, and react to each other.

An indirect relationship, in contrast to a direct one, involves the insertion of another position in between those that are indirectly related. In a direct relationship, the occupant of position A acts toward B who perceives A's behavior as it is being performed and responds. B's response is likewise perceived by A and responded to. In an indirect relationship, A acts toward X, who then acts toward B, who responds to X, who then transmits the effect back to A. Actually, indirect relationships need not even imply a feedback effect through the indirect-relationship chain. It is also apparent that indirect relationships can involve any number of intermediate positions as long as a continuous chain of relationships can be demonstrated. The two forms of relationship are diagrammed in Figure 9.1.

Groups are networks based on direct relationship among all of the component positions. Of course, in groups with more than two positions, there will also be indirect relationship chains to every other position. The number of alternative routes is determined by the size of the group and the number of permutations and combinations that number generates.

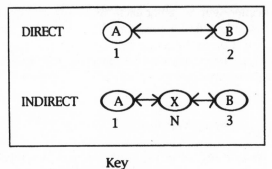

Key

1,2,N = Positions

A,B,X = Actors

⟷ Relationships

FIGURE 9.1. Types of Relationships.

The unique structural quality of a group derives from the fact that all positions are directly connected and also, as a consequence, are indirectly connected by a fully closed set of relationships, *closure* being defined as having direct and indirect connections among all permutations and combinations of positions. It is furthermore implicit in the definition of a group network that it contains (1) all positions that satisfy this condition, and (2) no positions that do not. In other words, group boundaries are reached when no other position can be found that is directly related to all the others that are included in the network. In interpreting this statement, it must be recalled again that the units of the network are positions, not people, and that *positions* are defined as sets of behavioral expectations subdivided into roles.

Because groups are comprised of behavior patterns rather than individual actors, we can observe groups whose membership, defined as particular actors, changes even as the network of positions comprising the group remains part of the structure of society. We can also find cases in which totally different groups defined as networks of positions are made up of identical sets of actors. An example of the first case is offered by the U.S. Supreme Court, which has existed for nearly 200 years as a set of rule-guided social positions whose internal network consists of a completely articulated, rule-guided set of direct relationships but in which the actual persons occupying the positions have turned over many times. An example of the second case is offered by a family that also runs a business, a small grocery store, for example. The family as a group contains a different set of positions, governed by a different set of self-referential rules than a grocery store group.

Membership sharing and membership turnover cannot therefore be considered as factors to be taken into account in establishing group boundaries or, for that matter, in assigning an identity to a group. A grocery store does not *become* a family because its personnel happen to be related by blood and/or marriage. The Supreme Court remains the Supreme Court even as judges come and go (see Bates 1957; Bates and Harvey, 1975).

9.3   Multigroup Systems: Organizations

If groups can be regarded as bounded networks, then it becomes possible to think of networks comprised of groups as the units of structure. To do so, however, it is logically necessary to introduce the concept of *indirect relationships*, because the definition of group networks makes all completely articulated sets of direct relationship automatically into groups.

In order to remain consistent with the definition of groups, it is necessary to posit the existence of structural mechanisms that use indirect relationships as a means of articulating separate networks of direct relationships. This can be accomplished in only two ways and still conform to the earlier definition. One way is suggested by member sharing among groups. The other is by the insertion of groups that perform the function of connecting other groups into larger networks. The member-sharing mechanism must be examined carefully, however, because, as I have said, social networks are not comprised of people. This means that member sharing must be required by the rules of the system or network and must stem from the structure of positions and their constituent roles, and not from the personal preferences or idiosyncratic associations of individual actors.

The basis for solving this puzzle lies in the notion of a division of labor. Group networks, in societies that are socially differentiated and comprised of many functionally specialized groups, are dependent on other groups specialized in other activities for the imputs they need to sustain their own internal functioning. This means that they must have access to the outputs of other groups to survive and operate. Their internal structure must therefore provide a set of rules that will generate linkages to these other groups and thereby provide the channels over which needed resources can be obtained. Elsewhere, the existence of a mechanism called "extramural roles" has been suggested as the solution to this problem (Bates, 1960; Bates and Harvey, 1975).

Extramural roles are roles whose norms require behavior inside the group in relationship to other members of the group that cannot, however, be performed using internally available resources. Extramural roles require that some position or positions in the group's structure contain behavior expectations that require the holder or holders of the position or positions to leave that group and participate in a permanent or temporary relationship in another group or set of groups from which the needed resources can be obtained. For example, urban families do not produce food, yet food is prepared and consumed in the household according to an internally applicable set of self-referential rules that vary from household to household. This means that some position or set of positions in the household group must contain a role, or roles, that require a position occupant, or several position occupants, to obtain food at such places as grocery stores, where a representative of the household occupies the position of customer in relationship to a grocery clerk.

We have already stated that this relationship may be contingent and nonbonded, but the point at present is that whether contingent or bonded, it is built into the structure of the group and the division of labor characteristic of that structure. The relationship is, in actuality, between the positions and positional networks, and people merely express that relationship in action (Bates, 1960; Bates and Harvey, 1975).

Grocery stores also require external resources and therefore contain extramural roles. Among other things, they are seeking a profit from the sale of goods to customers. Their structure therefore contains extramural role requirements that result in grocery-store representatives interacting with customers outside the boundaries of the set of directly articulated positions making up the grocery-store staff. The encounter between the clerk representing the grocery store and the customer representing a household brings into being an *interstitial group* that is neither part of the household nor the grocery store but exists in the social space between these two separate networks. This group contains the position of customer and clerk. This situation can be diagrammed as a network as shown in Figure 9.2 (Bates, 1956, 1957; Bates and Harvey, 1975).

The solution to the problem of conceptualizing the connections between separate groups given in Figure 9.2 necessitates a distinction between two types of relationships that link social positions to each other. One type of relationship is encountered within groups, between separate positions occupied by different actors. This sort of relationship is called a *bilateral relationship* to denote that it is two-sided and involves two different actors. In Figure 9.2, an example is given by positions 1 and 2 in the household group that are occupied by persons A and B. All relationships inside groups are always bilateral by definition.

Between-group connections are provided by the device of member sharing. In Figure 9.2, an example is given by the relationship between positions 1 and 7, or between positions 4 and 8. In these cases, the same actor occupies two different positions in two different groups. For example, a family member occupying position 1 becomes a customer at a particular store, occupying position 7. This sort of relationship is called a *reflexive relationship* to denote the fact that it does not involve the interaction of two different people; in-

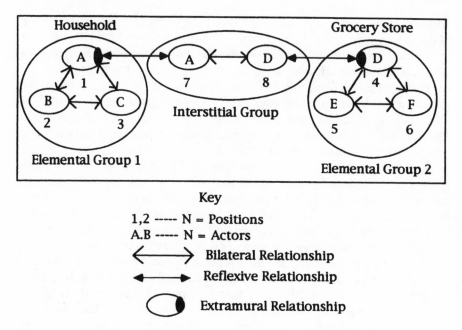

FIGURE 9.2. Types of Relationships and Groups.

stead, the relationship exists between two sets of roles played by the same actor (Bates, 1960; Bates and Harvey, 1975).

It is important to remember that reflexive relationships are produced by the rules embedded in the positions making up the social structure. These rules emerge to solve problems growing out of the division of labor that have the effect of allowing groups to be separate and bounded but at the same time dependent on their structural context.

It is useful to give separate designations to the types of groups shown in Figure 9.2. The household and the grocery store will be called *elemental groups*, and the customer–clerk group will be called an *interstitial group*. Elemental groups are fundamental units in the division of labor and constitute differentiated, bounded networks of relationships, organized in terms of a set of rules with reference to the performance of some specialized function or set of functions. In some instances, as in the case of families or households, there will be multiple, diffuse functions associated with the network, and in others, the functions may be quite restricted and explicit.

One of the functions of a bounded network may simply be to place boundaries around the set of positions to differentiate the network and its use of resources from other networks that use similar resources and have virtually identical internal structures. For example, in a simple, agrarian society, where most behavior takes place in household or family units, the structure of the network does not specialize the individual households in the products they produce so much as it differentiates the units in the network in terms of who has access to particular resources such as land, and who produces and consumes identical products. Under such conditions, one would not expect extramural roles to produce interstitial groups organized around trade so much as to produce interstitial groups organized around such things as mutual aid, common defense, religious observances, or marriage and kinship.

In more complex societies that involve an industrial division of labor as well as a division of labor along institutional lines into separate specialized governmental, educational, religious, and other institutionalized groups, the boundaries separating social units result in the necessity for complex forms of exchange. This means that the structure of the social network will contain social units whose function it is to connect other specialized units. Such "exchange" units are an emergent structural property necessitated by the specialization inherent in a functional division of labor. Interstitial groups exist to connect elemental groups and not to produce other outputs such as tangible products or services. Their function is to provide structural bridges, or channels, leading from one elemental group to another so that inputs and outputs, both tangible and intangible, may flow between parts of a larger network.

9.4   Bonded Networks

Interstitial groups may contain either bonded or contingent linkages among the positions they contain in their structure. Furthermore, they are not limited in their size except by the requirement that, in any group, all positions *must be directly linked*. In the example given in Figure 9.2, a dyadic network in which the positions are linked by a contingent relationship is shown. Each party to the relationship has alternative partners representing other groups with whom they could satisfy their extramural role requirements. The household representative could link up with other grocery stores, and the grocery stores with other households. There is no social bond that dictates the exact alter position that must be occupied to fulfill the extramural role requirements. For this reason, we say the relationship is temporary and contingent upon conditions in the ecological field and the preferences of the parties to the relationship.

Another example must be given to illustrate bonded relationships within interstitial groups. The case of a manufacturing organization that contains several shops or work groups will serve this purpose. Let us imagine a factory that produces some product using steel as one of the raw materials. Its structure contains a shop called the welding shop. The factory also has a supply room that stocks steel, welding rods, and the tools and supplies used in welding. This supply room is a separate, elemental group from the group called the welding shop. Each consists of a set of positions connected by a network of direct relationships. Furthermore, there are positions in each group's structure that have no direct relationship to positions in the other group, so that we must think of the two as separate, bounded groups.

Obviously, the welding shop has extramural role requirements, because it is not permitted to purchase and stock its own supplies. These activities are assigned to the supply room. A particular member of the welding shop is, however, assigned the duty of drawing supplies from the supply room. Similarly, a particular clerk in the supply room is assigned the duty of issuing supplies related to welding. These two individuals meet in an interstitial group as representatives of their respective elemental groups and occupy rule-guided positions containing rule-guided roles. This case could be diagrammed much like the household–grocery store case, except that in this case the relationships are *bonded and not contingent* (Bates, 1960).

The rules of the extramural roles require each party to deal with the other in order to obtain the inputs needed. There are no alternatives left open by the rules. The welding shop cannot go to some other supply room in some other factory and draw its supplies, nor can it seek them in the open market. Neither can the supply room issue its supplies to persons representing groups outside the organization's boundaries. In other words, the relationship inside the interstitial group is bonded and not contingent.

Because the supply room and welding shop are bonded to each other, we can think of them as being part of a single, larger self-referential system. Not only are the relations internal to the groups covered by a set of self-referential rules, but the relationship between them is also under the control of an overarching set of organizational rules. Organizations that are comprised of two or more elemental groups, joined by one or more interstitial groups, in which the interstitial groups contain bonded linkages, must be regarded as self-referential systems because the total set of rules, differentiated into subsets, constitutes a single *game* in which particular groups depend upon particular exact others under a set of common rules.

The bonding of groups together into an organization means that the subsystems of rules pertaining to individual group networks will necessarily evolve together as a larger set. Individual groups will be constrained by their bonded relationships not to evolve internal rules that are unrelated to, or in severe and continual conflict with, those of other parts of the same network.

This does not mean that such independent directions of development never emerge, but that they will tend to be "selected out" or "suppressed" by the interaction between the parts of the system, which contains bonded interdependence, *if the organization is to survive* as a single, integrated structure. Of course, we do not assume that organizations inevitably survive. They may break apart or fail if their internal self-referential system does not provide a stable, normalized, predictable relationship among their internal parts and between the organization and its environment.

9.5   Contingency Networks

In the case of groups connected by contingency relationship, it is necessary to take a different view. Because each side of such a relationship is independent of any given unit on the other side of the relationship, and is dependent only on establishing a temporary relationship with one unit out of a class of units, groups on each side of the relationship may change their internal rule structure independently of the other. Families or households may evolve internal rule changes independently of changes taking place in individual grocery stores.

Because of this, the parties to a contingent relationship represent separate and more or less independent self-referential systems. In the example given, this is like saying households constitute one self-referential system, and grocery stores a different one. Elsewhere, it has been pointed out that not only are there always two or more separate groups in a contingency relationship, but also their orientations in terms of the goals they seek and the functions they perform are separate and in a kind of structural conflict. Their survival interests are also separate. What is beneficial to the survival of one unit may be detrimental to the other (Bates, 1960; Bates and Harvey, 1975). That which promotes the survival and well-being of one group is quite distinct and independent of that which is beneficial to the other. Indeed, what benefits one may, in fact, hurt the other. What is in the interest of the household is good food at the lowest possible prices under the conditions that are most convenient to it. What is in the interest of the grocery store is the highest possible profit over a long period of time, which might mean higher prices and less quality and convenience than in the interest of households.

This lack of common interests is a product of the division of labor that separates groups and organizations into more or less specialized units that are nevertheless interdependent. It results, in the case where interstitial group relationships are left unbonded but contingent, in separately evolving systems of behavior.

9.6   Groups with Contingent Linkage
as Self-Referential Systems

The problem with relationships between and among such groups is to provide a set of self-referential rules covering interstitial group relationship that permits exchanges to take place under conditions into which the potential for conflict has been built by the division of labor inherent in the structure of the network. The customer–clerk interstitial group is not without rules, even though it is contingent and involves a conflict of interests among position occupants. As a matter of fact, we can regard the positions and roles contained within this group as being rule-guided behavior systems in and of themselves. But the structure of such interstitial groups has the effect of preserving the boundaries of independent elemental groups and of supporting the internal independence of their structure as separate, bounded, self-referential systems. This is why the linkage is contingent rather than bonded. If families were bonded to exact grocery stores by a set of rules, the independence of the family and the grocery store would be totally lost, and they would be welded together "permanently" in a totally dependent manner inside a single structural mechanism. Although households *as a category* are dependent on grocery stores *as a category*, individual families and stores are *independent* of each other. On the other hand, the welding shop in a factory is totally dependent on the factory's supply room for supplies.

The rules of relationship within bonded, interstitial groups have the effect of forcing cooperation between specific parties to an exchange, whereas those at the core of contingently connected interstitial groups exist to control the conflict inherent in the relationship, so that exchange can take place between structurally autonomous, temporary exchange partners. In the case of customer–merchant relationships, the rules of contract and of market exchange govern behavior. These rules have evolved as self-referential systems to permit independent (nonbonded) groups and organizations to develop separately and at the same time to obtain the inputs that they need from each other.

9.7   The Market as a Web of Contingent Interstitial Groups

The market can be regarded as a complex network of contingent interstitial groups that are activated and deactivated between and among exchange partners representing structurally separate self-referential systems, depending on the complex contingencies prevailing in the ecological field they inhabit. Complex industrial societies may also develop units that specialize in controlling interstitial group networks among categories of exchange partners. Examples of these sorts of units are wholesalers, brokerages, stock and commodity exchanges, banks, and insurance companies.

These units make a business of controlling aspects of the interstitial group relationships among categories of other units and may themselves be regarded as secondary forms of elemental groups. Wholesale grocers establish a network of interstitial group linkages with food producers and processors on the one hand, and with food retailers on the other. They sell the service of "batching" and then distributing specialized food products. Banks intervene in the same way between depositors and borrowers, and between depositors and the creditors of depositors. Stock exchanges perform similar functions for buyers or sellers of stocks and bonds.

These various devices provide separate, rule-guided self-referential systems that preserve the boundaries of other self-referential systems. Each must be seen as evolving separately and often in conflicting directions from each other. As a matter of fact, various units in such exchange networks may destroy each other as they compete for the establishment of more stable contingency-relationship patterns with their clientele, who, by following their own interest, may contribute to the destruction of one competitor in favor of another.

This sort of exchange network is characteristic of community- and societal-level exchange networks in modern capitalistic, industrial societies but not of the internal exchange networks inside organizations. To distinguish between exchange systems found within and between organizations, the terms *market exchange system* and *commissary exchange systems* have been proposed (Bates, 1974; Bates and Harvey, 1975). Market-exchange systems use contingent interstitial groups to connect independent, self-referential systems temporarily. Commissary exchange systems use bonded interstitial groups to connect structurally dependent groups together inside an organization. Market-exchange systems are characteristic of community and societal network structure in unplanned capitalistic economies, whereas the commissary form is characteristic of internal exchange relations inside complex organizations and associations, and perhaps within highly planned, centrally administered economies, where the distribution and consumption of goods and services is defined by a set of rules that determines the production obligations and consumption rights of every constituent social unit. Such a system seems to have been characteristic of advanced feudalism in Europe and may in some respects be regarded as the ideal implicit in "pure communism." It is at least worthy of consideration to entertain the possibility that societies could be organized in such a manner as to incorporate a commissary form of exchange system in which all social units are bonded together in a completely determinant set of relationships lacking contingency links (see Bates, 1974; Bates and Harvey 1975).

9.8   The Coordination- and Conflict-Control Functions

The division of labor within and between independent groups and organizations creates three structural problems whose solution requires the creation of an intergroup or interorganizational network. The first problem has been discussed in detail, that is, the problem of exchange. Differentiated social units require inputs from other social units to survive and function. Therefore, a network through which exchange can occur is required for a differentiated system to function. There are two theoretical possibilities through which this linkage system may be provided: (1) the market form, and (2) the commissary form. In real societies such as our own, there is the possibility of a mixed form. This occurs when governmental institutions intervene to establish commissarylike links that provide goods and services as a matter of rights (entitlement), for example, in the case of certain welfare institutions.

There are, however, two other structural problems that also grow naturally out of the division of labor. One can be called the coordination–conflict control problem, and the other the problem of common services. Certain parts of the structure of society or of its constituent parts grow out of attempts to provide solutions to these structural problems. In particular, a second type of interstitial group network arises to provide the necessary structural connections for solving these problems. The form that this new network takes also differs between organizations and communities.

The coordination–conflict control problem with respect to organizations may be stated as follows: Organizations are comprised of two or more separate elemental groups that are specialized in one way or another in the activities they perform. The groups, although specialized, produce a common function or output when their separate activities are combined by an organizational structure. Because they are part of a common organizational effort, it is important that their individual but interdependent activities be coordinated to some degree, so that a common output can result from their respective activities. This means that a structural mechanism must be inserted into the organization that can produce the necessary level of coordination. To do this, contact and communication are required between representatives of the constituent groups. In short, for coordination to occur, each separate, specialized group needs information concerning the plans and activities of the others. This need for information is similar to the need for any other resource or input and therefore can be regarded as an extramural role requirement. Some member or members of each group must be in contact with some member or members of the other groups, upon which it depends directly for information. Again, this requirement creates one or more interstitial groups that stand in between elemental groups and provide channels through which the necessary information can flow. Such an interstitial group is called a *coordination interstitial group* to denote its primary function (Bates and Harvey, 1975).

An example of such a group is given by the "management committee" in a manufacturing firm. Let us assume that a particular firm is comprised of five or six separate work groups, each of which has a foreman or supervisor, as well as a number of workers. This particular firm has formed a "management committee" comprised of the foremen or supervisors of each work group and includes the top executive in the organization. The management committee meets regularly to exchange information, make decisions and plans, and receive orders, directions, and instructions from the chief executive. In between full, regular meetings, pairs or triads of members constituting subgroups out of the management committee may interact to exchange information, make plans, transmit instructions, or to iron out problems.

This group is an interstitial group because it is comprised of representatives of elemental groups and is generated by extramural role requirements embedded in the structure of these elemental groups (Bates and Harvey, 1975). It is not, however, an exchange interstitial group like the one that connects the supply room and the welding shop. Its function is to solve the coordination problem. Furthermore, it has a definite internal structure, comprised of the positions occupied by the various members and the roles associated with these positions. The behavior that takes place is "rule guided" and recurrent. In short, the group has a stable existence as part of the structure of the organization that is preserved in the form of a subsystem of self-referential rules. This stability is partially the result of the fact that the relationships inside are bonded and not contingent. The reflexive relationships that connect the interstitial group to the elemental groups it serves are also bonded, noncontingent, and rule guided.

It is important to realize that in any given organization, many such groups may exist as part of the structure, depending on how extensively differentiated and elaborated that structure is. Each major division or branch of an organization must contain interstitial groups to join the individual constituent units of the branch or division. Many closely associated work groups within a division or branch may also form multiple interstitial group networks to bind the units together into subdivisions. The point to be made here is that organizations as systems will contain one or more coordination interstitial groups, whose functions it is to provide the channels through which information can flow and authority can be exercised among separate groups.

Power structures operate between groups through interstitial group networks. These networks provide a web of indirect connections between all positions in an organization's structure. Because of this, power can be exercised both directly and indirectly on persons occupying the positions comprising the structure, and thereby on the activities carried out by their occupants. Through this means, the operation of the various groups making up the organization can be controlled in relation to each other, and the rules governing their internal functioning can be enforced.

Communications networks may develop separately or take the same form as power networks, but they also use the device of interstitial groups to form connections between elemental groups. Through such networks, the information necessary to coordinated action can flow from one part of the organization to another.

Within organizations, specific representatives of particular elemental groups are thrust into specific interstitial groups by particular extramural role requirements. Their relationships are bonded and not contingent, in that there are no alternatives outside the boundaries of the organization that can be employed to satisfy the need for information, instructions, and other resources required for coordination. Furthermore, these interstitial groups are rule-guided, self-referential subsystems, subject, to overall control by the larger system. Power relations that are part of the organization's authority structure are bonded and specify which actors, by virtue of the positions they occupy, have power over which exact other actors. The rules further specify the limits of power and the methods by which it can be exercised. In short, the power structure of an organization operates through a bonded network of interstitial and elemental group relationships.

When we leave the boundaries of organizations and examine the relationships between organizations and structurally independent groups, an important difference emerges. Now the relationships between interstitial group members become contingent rather than bonded, and the need for coordination, temporary and highly restricted. This new network problem can best be discussed as the structural solution to the coordination- and conflict-control problem arising out of the division of labor at the community level.

9.9   Community-Level Coordination
of Interstitial Group Networks

At the outset, it is necessary to make certain assumptions about communities as social networks. The first is that communities contain independent organizations or fragments of organizations as units or parts. They also contain groups that are not attached to any organization but function as separate units. Under these definitional conditions, detached groups and organizations may be regarded as bounded, self-referential systems. Normally, these two types of units are specialized according to a division of labor in the functions they perform or the outputs they produce, as well as in the resources they control and the inputs they need in order to survive and function as systems. This specialized differentiation results in interdependence, in the sense that they require inputs from each other, but it also results in independence or autonomy. This seems paradoxical and contradictory at first glance but can be explained as follows.

If the interdependence among units is categorical rather than particularistic, then individual units are independent of each other as far as specific dependence upon exact partners is concerned. At the same time, they are dependent on a contingent relationship with some member of the category. As noted in the discussion of exchange networks in market-exchange systems,

individual units must obtain inputs, but they are not bonded to one source
of supply. This yields a degree of freedom or independence for individual
units to pursue their own interests separately. Out of this characteristic
grows the structure of the market or community-level exchange networks.

At this point, it is important to distinguish between communities in capitalistic societies that utilize a market-exchange system and communities
in noncapitalistic societies, where commissary forms of exchange are employed. We are forced by the logic of our argument to recognize that certain
precapitalistic societies, for example, tribal societies or feudalistic societies,
may have employed a different form of exchange system. It is also possible
to think of an extreme case of an advanced socialistic system in which every
social unit, and therefore every individual, occupies a fixed and bonded
place in an exchange network that functions much as that of a complex organization such as a manufacturing firm or an army. Here, everyone would receive the goods and services they need or consume through a bonded set of
relationships, which would be defined as a matter of "rules of the game,"
who would consume what, and where it would be obtained, as well as what
contribution each person would make to the processes of production and
consumption. This, of course, implies a totally planned economy, as well as
a totally managed social system, a situation that is far from being realized in
the present world except, perhaps, in small utopian or monastic communities. Nevertheless, there exists the theoretical possibility of communities
totally devoid of a market economy, and what will be said next must be understood against this theoretical possibility.

But we must now return to the question of coordination and conflict
control at the community level in societies with a market economy. In such a
system, we cannot justifiably claim that communities are producing a product or function other than providing an exchange network. That network is
a connective one rather than one that is part of a division of labor. I will take
the view, for the sake of argument, that communities in capitalistic societies
do not produce a product or function in the same sense that organizations
and independent groups do. They simply connect such groups together in an
exchange network and also provide two other structural mechanisms, one
directed toward conflict management, and the other aimed at the provision
of certain common services and the management of a common environment.
This latter function is performed by generating a set of public organizations
that are structurally like all other organizations, in that they produce a product or output, such as education or a water supply. The existence of public
organizations is therefore not especially useful in identifying the unique
structural qualities of communities.

Aside from the use of a market form of exchange system, it is in an examination of conflict control or management that we must seek the additional,
distinctive structural mechanisms characteristic of communities, at least in

modern capitalistic societies. The search for these mechanisms can best begin by returning to the earlier statement that the various units in the division of labor at the community level are simultaneously interdependent and independent. In order to survive and function, these various units must obtain inputs and outputs from each other, but at the same time, they are free to pursue their own interests. Furthermore, we have noted that the division of labor, in creating categorical dependence and, at the same time, unit-specific independence, creates a structurally built-in conflict of interests among the very units that depend upon each other.

Structurally derived conflict has two dimensions. First, it exists between the individual members of a category of social units that utilize and are therefore competing for the same resources or inputs. Grocery stores are competing for physical locations, for raw materials and products to sell, and for customers, as are auto manufacturers, steel mills, food producers, and so forth. In addition, there is structural conflict between and among categories of social units, expressed in relationships among particular members of the categories. What is in the interests of steel mills is not the same as what is in the interests of automobile manufacturers, building contractors, or farmers. Whereas those depending on steel to produce their own outputs need steel and therefore are dependent on steel mills in general, they are not dependent on a particular source of supply in a nonmonopolistic market. As a matter of fact, the tendency in capitalistic markets would be for each side of an exchange to seek advantage over the other to the extent that in the long run, some individual members of a category would be destroyed. This possibly exemplifies the underlying structural conflict among units that are functionally differentiated from each other.

There may be an abstract common interest in the survival of the community and the market upon which individual units feed, but the independence provided by contingency relationships allows conflict to express itself under conditions sufficiently *controlled* to permit the survival of the differentiated network. This control in exchange relationships is expressed in the rules governing exchange in exchange interstitial groups. But what if these rules fail to control conflict, and overt conflict arises out of the relationship among separate, self-referential systems in pursuit of their own individual interests? It is in the interests of the whole network to preserve the structure of the network, because each unit is, in some way, dependent upon it. It is out of this need to preserve peace and order and, consequently, to control and manage conflict that a second type of interstitial group emerges at the community level.

There are several forms of community-level-coordination and conflict-management interstitial groups found in modern complex societies. One form consists of judicial bodies, whose function it is to settle disputes and to enforce the rules governing exchanges between parties potentially in conflict.

A second form contains groups whose function it is to formulate the rules and to allocate the common resources in a manner that supports a common environment. The third form furnishes a basis for power struggles between categories of interest that are in conflict, and a fourth form manages the ongoing relationships among structurally conflicting units. Each of these must be discussed separately before the nature of the community-level social network is understood.

9.10   Judicial Bodies as Interstitial Groups

Civil and criminal courts amount structurally to conflict-management interstitial groups. In modern society, and to a lesser degree in simpler societies, they provide a highly evolved set of rules for controlling the conflict that grows out of failures of other systems of rules to manage the potential for conflict built into the division of labor. In American society, the civil courts contain representatives of parties from social units that are in dispute over such matters as the exchange of property or the fulfillment of a contract, or the observance of some law governing public safety or welfare. They also contain representatives of the political apparatus of the state, and often representatives of the citizenry.

Civil courts may be regarded as self-referential systems that have evolved a set of rules governing the conduct of participants in court procedures. These rules allow a dispute or conflict to be "acted out" under highly controlled conditions. They also provide a procedure for settling the dispute, at least temporarily. This is done by judging which party to the dispute has violated the rules pertaining to the relationship between the parties in dispute and arriving at a decision on what should be done about it.

The criminal courts pose a more difficult case to characterize, yet they too represent interstitial groups oriented toward conflict management and the maintenance of peace and order. In them, defendant, prosecutor, and their various representatives face a judge and jury and decide the guilt or innocence of a person or persons accused of a crime or misdemeanor. The various parties represent different interests and carry out a controlled conflict, supposedly in the interest of justice.

These oversimplified caricatures of the courts are not meant to be accurate descriptions of the great variety of matters that come before the courts or how these matters are settled, but to make the point that the courts at various levels and in various specialized forms constitute community-level conflict-control or coordination interstitial groups when viewed in terms of the cognitive apparatus being developed here. Again, it is necessary to point out that secondary elemental groups and organizations grow up around such interstitial groups and make a business of participating in and managing the relationship of other social units to them. For example, there are law firms, bonding companies, insurance companies, judges' staffs, including professional court officials, prosecutors' offices and staffs, and even law enforcement agencies, correctional institutions, and jails that surround the court as an interstitial group system. Indeed, the whole "system" of criminal and civil justice forms a community-level subnetwork organized around the judicial system. Units in this network perform specialized functions and are represented in various interstitial groups that constitute the courts and their connections to other organizations such as the police and prisons.

This network has yet to be adequately mapped using a well thought out cognitive apparatus even in a single community, and so there is little more that can be said about it at this point except to note that most of the units in the network represent different and conflicting interests and therefore are connected by interstitial groups that have what I have elsewhere called conjunctive rather than reciprocal relationships at their core (Bates and Harvey, 1975). This means that structural conflict dominates this network.

There is one other fact that needs noting. In the case of the courts, thought of as interstitial groups, there is usually not a whole class or category of potential relationship partners open to the participants, but only one. Plaintiffs and defendants may choose law firms, and courts may choose jurors, but the rules of jurisdiction normally dictate which court a case will be tried in. There is, however, the fact that no plaintiff or defendant is bonded permanently to the court, and the relationship to the court is on a case-by-case basis. This is a secondary form of contingency relationship that, once an issue arises, is limited by the principle of jurisdiction (a special form of political monopoly).

There are certain quasi-judicial bodies that may also be included in the structure of human communities. These groups share the characteristic with the courts of being organized around settling disputes or managing conflict. The best examples are labor relations bodies such as arbitration and mediation boards. Any group that judges a case in dispute between or among parties can be classified as a judicial interstitial group.

9.11   Legislative Bodies

Legislative bodies are a second form of community-level interstitial group growing out of the conflict of interest natural to the division of labor. These bodies are made up of representatives of various interest groups in the community or society and pursue the various interests of these groups under a set of rules that control and manage conflict. These rules develop or evolve as a set of self-referential rules covering the operation of an interstitial group having conjunctive relationships at its core. County commissioners, city councils, state legislatures, national and international congresses and parliaments, as well as various boards such as school boards, fall into this category of conflict-management interstitial groups.

They contain members who represent various constituencies, these constituencies having differentiated vested interests. They are usually thought of as representing population groups defined by territory. However, these constituencies are differentially connected to the social structure in terms of such things as occupation, industry, local territory, sex, race, age, and so forth, all of which, because of the division of labor, are associated with different interests. The senator from an oil state represents the interests of the oil industry, and the senator from a farm state represents the interests of farmers. Furthermore, representatives in legislative bodies, in order to maintain their seats, normally represent those who contribute most heavily to their campaigns, or who can do the most for them as individuals.

A well thought out, empirically based model of the legislative subnetwork in any society, much less American society, is beyond the scope and capacity of this discussion. The point to be made here is that such bodies permit the representatives of various interest groups to pursue the interests of their constituencies under a set of rules that controls the potential for open, possibly violent, confrontation. In the interest of those elements most heavily or powerfully represented, they make the laws or rules and allocate the public resources for the communities or societies in which they function. What the outcome is in terms of the various interest groups involved is determined by a power struggle through which issues are temporarily resolved in favor of one interest group or another. In short, the outcome is determined by a conflict process carried out in terms of a set of self-referential rules (i.e., parliamentary procedure, etc.). Again, it must be recognized that whole groups or organizations may form around legislative bodies and constitute a newer and derived layer of elemental groups or organizations than those that represent the primary division of labor that fostered the need for the interstitial group (the legislative body) to begin with. Representatives to the legislature may have office staffs. The legislature may create its own budget office or its own legal department or library. Lobby groups and organizations, as well as consulting firms, and so forth, may make full-time businesses of serving or exploiting the legislature. The extensiveness and complexity of the network elaborated around the legislature as an interstitial group, like that which surrounds the courts, depends on the size, complexity, and historical background of the community or society in which it is embedded.

This discussion and that which went before it lead to the hypothesis that (1) the division of labor in society, because it brings structural conflict into being, requires the insertion of conflict control or management mechanisms into the ecological field in order to increase the probability of survival of the members of the field; (2) interstitial groups such as courts and legislatures evolve to provide specialized parts of this mechanism; (3) around these interstitial groups, a secondary layer of specialized elemental groups evolves, either to provide services to interstitial groups or their members, or to influence and control what goes on inside them. These derived groups and the interstitial group they surround, as well as the constituencies they represent, form subnetworks in the structure of the community or society. These subnetworks comprise separate, self-referential systems as parts or units and the dominant process within the networks among units, rather than within units, is conflict.

9.12 Political Parties, Unions, Coalitions, and Special Interest "Groups"

As pointed out earlier, the division of labor brings two types of structural conflict into being as a natural and inevitable product of specialization in function. One type is among the members of the same category of social units who are in competition with each other for resources and other inputs. The second type is between one category of social units and other categories specialized in other aspects of social life. This second type of conflict is the basis for the formation of interstitial groups designed to pursue the interests of one sector of the division of labor in opposition to those of other sectors.

Political parties, labor unions, professional and trade associations, and certain other civic groups and temporary coalitions or voluntary associations are of this type. If the proletariat and capitalists referred to by Marx organized themselves into political parties or associations, they would be of this type.

In such interstitial groups or organizations, representatives of social units having a common interest in opposing other social units, or in furthering the advantages they have with respect to the resources of the community or society, form temporary or sometimes relatively permanent alliances or coalitions. In these associations, they continue to represent the interests of their individual, self-referential systems but work together under a set of common rules for whatever is defined as the collective interest. Because they remain in competition at another level of the division of labor, their relationships in such interstitial groups remain conjunctive and contingent. They are, in other words, not bonded to such groups but may withdraw.

Such coalitions or alliances may become very elaborate as they span large territories and encompass related but quite different social units. For example, the American Association of Manufacturers spans a continent and takes in many types of manufacturers whose interests are at some level in conflict. The American Federation of Labor and Congress of Industrial Organizations (AFL–CIO) is similar in complexity, but at a very general level, the conflict of interests between these two associations is quite clear. Certain civic groups such as the Rotary and Lions Clubs and Junior Chambers of Commerce, as well as others, must also be considered of this type because they usually represent one rather narrow range of interests in a community. Also included here should be the National Association for the Advancement of Colored People (NAACP), the National Organization for Women (NOW), and the American Association of Retired Persons (AARP), which represent population groups with special interests.

All of these groups that are, in actuality, based on the recognition of their metaphenomenological similarity to each other represent coalitions organized around presumed common interests in opposition to other interests. They bring together representatives of various separate groups or organizations, or representatives of population categories, for example occupations (that in other respects have conflicting and competing interests) to form interstitial groups whose aim it is to further the common interests of the social units or categories they represent.

9.12.1   Buffers and Fronts

Another type of interstitial group performs the function of buffering or screening an organization or interest group from the criticism and pressure that arises because it takes actions that are in conflict with the perceived, if not actual, interests of the public in general or of the clientele it serves. Such interstitial groups are designed either to diffuse responsibility for a given action or set of actions, or to hide the real process of decision making behind a screen created by an interstitial group. Such groups often operate by claiming that everyone's interests are, underneath it all, identical to those of the unit responsible for creating the buffer interstitial group to begin with.

A good example of this sort of group emerged during the early stages of the Civil Rights movement in the American South when interracial citizens committees were created to convey the impression that the white power structure of communities under pressure to integrate was actually listening to black leaders. In many cases, the black leaders chosen for participation on interracial committees were individuals considered "safe" by the white power structure, who did not want to integrate but wished to diffuse public demonstrations and lower the pressure for change. These groups were often meant only to "buffer" vested interests from the criticism of outsiders and from the growing demand for change.

Another example of a buffer interstitial group is offered by a device often used by voluntary organizations such as the Red Cross in distributing aid to disaster victims. Such organizations are often faced with making potentially unpopular decisions concerning who will receive aid and who will not. Because they live off of public donations, they cannot afford to offend the public. They therefore create "citizen committees" of local leaders who are asked to make the potentially unpopular decisions. Normally, such committees are given a set of guidelines that are so detailed and specific that the committee really makes the same decisions the agency itself would make if operating alone, but the important thing is that the committee, not the voluntary organization, is held responsible for the decisions. The committee takes the "heat" and the voluntary organization can claim the credit!

9.13 The Place of Governmental Units in Community Networks

It is often assumed that the government of a community or society plays a role with respect to the various parts of these networks similar to the role played by the power or authority structure in an organization. Accordingly, the government is assumed to exercise power or authority over the various units of community structure in such a way as to control their various activities. On the basis of this, communities are assumed to be systems capable of responding to their environments as more or less integrated units. In other words, the government, particularly through its executive branch, is thought of as leading or directing the community or society toward common goals and objectives. This common goal seeking is taken as evidence that the community or society is a total system rather than a set of separate and competing systems organized as an ecological field, as proposed in this book.

It is contended here that in a capitalistic society that employs a market form of exchange system, governmental units constitute a separate subset of bounded, self-referential systems that perform certain specialized functions within the societal network. Governmental organizations do not constitute the directorate of a corporate body called, for example, "American Society," but instead exist as just another set of social units with particular specialized functions to perform.

The sovereignty of the "state," and therefore the powers of governmental organizations, are severely limited. In particular, governmental organizations lack the power to exercise detailed control over the internal affairs of nongovernmental units. The control actually exercised is accomplished through regulatory law, largely directed toward managing the potential conflict that grows out of the division of labor and out of the market form of exchange system. In addition to its regulatory function, which is quite different from the function of "managing" the whole community or society, government operates a set of public organizations that produce products or services not offered by nongovernmental organizations. These services are usually those so essential to every other unit in the social structure that they cannot be left to market forces to provide without a high risk to the society, or they are services subject to monopolistic forces that, if left to the market, would result in inordinate power falling into the hands of a few social units. This latter category includes such services as public roads and highways, public water and sewage systems, military defense forces, jails and prisons, the monetary system, and so forth.

As has been seen, judicial and legislative bodies form interstitial networks whose function it is to control and regulate conflict and to provide a means of reaching temporary agreements between units and elements of the social network that stand in conflict relationships to each other as a result of the division of labor. Legislative and judicial bodies *do not* join the separate elements of society into a single, self-referential system but instead preserve their boundaries and therefore the separateness of specialized independent units that are categorically interdependent from each other.

In a capitalistic society, the executive branch of government, in contrast to legislative and judicial branches, operates a set of organizations that perform services or produce products that provide a common environment within which other units operate. At the community level, city government runs the waterworks, the fire and police departments, the schools, and the public works departments as well as others, but the mayor does not *rule* the city as its chief executive in the way the chief executive of a corporate bureaucracy, such as an automobile company, "rules" the company. These government bureaus constitute a set of public organizations that are not unlike private organizations, in that each represents a separately evolving system. Furthermore, they stand in a structurally produced conflict relationship with other organizations that are part of the same network, because they have separate interests and separate processes of evolution and development.

It has been customary in Western democracies such as the United States to believe in the fiction that national and local governments, since they are headed by officials elected by the people, represent the people in carrying out their joint will. What is being suggested here is that the structure of the state in Western capitalistic democracies is such that it actually prevents the executive branch from managing or "ruling" the whole society as a unified system, and limits the functions of government to the operation of a few public organizations that provide services to or for other units in the social structure.

At the national level, these services include the maintenance of a military establishment and the conduct of foreign relations through a network of embassies and bureaus. The "joint will" to which these agencies are supposed to be responsive expresses itself through processes of conflict that occur politically and economically as the various units embedded in the social network pursue their own separate interests. The direction taken by the national or local government in pursuing the "common will" is determined by the developing, temporary outcomes of the process of conflict. In other words, the public will is defined by the outcome of an ongoing power struggle among the various separate, self-referential social systems that form the corpus of an ecological field.

In capitalistic societies, the various units of government may be regarded as part of the total population of separate, bounded, self-referential systems that form the units in the network of relationship constituting the structure of society. That structure takes the form of an ecological field.

It is possible that careful examination of centralized states, with authoritarian governmental structures that attempt to manage and control all aspects of life, from kinship relations to industrial production, will require a different view of government in relationship to the other parts of society. Indeed, such societies may approach self-referential-system status as total entities. This would appear to be theoretically necessary in a society with a centrally planned economy involving a commissary form of exchange system, because such a system would require centralized decision making and control over virtually every detail of life in society.

It may also prove true, after careful study, that medieval kingdoms with feudalistic political economies, as well as ancient empires subject to despotic power structures, might best be modeled as having different, more integrated structural patterns than modern, Western, capitalistic industrial societies. What has been said previously about government furnishes a cognitive model of societies with market economies and governments with constitutionally limited sovereignty. Even in this model, governmental units are seen as attempting to regulate the relationships among other units in the social structure and to control aspects of their internal functioning. Nevertheless, they do so within the context of a structure that sets up a kind of structural conflict between the units regulated and those conducting the regulation, and also between the units whose interests are being served by the regulatory rules and those whose interests are being hurt by them.

At the very least, it must be recognized that the system of "checks and balances" built into the U.S. Constitution was designed to prevent anyone from achieving enough power to actually control the affairs of the society in detail. The U.S. Constitution, and others similar to it, can be interpreted as being designed to preserve the separateness and independence of separate, nongovernmental, self-referential systems, and at the same time to preserve the integrity of the total social network by providing the means for controlling conflict on the one hand, and serving the dominant interests in the society on the other. Here, *dominance* is defined as the ability to protect and possibly achieve one's interests through the use of economic and political power in the conflict process that occurs constantly among separate, self-referential social systems in complex, highly differentiated, capitalistic industrial societies.

The very structure of such societies favors the interests of the economically powerful, because social units with power resources will be able to impose their will in the conflict among competing interests on those units of structure without such resources. It is a mistake, however, to think of this conflict as being waged among individuals or social classes. The conflict is among corporate bodies, by which I mean economic enterprises, as well as public and private organizations, and is structural in character. Individuals occupy positions and play roles in such bodies and, as a result, exercise power and control resources, but it is the structure of the social network itself that accounts for the outcome of the process of conflict and competition.

9.14   Summary

This chapter employs a structural strategy to establish a language through which cognitive models of the organization of social systems and of the ecological subfields comprised of social units may be constructed. The language employed is that of role theory, as it was elaborated some years ago in *The Structure of Social Systems* (Bates and Harvey, 1975). This chapter attempted to remain consistent with the ideas presented in earlier chapters as it went about the job of applying them specifically to the structure of human systems, using the language of "structural role theory." The result is an ecological view of social structure. This structure must be placed in the context of the nonhuman environment to arrive at a comprehensive cognitive picture of the total, global-level ecological field.

10

Individual Actors and Social Systems

10.1   *Introduction*

Ecological fields contain both individual actors and social systems. Because both are defined as elements in ecological fields, there is the need to conceptualize how the two types of systems are related to each other in forming the structure of the field. This need is made more pressing because our culturally derived cognitive systems lead us to assume uncritically that social systems such as groups and organizations are comprised of individual actors and the relationships among them as they interact. Thus, individuals are regarded as the obvious "natural" units from which the structure of social systems are constructed.

This rather naive, but common, view ignores the fact that individuals as conceptual realities are constructed images created by cognitive action and not empirical realities seen in the same way by all careful observers. The actor as a concept is no different from the concept system as far as its cognitive standing is concerned. It therefore depends on the contents and organization of the cognitive apparatus used by the observer to construct mental images of social systems, whether a social system is regarded as being made up of actors or of some other units of conceptualization.

Within the context of the earlier analytical discussion of the concept *system*, in which systems were regarded as bounded, autonomous, self-referential entities comprised of parts bonded together in determinant relationships, the notion that both individual actors and social systems are types of systems included in ecological fields presents a cognitive dilemma. If individual actors are regarded as bounded, self-referential systems that are self-governing and autonomous, it would appear that they cannot at the same time (as total actors) function as parts of social systems. To do so would imply a loss of autonomy and self-reference, and with it the boundedness required to be a system. It would appear, therefore, that we cannot regard both actors and social systems as systems and at the same time assume that social systems are comprised of social actors as units of structure. To do so would abandon the assumptions made earlier concerning the difference between ecological fields and self-referential systems.

Within social units that are usually thought of as social systems, such as freestanding groups and organizations, relationships among units of structure are by definition, *unit specific* rather than *categorical* in nature. After all, this is a characteristic that distinguishes the structure of systems from that of ecological fields. For example, in human families (a type of social system), specific husbands, wives, and children are joined in a unit-specific web of social relationships, within which mutual obligations are highly specific among actors. A husband as an individual member of a species of actors called "husbands" is not tied by a *categorical relationship* in a division of labor to classes of potential alter actors called *"wives," "sons,"* and *"daughters,"* but instead to *particular individual actors.* This being true, it would be incorrect to say (within the cognitive architecture used to define systems and ecological fields) that families are, in fact, ecological subfields characterized by contingent categorical relationships among units of structure. At the same time, if we regard individual actors as autonomous, self-referential systems, we cannot say that families are social systems without seeming to contradict this statement.

The trouble lies in how we conceptualize the individual as an actor, and in how we conceptualize the participation of the individual in social systems. For the most part, social scientists, following the general cultural tradition, think of the individual as a bounded, unitary object that includes all of the biological and social psychological traits and characteristics of a distinct and separate organism and personality. In terms of systems reasoning, the individual is treated as one unified biosocial-psychological system. When the actor is treated as a member of a group or organization, or, in other words, as a participant in a social system, the tendency is therefore to think uncritically of the whole actor or the whole person as a being, a participant in the system under consideration. Thus, whole people, or total individuals, with all of their biological, psychological, and sociocultural traits and characteristics are thought of as the units that form the parts of social systems. Implicitly or explicitly, the actor is therefore treated as if he or she constitutes a single, organized behavioral system. As a consequence, all aspects of the individual as a living, acting social organism are taken to be relevant to the individual's participation in any particular social system.

It has, however, always been recognized, either implicitly or explicitly, that individual actors belong to or participate in many different social systems. For example, the same person may participate as an actor in a family, a work group, several friendship or neighborhood groups, and so forth (Linton, 1936; Bates, 1956; Merton, 1968; Gross, Mason, and McEachern, 1958). In addition to this, the individual actor may, at times, act completely outside the boundaries of any organized group or organization as a solitary actor. One reason the inconsistency inherent in viewing both actors and human groups, and organizations as systems, has not been recognized more clearly and become the subject of more frequent theoretical debates lies in the fact that whole societies have been regarded as the relevant systems for sociological analyses, and groups and organizations have been thought of "subsystems" within them. If this is the case, then there appears to be nothing inconsistent about thinking of the complete individual actor as a kind of subsystemic unit in the structure of a single, larger system called *society*. This view is defensible on the grounds that the behavior of most individuals takes place within the boundaries of one particular society, even though it may be distributed among many groups within that society. The participation of an actor in a particular group can be thought of as a subsystem under these conditions, and the whole actor as an organization of subsystems.

However, as pointed out in earlier chapters, the assumption that societies form single, unified systems does not stand up well under close theoretical scrutiny because they lack unit-specific links among most social units. Furthermore, if we are to take the alternative approach and regard society as an ecological field, as is the case in this book, then social systems such as social groups and organizations constitute the smaller elements that comprise society as an ecological field, and under these circumstances, each individual will belong to many different social units.

The tendency to treat the actor as a single, bounded behavior system, and at the same time regard the whole actor as being a participant in many different social systems contained within the same ecological field, is the basis of the dilemma mentioned earlier. In an attempt to solve the dilemma, the question arises, "What exactly is it about the actor that constitutes the actor's participation in a social system?" Stated differently, if whole actors constitute systems, and they constitute the microunits of social structure, and if, at the same time, we wish to think of groups and organizations as systems, how can we sustain the core meaning of the concept *system* without, in the case of groups and organizations, thinking of them as ecological fields? After all, the essence of the idea of an ecological field as defined in earlier chapters is the idea of the interrelationships between and among separate systems. If each individual must be regarded as a bounded system, and groups and organizations are comprised of interacting individuals, then what we have previously called social systems, themselves, must be thought of as ecological fields or subfields.

10.2   An Alternative Conceptualization

The cognitive problem is to create a theoretical apparatus that provides an internally consistent, logically integrated view of individual actors and social systems, and their relationships to each other. In proceeding with this task, there are alternative paths that can be followed. One approach is to model the individual first, using the systems concept to provide a set of cognitive guideposts. Having modeled the individual, the next problem is to create a cognitive means of modeling groups and organizations that is consistent with the prior conception of the individual. If we remain consistent with a self-referential systems approach, social units such as groups and organizations are likely to be regarded as something like what we have earlier defined as ecological fields. This view might easily fit the theoretical apparatus used by symbolic interactionists, who tend to treat the actor as the ultimate unit of social interaction, and social structure as a kind of plastic product subject to constant change and recasting as actors continuously redefine their relationship to each other. Under such a view, ecological fields will themselves be reduced to objects comprised of individual actors as systems, and social units, such as human groups, as well as social grouping made up of other animals, such as herds of mammals, flocks of birds, or insect colonies will become special types of subfields within a larger ecological field. The "social world" will thus be reduced to the level of the individual and to the relationships among individuals by a form of cognitive reductionism. All social relations will become contingent encounters among separately acting self-contained, self-governing systems called *individuals*. There are other consequences that flow from such a decision, but before they can complicate the discussion further, let us consider the second alternative.

Instead of cognitively modeling the individual first and then the social system and ecological field in such a manner as to conform to this prior conception, the reverse procedure can be used. We can first model ecological fields and the nature and place of social systems within such fields, leaving aside the question of how the individual actor is to be conceptualized, and after this, a model of the individual may be formulated to fit into this prior conception. Intuitively, it would appear that when this procedure is followed, and if we remain consistent with our earlier stated conception of systems and their place in ecological fields, the concept *individual actor* will lose its customary unity and, with it, the characteristics necessary to think of the actor as a unified, self-referential system. In other words, the individual, thought of as an actor, will become more like an ecological field in conceptualization and less like a system. This is the procedure that we will follow in the next few pages.

10.2.1   Human Systems as the Generators of Action

Before the question of how to conceptualize the individual in relation to the social system can be approached fruitfully, it is essential that the phenomenological domain within which these concepts take on their meaning be specified more clearly. Very early in this book, "behavior" was identified as the phenomenological target for which a cognitive system capable of generating models of ecological fields would be constructed. At that time, it was pointed out that we will regard behavior as the means by which human systems adapt to and impact upon their environments. It was also pointed out that the behavior of self-referential systems is defined as being generated by the system itself, from within its own boundaries.

It is now time to consider the meaning of these statements in terms of how they related to the concept *system* when that concept is applied to individual, human social actions. In particular, it is important to consider what they mean for the conceptualization of the individual as an element in an ecological field that also contains social systems. The most important point that needs immediate recognition is the implicit distinction contained within these statements between a system and the output of that system. The behavior of a system in real time, as it is being performed, can be viewed as the product or output of the system as the system operates within itself as a systemic mechanism to adapt its user or users to an environment it recognizes by means of its own mechanism. Thus, there is a conceptual distinction made between the behavior of a system and the system as the generator of behavior. The system is the generator, and behavior is its output or product. If this is granted, then systems are not themselves comprised of actual behavior but, instead, of the elements that comprise the mechanisms that shape and produce behavior as an output.

Any human system, whether an individual actor or a social system, is capable of generating more types of behavior than those that actually take place in any finite, real unit of time. Furthermore, they are capable of producing a greater variety of episodes than are ever generated in the lifetime of any given individual or social system. Thus, the generator is more complex and more inclusive than the finite output it produces. Behavior is not a mere playing out of a kind of cognitive tape recording in which the recording contains the same message, in coded form, that is heard when it is played on a record player. Instead, behavior is the output of a generative mechanism that is able to produce many different outputs in response to different cognitive demands, no one of which is given as a preorganized, predetermined performance by the generative mechanism itself.

Using language as an example, an actor who knows a language such as English is equipped cognitively to utter an enormous number of sentences, each of which is grammatical and meaningful. Yet only a few out of this huge potential set ever occur as real utterances. The generator of speech, the language as a system, is more comprehensive and more complex than the particular, discrete real utterances that emerge from the linguistic machine as episodes of verbalization. The linguistic system contains the rules for speech and the code through which the rules are expressed, but not the content and organization of every utterance ever uttered, or ever to be uttered.

The total linguistic apparatus contained in the mind of the speaker constitutes a kind of cognitive generator that, when activated in interaction with other contents of the mind, produces verbal utterances as an output. These actual verbalizations are the products of the linguistic system (a cognitive mechanism) as it operates in interaction with other cognitive systems contained within the mind of the speaker. Thus, there is a distinction between the generator (a language) and the generated (utterances).

Given this distinction, how shall we conceptualize the individual actor as an object contained within an ecological field? Shall the actor be conceptualized as action or as the generator of action? Our choice will be the latter. As far as individual behavior is concerned, the actor, seen as an organism, contains a "cognitive machine" that, along with the organism, functions as the generator of action. Given this view, the question immediately arises, "How is the cognitive generator itself to be conceptualized?"

In answering this question, we need not formulate a comprehensive, empirically based theory of human personality and, along with it, an explanation for how the individual actor comes to contain the behavioral generators we conceptually construct. To do so would shift the discussion away from ecological fields and entangle us in a different task than the one we are pursuing. It would also shift us from a constructivist agenda to an empiricist one. What is needed, instead, is a conceptualization of the individual actor that is constructed in a manner consistent with and logically linked to the conception of social systems and ecological fields discussed earlier. Eventually, this discussion will demand a further clarification of what constitutes a social system. It seems apparent at this point, however, that the distinction between the generator of behavior, or action, and the generated actions must also apply in the case of social systems. But now let us return to the task of conceptually modeling the individual actor as a cognitive machine.

I have said earlier that societies may, from one perspective, be viewed as special cases of ecological fields. As such, they consist of a population of bounded, self-referential systems that are differentiated into a division of labor according to the outputs they produce and the inputs they utilize or consume. Each social system is an autonomous actor, confined or constrained in its behavior only by its own internal capacity to function and by the web of interdependencies built into the division of labor present in the ecological field, and the supply of and demand for resources within that field.

If the ecosocial field is comprised of numerous differentiated social systems and if, in order to satisfy their needs and wants, the individual actors making up the population of actors in the field are conceptualized as participating as actors in subsets of these systems, it is apparent that actors must be conceptualized as containing within their internal cognitive structure generative mechanisms that enable them to produce actions that fit into the structures of many separate, self-referential social systems. But because the social systems are themselves bounded, self-referential systems operating in an ecosocial field, and thus are autonomous systems, then each of the cognitive generators of action contained within the individual that fits social actors into separate, bounded social systems must also stand as autonomous units in the organization of the actor's internal cognitive apparatus. In fact, these cognitive generators may be regarded as fragments of social systems that are housed in the mind of an actor, where they can operate to generate behavior in interaction with the behavior of other actors, thus furnishing part of the larger generative mechanism whereby the social system operates.

At this point, we must proceed in several directions at once, but, unfortunately, the written word permits only one line of reasoning at a time. First, we must find a place in a cognitive code that will allow us to describe the "container" of the generative structure we wish to model and then distinguish it from the generative mechanism itself. We must also create a language for describing the internal organization of the container and at the same time create a logic that allows us to think about how it operates that fits the image we have created of social systems and ecological fields. Also we must have at least a general, if inexact, conception of how the contents of the container are, themselves, generated and become organized. All of these tasks need to be completed simultaneously or in reference to each other. Otherwise, the fit among concepts will be faulty, and the cognitive apparatus we are constructing will fail to function properly as a kind of thinking machine.

Even so, we are required by the constraints of exposition to proceed one step at a time, but we should do so, recognizing that it is a circular path with many back-spiraling crosspaths we are following. That path loops back upon itself time and again, and the meaning of each step along the way is given only by its relationship to all of the others. All of this must be accomplished without the implication of a step-by-step progression, but rather with recognition of the notion that all strides are made simultaneously in all directions as multiple conceptualizations coemerge!

10.2.2   Mind as the Container for the Generator of Action

In the case of the individual actor, the "mind" constitutes the container of the cognitive systems that operate as generators of action. The word *mind* in this particular enterprise of cognitive construction does not refer to a reality, knowledge of which was arrived at by observation, but it refers to a *theoretical construct* created to fit into a cognitive system comprised of other cross-referenced abstract constructs. It refers to that object of conceptualization within which cognitive action takes place, and within which information (as defined earlier) is generated, stored, organized, given meaning, and utilized. It is a conceptual container filled by and constructed out of mental representations that are organized in terms of cognitive codes. From this perspective, the *mind* as a concept is distinct from the brain, nervous system, and other organic parts of the total organism that contains it. It is the locus of the cognitive systems that guide perception, thought, and action. It is built up as an artificial, self-constructed entity contained within the organism as the organism interacts with its self-perceived environment.

For present purposes, it is useful to assume that the mind, once formed through interaction between the organism and its environment, contains a population of bounded, self-referential cognitive systems or subsystems that develop autopoietically. Each of these systems or subsystems, which are comprised of encoded information in one form or another, is related to a set of recurrent, adaptive problems cognitively defined as demanding action from within the mind of the actor. These cognitive systems or subsystems furnish the actor with a mental image of situations demanding adaptive behavior, and with a repertoire of possible behavior patterns that fit these situations. They also furnish the actor with the basis for generating the information by which the actor defines his or her environment and situation with respect to it. It is well to remind ourselves at this point that the environment of a human actor contains other actors and the social systems these actors participate in.

If this is granted, then the actor, in adapting to his or her environment, will be forced to develop cognitive systems that allow the actor to deal with the social systems in his or her environment that control desired resources or present potential threats to the actor's well-being. Although it remains true that the environment only exists for the actor as a self-generated image, actors who survive or prosper will be those who generate cognitive systems that fit the environment well enough to allow them to survive.

In the previous statements, the issue of whether the contents of the mind must be regarded as consisting exclusively of complete, bounded systems or can also include fragments of such systems in the form of subsystems that are taken from the structure of social systems was left open for future discussion. Thus, for the moment, we will think of the mind of an actor as containing a population of cognitive systems and/or subsystems.

In an earlier chapter, the organically inherited program for building up these cognitive systems was discussed. The assumption was that the minds of learning organisms are autopoietically constructed, having within themselves a biologically based program for building their own cognitive systems and subsystems. These cognitive systems, once formed, are the generators of particular episodes of action in the same sense that a linguistic code constitutes the generator of verbal utterances. The cognitive systems do not furnish a rigid script for action but provide a dynamic cognitive mechanism that is capable of generating many different outputs that are meaningful within the context of the system's own rules, and within the context of its self-generated image of itself and its environment.

The most important point with respect to the current discussion is the idea that each of these cognitive systems is a bounded, self-referential entity that generates its own internal organization that, once formed, generates its own episodes of behavioral performance in relation to its own self-defined environment. The mind therefore, as Bateson has suggested, takes the form of an ecological field containing many separate cognitive systems and subsystems that, though autonomous, upon occasion interact, because they are part of a common mental ecology. But more important still is the implication that the mind lacks the unity necessary for us to think of it as a single, integrated, self-controlled system operating under the control of a single mechanism, for example, a mysterious thing called an "ego" or a "will" or "self"! If each cognitive system contained within the mind is bounded and self-referential, then the mind is an ecological field populated by many separate autonomous systems, each of which generates its own behavior, and there is no master controlling mechanism governing the whole field of the mind.

If we think of the mind as an ecological field, we will view the relations among the various systems comprising the mind as contingent relationships, and the actual interactions among cognitive systems within the mind will be viewed as probabilistic mental encounters and not as interactions ordained by a structural mechanism that compels a deterministic order in their interaction. It is on the basis of this conceptualization that the metaphor between the mind and a garbage can was utilized earlier. That metaphor suggests an object containing objects more or less randomly thrown into a container, without reference to their relationship to, or relevance for, each other. It also suggests that the contents of the mind, like the contents of a garbage pail, may interact and pick up elements from each other without there being a rational or deterministic basis for doing so. It is assumed, for purposes of this discussion, that each system or subsystem in the mind arises autopoietically out of the operation of a primitive program for self-construction. This primitive, biologically inherited program automatically generates differentiated cognitive systems as it interacts with differentiated environmental-adaptation problems. It thereby constructs a complexity of mind that reflects the complexity of the organism's perception of its social and nonsocial environment. Without reflecting this complexity, the mind, as the generator of behavior, would fail to generate actions that would adapt it to its environment, thereby exposing it to failure as a living system (Luhmann, 1986).

There is the further connotation that if the mind contains populations of independent and often unrelated systems, there is the possibility that these systems may be in conflict with one another and compete with each other to dominate the output of the organic machine they inhabit. Such cognitive dissonance could threaten the survival of the organism, or it could provide it with a mechanism that is capable of producing innovation.

It is important at this point to recognize that the autopoietic nature of cognitive systems does not assure they will construct themselves in a manner that will match or correspond to the environmental situations and adaptive problems out of which they evolved. After all, the environment as an objective reality, and the adaptive problems associated with it, still exist for the mind of an actor only as a self-constructed image. This image does not necessarily match "reality." The organism utilizing its own self-constructed cognitive apparatus can survive and elaborate itself, even on an illusory basis, as long as it provides a means of averting its own destruction. It can survive if it, in von Glasersfeld's terms, unlocks the door to survival, even if its conception of the door is faulty and its key, is not perfect. It need not provide a perfect key, nor must its definition of its adaptive problem reflect "true reality" for it to have survival value (von Glasersfeld, 1987). Presumably, there are many alternative cognitive systems that, within a given set of environmental conditions, can serve these purposes.

10.2.3   The Relationship between the Actor and the Social System

We have said that the mind of the actor contains a population of cognitive systems and/or subsystems, each of which has emerged out of interaction between the actor and the environment as the actor's primitive program for learning has generated information on the basis of raw sense impressions. Let us suppose, for the moment, that some of these self-generated cognitive structures have emerged as the actor has acted toward and in response to other actors in the context of a particular type of social system, for example, a family or a work group. In a very general sense, we can refer to the cognitive structures that have arisen as the actor generates behavioral response patterns that fit into the context of a particular type of group as "roles," because they represent the cognitive structures that generate the behavior an actor performs in a particular set of social relationships. If we use the term *role* in this particular way, we can say that the mind of the actor contains a population of cognitive structures called roles, and each role represents the mechanism that, in interaction with other contents of the mind and with incoming information created by the mind to represent the environment, generates behavior performed in interaction with other actors in the context of a particular social system, for example, a work group.

Thus, the cognitive structures here referred to as roles simultaneously constitute elements in the ecology of the mind of the actors participating in various social systems and units incorporated within the structure of these social systems. For example, the cognitive structure that defines the role of father–husband for a particular actor also forms an element in the structure of a particular family group that contains other roles that generate behavior for other members of the same group, for example, the roles of wife–mother and son or daughter.

The roles discussed here as elements in the structure of a social system such as a family must be regarded, at best, as subsystems or incomplete systems, because the whole group seen as a bounded, cross-referenced, interrelated network itself constitutes a social system made up of several parts (subsystems) called roles, each of which refers to a different actor's participation in the group. If this is true, according to the internal logic of the conceptual apparatus being developed here with respect to social systems, it must also hold true for roles as elements or units contained within the ecology of an actor's mind. In other words, at least some of the roles built up in the mind of the actor are *incomplete systems* or subsystems, because they are only one among many parts contained in the structure of a social system and depend upon these other roles for the conditions of their performance. They are, in other words, only fragments of social systems rather than systems in their own right. Such fragments of social structure are incomplete generators of behavior because they can be performed only in interaction with specific alter actors. One cannot act out the role of husband without someone to play the role of wife! At best, therefore, the complete generative system must include the roles of both husband and wife in order to constitute functioning elements in the structure of a social system.

A characteristic of a subsystem is that it cannot survive (i.e., maintain itself) or function unless it is combined with other subsystems in a relationship network that defines a complete systemic mechanism. As noted earlier, a part of a system, being only one element in a larger systemic mechanism, can function as a part only in the context of the whole from which it draws the inputs necessary to its own functioning. A man can only perform the role of father and husband in a context that includes others performing the roles of wife, son, and/or daughter. Without these other roles, the cognitive system that generates father–husband behavior has no meaning and cannot yield the adaptive consequences that flow from the performance of the behavior it is capable of generating. By analogy it is like a person who is the only speaker of a given language (e.g., the last of the Mohicans). The language is entirely private, and uttering sentences using it is meaningless except to the speaker. Such utterances cannot produce a social response worthy of the designation communication.

The notion that roles representing parts of social systems must be regarded as subsystems and therefore as partial behavior generators can be understood best by returning to the *division of labor* concept. Within a group-level social system, a work group for example, there is a *division of labor* among group members that is reflected in the differentiation among the contents of the cognitive structures that define roles. As a consequence, in order to obtain inputs from the division of labor, or to produce outputs that are utilized elsewhere in the division of labor, an actor must associate with others who complete the performance of the episodes of behavior characteristic of the total system and thereby supply their behavioral contribution to the operation of the group as an acting system. The roles contained as cognitive structures in the mind of an actor, that generate behavior within social systems, contain within their cognitive structure not only information that defines behavior appropriate to a given context but also information that defines the types of alter actors, or even the particular alter actors and systems within which they have meaning. These cognitive structures allow the actor to construct or interpret an environmental reality that contains the necessary systemic context for the generation of social behavior.

From what has been said earlier, it is apparent that *social systems* as the generators of *social behavior* consist of cognitive subsystems, which we have so far referred to as *roles*. They are *not comprised of actors* as biological or social entities, nor are they comprised of *the behavior of actors*. Instead, as behavioral generators, social systems are comprised of the cognitive subsystems that operate to generate social behavior and, through behavior, utilize physical and biological objects and produce physical products or impacts. From this perspective, social systems are in no respect physical or biological. They are entirely comprised of what, in a generic sense, can be called information, if information is interpreted to include all ideas that are interpretable as having meaning within the context of a cognitive code. As structures comprised of cognitive systems, social systems operate as the generators of social behavior.

Given the previous discussion, we appear to have encountered a new form of our old paradox. Two separate conceptual objects, actors' minds and social systems, appear to contain the same objects, so that actors and social systems overlap. If we continue, for the moment, to use the concept *role* in the very crude sense in which it is employed above, the mind of a particular actor contains some, though not all, of the roles that act as the cognitive generators of action inside the boundaries of social systems, where they are regarded as substructures contained as parts within the bounded structure of the social system. Thus, part of a particular actor's repertoire of roles penetrates the boundaries of a particular social system, and part of a particular social system's collection of roles penetrates the boundaries of the actor's mind. If this is the case, it appears to violate the assumption that systems are by definition closed and bounded, and therefore autonomous and self-referential.

This view would seem to make social systems objects comprised of fragments of the ecological fields found in minds of particular actors. Thus, social systems seem to depend upon the minds of particular actors for their existence and for their functioning. They, therefore, seem to have no independent existence that transcends the life or participation of particular, exact actors and no existence that continues to reproduce itself, even as particular individual actors leave the social system and are replaced by others.

The problem of conceptualizing the independence of social systems from the particular actors who enact roles within them at a particular time can best be solved using an evolutionary (diachronic) perspective toward social systems and the life careers of individual actors. We need to redefine how social systems are conceptualized as generative structures that operate through a sufficient period of time so that many generations of actors can pass through them without these social systems dissolving into their environments. We need a perspective that allows us to conceive of how social systems come into being, evolve by differentiation and elaboration of their structures, and maintain themselves as systems in an environment that has the potential of destroying them.

10.2.4   The Origin and Evolution of Social Systems

Before we can arrive at a solution to the paradox created by the assumption that ecological fields can contain both individual actors who constitute organically based behavioral units and also social systems that generate at least part of the behavior of actors, it is necessary to formulate at least a crude conception of how social systems can emerge as independent entities out of the interaction among individual-level systems. For purposes of logical analysis, let us begin by positing an ecological field populated entirely by individual organisms that act toward each other entirely as individual, bounded, self-referential systems. In the organization of the field, there are, in other words, no social systems that require the bonding together of individual actors in unit-specific relationships as they adapt to their environments. All relations among individual actors are therefore contingent upon their own interests and their own constructed images of their situations.

Interaction among individuals in such a field grows out of the categorical interdependencies among species of systems that are built into the structure of the ecological field. Relations among individual actors are, in other words, like those described among lions and zebras in an earlier chapter. Now, the question is how can the relations among the autonomous, self-referential behavior systems (individual actors), characteristic of relations among systems in an ecological field, evolve into relationship patterns characteristic of those within, rather than between, systems. How, in other words, could a social order evolve out of the social chaos characteristic of ecological fields that are made up entirely of independently acting individual-level systems?

In attempting to answer this question, we will be engaged in an entirely speculative, theoretical endeavor in which we are expanding the cognitive apparatus already presented to incorporate a self-consciously designed longitudinal or evolutionary dimension. We must constantly keep this in mind as we engage in this discussion, lest we slip into thinking we are engaging in some form of empirically based speculation and are attempting to represent some dimly observed reality. We are not attempting to describe a historically correct evolutionary progression that started with individual systems alone and developed social systems later. Instead, we are attempting to present a hypothetical argument based on convenient but entirely theoretical assumptions.

We can begin to build our hypothetical argument on the basis of the earlier discussion of how cognitive systems construct themselves in the minds of individual actors. That discussion assumed that any organism that utilizes its behavior as a means of adapting to an environment must be capable of "learning from experience." It was assumed that in order to learn, in the sense of accumulating information in the form of cognitively coded materials rather than genetically coded ones, an organism must be able to transform raw sense impressions into information and to accumulate that information in a form that makes it possible for the organism (within survival limits) to predict the effects of its own behavior on its environment and upon itself.

In the discussion of learning, it was assumed that a learning organism will evolve behavior patterns it perceives as having a higher than chance probability of success. Thus, the organism's cognitive apparatus will come to contain a population of behavior patterns stored in the form of cognitive systems or subsystems that have grown out of more or less successful attempts of the organism to adapt to a self-defined environment. In the immediately preceding discussion, I referred to some of these patterns as *roles*. The point here is that roles, as information systems, define behavioral patterns that, on the basis of experience, have been perceived by the acting organism as providing at least minimally adaptive behavior patterns. Again, we must recognize that there is nothing inevitable about the tendency to evolve adaptive behavior patterns, nor is there a tendency for them to move toward higher and higher levels of adaptation. The learning organism may create cognitive systems that result in failure as well as success. In order to survive, the patterns evolved need only fit within the limits that allow survival and need not be a perfect and exact fit. The only proviso is that patterns falling beyond the tolerance limits of the environment will result in negative selection.

Having applied these well recognized provisos to the assumption that organisms will tend to evolve patterns of behavior they perceive as adaptive, we can now move on to a proposition with relevance to social behavior. Let us assume that social behavior, that is, behavior that involves two separate actors interacting in the process of producing a common output, has a higher probability of success in satisfying many of the needs or wants of individual actors than solitary behavior. The focus here is upon social collaboration, or social cooperation, rather than upon conflict or competition. Two lions hunting together have a higher probability of killing a zebra than each would have hunting alone. A group of humans, each specialized in the performance of a given task, has a higher level of production of a given product than each would have working alone. Thus, more products that satisfy human needs will be produced by social systems than by solitary actors.

This proposition refers to the bonding together of a set of actors in unit-specific relationships through which they act in concert to produce a common outcome. The assumption is that there are "survival" or "competitive" advantages in social collaboration that arise out of a division of labor that allows specialization and collaboration among or between actors. If we accept this rather well-known assumption, then it is apparent that individual actors will tend to learn (evolve) behavior patterns that call for performance of behavior as actors occupying positions within the structure of a social system. Occupying social positions and playing social roles within group structures yields the adaptive advantages assumed earlier.

Given this reasoning, then, the structures of social systems will gradually evolve out of interaction among individuals as they construct adaptive behavior patterns as cognitive systems and subsystems within their minds. Over long periods of time, populations of actors who adopt a social solution to various adaptation problems will survive and tend to expand, and come to dominate the environments inhabited by less socially developed populations. Thus, the evolutionary process will tend to push human populations toward the development of a complex social division of labor containing a wide variety of social systems.

We should not assume that this means there is an inevitable one-directional movement toward complexity that will continue forever or for every society. It must be remembered that each evolutionary development in each system produces a change in the ecological field and affects its impact upon the substratum of resources that supports life itself. As a consequence, there are always limits that operate to confine and negatively select innovations that at an earlier stage in the development of the ecological field would have been tolerated. If we assume, nevertheless, that the average probability of success in satisfying biological needs and social wants will be increased as the division of labor within and between social systems becomes more complex and specialized up to some as yet unrecognized level is reached, whereupon this trend will be reversed, then we can assume that continued interaction among actors in a social context will lead to further differentiation and elaboration of the structure of social systems and of the ecological field containing them.

So far, in order to discuss the origin of social systems, we have reasoned as if all of the actors involved in interaction enter a world that is unstructured socially. But once a social structure has evolved, actors enter an already structured ecological field that contains already formed social systems, differentiated into an intersystemic division of labor. In such a world, the task of the actor is to adapt to an environment that contains an existing social order.

10.3   Culture as the Container for Systemic Structure

In order to conceptualize a division of labor among species of social systems and at the same time contend with the persistence of social systems as operating entities, even as individual actors come and go, it is necessary to think in terms of a mechanism that operates as the container for social structure and for the behavior patterns associated with it. The traditional solution to this problem has been to introduce the concept *culture* in one form or another, and to say that the behavior patterns associated with social systems are generated by cultural patterns that are shared by the population of actors who participate in those systems. Culture, therefore, becomes a superorganic cognitive apparatus and constitutes the storage mechanism that generates the recurrent patterns of social action in social groups, organizations, and communities.

This solution, however, is not satisfactory for our purposes unless we are willing, in some way, to ignore several previous assumptions or to revise rather radically the meaning usually given to the concept *culture*. For example, we are working toward developing a conceptual apparatus that will yield a clear image of an ecological field. I have said that such fields contain populations of self-referential, autopoietic systems. Each such system is self-generating and self-governing, thus operating as the generator of its own behavior. Since the field, as I have stated earlier, contains individual organisms as well as social systems, and each constitutes a bounded system in and of itself, the question arises: "How can each separate system, which, by nature, defines its own environment, and develops its own cognitive generator of action, be controlled at the same time by an external, independent superorganic thing called *culture*?" We cannot remain faithful to the assumptions that define bounded, self-referential systems and at the same time see them as under the control of forces or influences outside themselves. If each system acts on its own, at the very least, we must be prepared to say that it generates and employs its own internal culture in the form of its own self-evolved cognitive structure. When this is done, however, we are back where we began.

We have assumed that individual actors are separate, self-controlled systems, and we wish to treat social systems also as self-controlled systems. This being so, there remains the problem of boundaries between them. Actors cannot penetrate social systems and be controlled by them without losing their self-referentiality, and social systems cannot exist as systems if they consist of separate, self-referential systems called actors. I shall propose a revision of the concept *culture* that can make it possible to overcome this difficulty, and then apply the revision to both individual actors and social systems.

10.3.1   Culture as a Metaphenomenon

When social scientists speak of the culture of a particular society, for example, "Chinese culture," they are usually referring to the complex collection of beliefs, values, patterned social relationships, and activity patterns that are characteristic of a particular human population. From this perspective, culture contains the cognitive guidelines that supply a population with an ideology, a technology, and patterns of social organization.

To think of an item of technology, a behavior pattern, a value, or a belief as being an item of culture, it has been the usual practice to think of it as being "shared" or "held in common" by most, if not all, of the members of the population under consideration. It is the quality of being characteristic of many members of the same population and of being passed on from one member to another, possibly over many generations, that has given culture its central meaning in the minds of most social scientists. This quality of commonalty among the members of a population raises the concept *culture* above the individual level and makes it into an object of thought that is, in a sense, superorganic. It becomes a collective reality, a kind of categorical substance held together in the mind of the observer by the notion of similarity in behavior patterns among actors making up a population.

Culture functions as a concept with respect to social behavior in much the same way that genetics functions conceptually with respect to organic structure. It furnishes a ready-made explanation for the similarity in behavior among the members of a population who are faced with the same situation. The Chinese eat their food using chopsticks, because chopsticks are part of Chinese culture! Each Chinese individual has within him or her that piece of Chinese culture that generates chopstick using. In contrast, Europeans use knives and forks, and a similar claim can be made. It is the sharing of the pattern that prompts Chinese restaurant owners and their employees to supply the chopsticks that are then used by customers, and Europeans to supply the knives and forks. The social transaction among customers and restaurant personnel is an acting out of cultural patterns.

In the same way, Chinese people are similar in physical appearance as compared to Europeans, because they are genetically alike. They share genes from the same gene pool. The *gene pool*, as a collective concept, accounts for physical similarity among the members of a Chinese population and the *cultural pool* accounts for their similarity in behavioral practices. Both use *metaphenomenological concepts* in a circular argument to account for similarity and difference. Categories of organisms or behavior systems comprised of similar units of observation are said to contain the mechanism that generates the very similarity they are based on: genes or cultural norms!

Given this all too brief discussion, it is apparent that it is the idea of similarity in genes or cultural norms that operates as the key to "explaining" similarity in physical appearance and behavior. In so doing, it furnishes a circular path that, by itself, offers only a useless repetition of itself. However, there is a facet of this circular path that may offer a more useful perspective in the case of culture. The use of similarity among the members of a population as one of the most important defining characteristics of culture raises the level of abstraction of the concept above the phenomenological level and creates a metaphenomenological concept. Culture, as far as the mind of the user of the concept is concerned, is a metaphenomenon. If this is the case, the question is, what are the phenomena used as the basis for arriving at culture as a categorical concept, which, because it is categorical in character, is metaphenomenological? Since it is an abstraction that refers to a category and not an individual object that can be thought of as existing as a noumena, we cannot think of it as operating to produce phenomenological results.

In answering this question, we are led to pay attention to another, and possibly more important, defining characteristic of culture. At the phenomenological level, culture may be thought of in terms of cognitive systems, in fact, as consisting of the same cognitive systems that I have earlier said populate the minds of individual human actors. If we think of a single individual, a Chinese restaurant customer, for example, and we think of the use of chopsticks as eating tools, then we are back to the question of the behavior of actual chopstick use and the generator of that behavior. We can say the individual we have reference to contains within his or her mind a cognitive apparatus that includes the mental rules that generate chopstick use as a behavior. The mind is comprised, as we have said, of many such cognitive systems, and each is comprised of relatively complex, encoded information.

We can take the position that the total culture of a population of human actors amounts to the total population of cognitive systems held in the minds of all of the members of the population. An observer, with a cognitive apparatus that allows it, can imagine the possibility that many of these separate cognitive systems are similar; that is, many millions of Chinese people contain cognitive systems that generate chopstick use. This similarity is in the mind of an observer, who has first conceptualized chopstick use at the individual level and then, by comparison, constructed a conception of similarity, thus arriving at a metaphenomenological concept, the cultural practice of chopstick use. *But what makes a thing a part of culture is, according to this definition, the quality of being a cognitive generator of behavior.* Sharing has nothing to do with thinking of a cognitive object as being part of culture!

This is like saying that what makes a thing a part of a genetic pool is its nature as a gene or chromosome, comprised of DNA–RNA, that operates or functions to generate the growth and organization of an organism. It is *not* that the genes are "shared" that makes them "genetic." *It is how they function.*

The fact that skin color is similar among Chinese and different from Africans is a metaphenomenological conception. All genes in all individuals, regardless of similarity to others, are thought of as part of the gene pool.

10.3.2   Social Organization as the Organizer of Culture

As roles and systems of roles evolve, simultaneously, as part of the same process, a division of labor coevolves. This division of labor organizes the metaphenomenon called *culture* by allocating it differentially to the members of a population. Certain categories of the members of the population acquire certain roles as their particular fragments of culture, and others acquire different fragments. Because roles are such that they require other actors for their performance, they have the effect of organizing a human population in terms of two types of interdependence: unit specific and categorical. One type of interdependence creates a division of labor in which specific actors are forced to associate inside the boundaries of social units, and the other forces categories of actors into association as they interact in the interstices between social units. Conceptually, one form of interdependence brings social systems into being, and the other, ecological fields.

10.4   Person-Centered and System-Centered Analysis

When we say that ecological fields contain both individual actors and social systems, and recognize that this seems to represent a paradox, and if, at the same time, we assume that both individuals and social systems are regarded as self-referential systems, we have created a self-inflicted enigma that is more a product of the language than the logic we use. If we allow the concepts individual actor and social system to *coemerge*, then, as suggested earlier in *The Structure Of Social Systems*, there is really no contradiction except that produced by changing the object of structural modeling (Bates and Harvey, 1975). If we start with the individual and force our conception of the social system to conform to this preconception, or if we reverse this procedure and model the system first and the individual second, then this paradox emerges. However, if we allow the two concepts to *coemerge*, so that they are like the two sides of the same coin, the dilemma is resolved. Now, it lies only in the choice of analytical problem made. The observer can proceed to keep a cognitive eye on the individual actor and screen out the structure of social systems and ecological fields, or pay attention to the social structure, be it that of a system or ecological field. The two procedures produce two types of structural models using the same conceptual elements. One model is *person centered* and the other *system centered*. There is no paradoxical inconsistency except that produced when the observer attempts to use one model to supply the basis for forming the other.

10.5   Summary

It should now be apparent that the dilemma referred to earlier in this chapter has been resolved by redefining the concept *individual actor* in such a way as to allow it to coemerge along with our conceptions of social systems and ecological fields. As our conception of ecological fields has evolved, we have adopted the view that individual actors, as actors, are not to be thought of as bounded, self-referential systems but instead must be viewed as a type of cognitive ecological field. Otherwise, they could not be seen as participants in such fields. The various elements in the cognitive ecology of the actor fit the behavior of the actor into niches in the divisions of labor found in social systems and ecological fields.

Even with this conception, it is still necessary to make provision for the possibility that individual actors sometimes act as individuals not included in any interaction with other actors. When we do so, however, we need not assume that the total individual, as a total system, is acting. Again, we can assume that only a fragment of the ecology of the individual's mind is involved in such interaction.

11

An Overview of
Sociopolitical Ecology

11.1   Introduction

This book was written to present a theoretical and conceptual apparatus that supplies a basis for integrating selected aspects of the biological and social sciences. In particular, its objective is to develop a theoretical approach through which the relationships among human systems and between them and their nonhuman environments may be interpreted and understood using a known and well-defined viewpoint. In a broader sense, it was written with the hope of founding a new school of thought concerning the relevance of the various social sciences to general ecology and of biological ecology to the social sciences.

The name *sociopolitical ecology* was chosen to designate this point of view. This was done in order to distinguish it from older subdisciplines such as social or cultural ecology, environmental sociology, human geography, and so forth. This new approach is meant to concentrate attention on the relationships among human systems in the context of their environments and, in so doing, to concern itself with the impacts of human systems on their environments. At the same time, the objective is to explore the impact of environments on human systems.

Encompassed within this statement is an understanding that sociopolitical ecology is meant to deal with social, cultural, economic, and political relationships among human systems as they interact with each other, and to provide a means of examining how environmental factors impact upon these relationships, and how these relationships impact upon the environment. Also assumed is a clear recognition of the dependence of human systems upon their nonhuman biotic and physical environments.

This rather ambitious theoretical enterprise was undertaken on the basis of an explicitly recognized neoconstructivist epistemology. Within the constructivist tradition, it takes a "cognitive science" orientation. Thus, from the beginning of this project, it has been assumed that scientific observers (like

227

lay observers) "see" (in their "mind's eye") what their conceptual and theoretical apparatuses generate from within themselves. They encounter their environments through self-controlled sensory mechanisms. Therefore, if we, as observers, are to envision the relationships among human systems and between them and their environments, we will inevitably do so through the use of cognitive processes that employ a kind of cognitive machine to generate the images our minds see. It follows, therefore, that if we change the contents or organization of the cognitive machines we employ, we will simultaneously change the way we perceive the world, and if, as human actors, we adapt to the world *as we see it* rather than *as it actually is,* changes in our cognitive machines will just as inevitably affect our behavior and our chances of adapting successfully to the world we live in by use of them. Furthermore, if human systems are the subjects of our concern, changes in the cognitive apparatus employed by human systems themselves to generate their own behavior will produce changes in the relationships among these systems and between them and their environments.

This constructivist foundation implies a basic scientific need to understand the cognitive machines we use to construct our images of the world, so that we can experiment with revising them to serve our purposes more satisfactorily. If we need to understand our cognitive apparatuses in order to make them more useful, it seems apparent that they must be clearly and self-consciously defined. For this reason, a great deal of effort has gone into clarifying concepts and defining their relationships to each other in this book. In particular, I have attempted to remain consistent with my conceptualizations, once they have been formed, and have worked hard not to sidestep theoretical problems by simply relaxing or ignoring definitions and assumptions, thus using a cognitive trick to give the appearance of solving a logical problem without actually doing so. In particular, the term *system* is central to the discussion in this book and I have attempted to give it a particular, bounded, well-specified meaning, and to stick with that meaning, even though it forces redefinitions of other well-established concepts.

This strategy of making the concept *system* central to the development of the cognitive apparatus has resulted in reconceptualizations of many related concepts. The net effect of all of this cognitive labor has been the emergence of a different way of perceiving human systems in general, and human societies in particular. Specifically, one innovation presented in this book is to see at least some societies as "nonsystems." Instead, they are viewed as particular types of ecological fields.

This theoretical exercise has also led me to rethink the concept *ecosystem* and many of the ideas associated with it, putting in its place the concept *ecological field,* which seems to fit a precisely limited concept of *system* and, along with it, a consciously adopted evolutionary perspective, better than the notion of ecosystem. Given this broad introduction to this summary chapter, I proceed to give a methodical recapitulation of the major features that define sociopolitical ecology as a theoretical perspective.

11.2   The Systems Perspective

This book uses the concept *system* as the cognitive cornerstone around which a larger cognitive edifice is constructed. It, however, employs a particular variety of systems theory and develops its own restrictions with respect to its use. First, it assumes that all systems are objects made up of subelements called *parts* that operate or behave with respect to each other inside a boundary that seals them off from their environment in such a way that the system itself controls its own intake of resources, and its own generation of information from the environment. Thus systems, to be systems, must have the characteristic of controlling their own actions or reactions to external events or conditions. They are, in other words, *closed and self-referential automatons.*

Each system is comprised of a specific set of parts assembled into a unit-specific division of labor that forms an operational mechanism. This independently functioning mechanism differentiates each particular system from all others and from nonsystemic elements and conditions in its environment.

Systems are structured in such a way that they supply a whole or complete mechanism containing all of the elements necessary to the system's continued functioning, assuming that the system succeeds in obtaining the resources it seeks from its environment by means of its own behavior. This statement is meant to call attention to the fact that there is a difference between a system and its environment, and also between a system and a subsystem. Subsystems are parts of systems and, as incomplete systems, cannot function except in relation to the specific other parts that make up the rest of a particular systemic mechanism.

I have differentiated between active and passive systems rather than between open and closed systems in order to make the meaning of self-referential systems clearer. *Self-reference* refers to a particular type of closure that stems from the fact that self-referential systems generate their own information and control their own behavior from within themselves, and through generating information and controlling the behavior they generate on the basis of it, systems control their input–output relations with their environment. Self-referential systems are therefore active systems because they respond to their own self-constructed environments. They may also be autopoietic, if they are so structured that they can take in resources from their environments and use them in such a way as to continually reconstruct themselves, thus resisting both structural and functional entropy. Passive systems lack the internal controls necessary to regulate their intake of resources and their output of products, as well as the capacity to repair or reconstruct themselves in order to defy entropy.

11.3   The Utility of Systems Reasoning

In this book I have argued that the utility of systems reasoning lies in its use in arriving at a type of explanation that employs a kind of "systemic mechanics" to understand how a "systemic machine" operates as a causal or determinant mechanism for its own behavior. For the idea of system to yield this theoretical benefit, it must be kept "pure" by ruling out of its conceptual apparatus those qualities that would make mechanistic (or for that matter, organismic) causal reasoning impossible.

This proposition has led me to describe systems as "islands of order in a sea of chaos," or in terms used by Miller (1978) and many others, as examples of negative entropy. On this basis, systems are conceptualized as entities that function within themselves in a nonrandom, nonchaotic fashion, even as they draw resources from an environment that is more or less chaotic and characterized by high levels of randomness rather than order.

By using this particular view of systems, it is possible to envision an object of conceptualization that consists of many separate, self-referential systems in interaction with each other in the context of a common space where a substratum of resources and conditions are present. Each system in the population of systems operates as a self-controlled actor whose behavior, being self-generated, is independent or autonomous of control from outside itself. If this is granted, and if the population of systems is undifferentiated and unstructured, then the behavior of all of the systems taken together as a set will appear to be random, even chaotic, with respect to each other.

This is like saying that if we let a number of dice represent a number of systems, each die being an independent object, when a large population of dice are cast many times, the results will be a random distribution of possible outcomes. Even though we can describe, even predict, the characteristics of the distribution on the basis of probability theory, the behavior of each die on each throw is independent of all of the others. Of course, this is a requirement of the very probability reasoning that makes it possible to know the characteristics of the distribution. Thus, the stability that seems to characterize this distribution of outcomes, because over many trials at casting the dice the form of the distribution does not seem to change, is a stability based on randomness, a form of collective chaos. Such collective randomness can be cognitively modeled if we can imagine the types of events that are possible when we throw the dice. In actuality, the structure of the dice themselves, and the size of the population of dice, limit the possible outcomes, thus departing from complete chaos.

If we allow the structure of the field, thought of as the characteristics and potential behaviors of the population of systems inhabiting it, to be represented by the faces on dice, then we can predict that some form of stability will prevail in an ecological field as long as the way its population of systems is structured remains unchanged.

11.4   Ecological Fields

The term *ecological field* was chosen to represent the object referred to earlier and to differentiate it from a system. An ecological field is an object comprised of a population of autonomous active systems that interact within the context of a common space containing resources and characterized by a set of conditions. *An ecological field is a nonsystem made up of systems!*

Essentially, this perspective sees *ecological relationships* as the relationships between and among autonomous systems, whereas *systemic relationships* are those that take place inside the boundaries of a particular system among its parts or subsystems. Systemic relationships are always, by definition, between and among the specific parts that are found inside the boundaries of a particular autonomous system. For the sake of communication, such relationships were referred to earlier as unit specific, to point to the particular type of division of labor among social units characteristic within systems.

Systemic relationships were contrasted to ecological relationships, which in a structural sense, are between or among categories of systems. Here, we have the case in which the organization of the field is characterized by a differentiation of systems into "species" that occupy "niches" in a categorical division of labor, such that specific categories or species of systems are dependent on each other for resources, or vulnerable to each other in terms of threats to their survival. Thus, an ecological field is organized into a categorical division of labor that differentiates systems into niches and results in competition for resources among the members of a particular species, or among species occupying similar niches, and conflict between species that are interdependent for resources.

Which particular systems actually interact at any given moment and what the outcome of the interaction will be cannot be predicted from knowledge of any nonrandom mechanism. The reason is that each system located in an ecological field is self-referential and therefore is defined as being able to act on its own to pursue its own ends, or to avoid distruction or damage by other systems in its environment by use of its own defensive behavior. The outcome of the interaction of all of the systems forming a particular ecological field can therefore be predicted only on an actuarial basis, or upon the basis of probability theory applied to models of the field's structure.

The structure of ecological fields must be modeled using concepts that fall at the metaphenomenological level. Such concepts employ other concepts standing for phenomena (objects believed to be *noumena* or "real" objects) as their referent. Phenomenological concepts, on the other hand, refer to objects or events assumed by an observer to be the source of sense impressions that, themselves, originate with noumena in the environment of the observer's mind. This means that phenomenological concepts refer to objects thought of as occupying space and transpiring in time and presumed to have particular discrete, individual identities as separate objects of observation. In contrast, metaphenomena are referred to by concepts that in turn refer to categories or classes of phenomena. Individual animals are seen in the mind as phenomena, but species are metaphenomenological. The division of labor in an ecological field is conceptualized at the species, or metaphenomenological level, not at the individual system or phenomenological level. In contrast, the division of labor within a system among its parts is conceptualized at the phenomenological level.

The stability or "negative entropy" found inside systems is perceived by an observer by use of phenomenologhical concepts, because it is concerned with the persistence or autopoiesis of a structured pattern of relationships among particular parts having an identity as real objects. These "real" parts of "real" objects called *systems* are referred to by conceptions at the *phenomenological level*. The stability or, for that matter, the lack of stability perceived in an ecological "field" (in contrast to the stability inside a system) is constructed cognitively by an observer using metaphenomenological concepts as the cognitive tools employed by the mind.

The relations among species of systems remain stable or become unstable as the mind of the observer moves the structure of the field through time. As the mind attends to the relative size of species populations through time, the structure of the field seems to change and with it, the conditions for survival of the species themselves. The aggregate effects of the behavior of systems (seen through metaphenomenological constructs) are perceived by an observer as producing alterations in the collective environments of the species in the field, and these changes are perceived by an observer as feeding back upon systems and changing their relationships to each other at the categorical level.

From this brief summary, it can again be seen that ecological fields can be conceived as "nonsystems," because they are conceptualized on the basis of categorical reasoning that employs metaphenomenological constructs. When this is done, the basis of the "mechanistic" form of explanation embedded in systemic reasoning is lost and a form of *limited* or *bounded indeterminacy* is introduced—a kind of structured chaos. It is for this reason that I have abandoned the concept *ecosystem* and put the concept *ecological field* in its place.

11.5   Societies as Nonsystems

The usual sociological perspective implies that societies are conceptualized at the phenomenological, not the metaphenomenological level, and therefore they may be viewed as systems. From the perspective employed in this book regarding the defining characteristics of a system, this would mean that societies are made up of specific parts that stand in a set of unit-specific relationships to each other and form one, single, autonomous operating mechanism in which the various parts are controlled through their placement in the structure of the whole by a single systemic mechanism. The parts are sometimes conceptualized as institutions and at other times as social groupings (such as families or work organizations) but, in any case, they are thought of as functioning as units in a larger "social machine or organism."

The argument presented in this book is contrary to this view, because it models societies that contain market-exchange systems and democratic forms of political organization as ecological fields because, when they are modeled using the rules implicit in our definition of self-referential systems, such societies lack the qualities necessary for us to regard them as systems. Instead, the division of labor characteristic of market economies with democratic political institutions establishes autonomy among economic and political units and places them in an ecological field, where they compete for resources and for survival in an economic or political market place.

In such markets, categories (species) of social systems, specialized in the niches they occupy in the political or economic order, compete with each other for supporting resources and defend themselves against disruption or destruction by other systems operating in the same field. There is, therefore, a categorical division of labor within the socioecological field that structures it and limits or constrains the behavior of individual systems as they generate their own behavior on the basis of their own autonomous, autopoietic, self-referential orders. A difference exists, however, between the idea of a set of limits within which behavior takes place and the idea of determinants that operate within a mechanistic or organic structure to "cause" or "produce" specific outcomes. The structure of ecological fields limits or constrains the behavior of systems. Systemic structures, in contrast, cause or determine the behavior of the system as it operates within the limits placed on it by the field.

11.6   Government in the Context of Ecological Fields

From the perspective presented in this book, governmental units (such as legislative or judicial bodies, or administrative bureaucracies) are modeled as separate systems that interact as autonomous actors in a common field. As in the case of all systems, they control their own behavior from within their boundaries and resist intrusions from outside their boundaries. What has been described by others as a *political system,* under this reasoning therefore becomes the ecological subfield of political behavior.

When social systems function according to their own self-referential mechanisms, they take in resources from their environments, process them internally, and produce outputs back into the environment, some of which are utilized as resources by other systems, and some of which constitute "trash or waste " as well as the by-products of systemic functioning. The aggregate effects of systemic functioning seen by means of metaphenomeno-logical constructs are perceived by an observer as transforming the environment in which all of the systems occupying niches in the field operate, thus affecting the conditions of their functioning and survival.

11.7   The Global Ecological Field

At the global level, the consequence of this point of view is that the systems forming the global ecological field are no longer automatically defined as whole societies or nation states, but instead, as individual social groups and organizations. If societies are regarded as ecological fields or subfields, then a world containing many societies would contain many subfields, and the total global field would be comprised of the same differentiated, bounded social systems that comprise the subfields now called societies. Now, however, we must think in terms of a global division of labor among species of social systems and of these species of systems transcending the boundaries of nation-states. For example, we could illustrate this point by saying there is a species of social systems called automobile manufacturers. This species contains individual systems (automobile companies) as the individual members, and individual units falling within the species operate in many different countries as parts of socioecological subfields. At the global level, these individual systems (automobile companies) compete with each other and with other species of systems that occupy niches in the transportation category for passengers, resources, governmental favors, and so forth.

Similarly, the global ecological field contains species of systems called "foreign offices" or "departments of defense," "parliaments," and so forth. These political units operate in the field as autonomous, self-referential political systems rather than as subsystems contained within a larger political system. In so doing, they interact selectively with other systems, competing for resources, defending themselves against external threat, evolving and adapting to their self-defined environments.

From this perspective, the significant actors on the world stage are the autonomous, self-referential social systems that constitute what were formerly thought of as the parts (subsystems) of society. Nation-states under these conditions become ecological subfields. The autonomous, autopoietic systems that make up separate societies form a global economic, political, and sociocultural marketplace that is organized as an ecological field and not, as Wallerstein (1974) would say, as a "world system." Just as societies are seen from within the perspective of sociopolitical ecology as nonsystems or as ecological subfields, the global, planet-earth-level object of conceptualizations is also a nonsystem, a global ecological field, both in the sense of human and biological systems.

11.8   Differences between the Sociopolitical-Ecology Approach and Other Social-Science Perspectives

From the perspective of constructivism, no theoretical system can claim exclusive rights to the truth or even to clearly superior utility. Each theoretical system yields its own cognitive construction of reality relative exclusively to itself. Each such orientation also has the potential to yield benefits to its user, although the utility of each system is limited by its own internal order. Both the benefits and limitations of various theoretical approaches are, in other words, relative to the cognitive systems that produce them.

Ultimately, the test of any cognitive apparatus comes when it is used to solve either an intellectual or practical problem. Those cognitive systems that fail to provide solutions to the problems they themselves pose from within themselves will be judged by their users to be less desirable than those that provide at least partial solutions and will eventually be abandoned, not because they are judged to be false views of reality, but because they are not regarded as being useful.

Sociopolitical ecology, as developed in this book, must compete for survival (to use its own metaphor), in the intellectual marketplace with other perspectives. Indeed, because every theoretical system is limited and therefore always incomplete, each system must exist in a field that contains other theoretical systems that are themselves specialized in the problems they pose and attempt to solve. It is therefore indefensible for adherents of any perspective to claim ultimate superiority for one theory over another, because each cognitive system creates the intellectual arena in which it functions, and it cannot therefore be judged outside its own boundaries.

It is, however, possible, and indeed legitimate, to specify how various systems differ in the way they construct their self-referential realities. Accordingly, the next few pages will be used to point out some important differences between the sociopolitical-ecological perspective and other recognized approaches.

11.9   Differences from Miller's Living Systems Theory

Sociopolitical ecology explicitly recognizes the need to define the concept *system* against a background in which nonsystems are recognized not only as a practical possibility but also a theoretical necessity. Of course, virtually everyone who has used the term *system* has recognized that concepts such as randomness, chaos, and entropy are characteristics of nonsystems, but this fact has been treated more as a theoretical or definitional given than as a "reality-generating construct." Once the idea of *system* is associated with the ideas of *order* and *negative entropy*, the tendency of most "systems theorists" has been to see every knowable object either as a system or a part of one, because for an observer to recognize an object or a process and give it a name, it is necessary to think of the object using a symbolic code that implies an entity that has more than a random, momentary existence.

Being able to recognize an object and give it a code name implies that it is one case among many similar cases designated by the same symbol. Thus, when I use the word *society* to refer to an object believed to be recognizable as coming from a class of similar objects, the very use of the noun *society* implies a kind of stability, or a specific type of order that is an example of nonentropy. If this is the case, it becomes almost irresistible to think of all objects that are given verbal designations (e.g., societies) as being systems or parts of systems, because, in order to recognize them, an observer must also think of them as being stable and nonentropotic.

Whatever the reason, the tendency in the social sciences, indeed, in science in general, has long been to see everything "in nature" that we can recognize through empirical observation and give a name to as being a system or subsystem. To do this and at the same time preserve at least a modicum of consistency in the meaning of the concept system, theorists have used the device of thinking in terms of a hierarchical ordering of systems. Such hierarchical ordering, although allowing many characteristics of randomness and chaos to creep into the picture between levels in the hierarchy, does so by blanking out perception of such nonsystemic characteristics by using metaphenomenological constructs that appear to raise the level of scale of the objects being examined rather than the level of abstraction of the concepts being employed. Thus, what appears as randomness at one level of a hierarchy becomes order at the next. For example, the randomness in the behavior of individual animals in relation to each other, at the level of the individual actor, becomes regularity at the level of the species. For example, there is an appearance of systemic order created by the statement that lions (as a general category) habitually eat zebras. Although this statement is true at the categorical (metaphenomenological) level, at the level of predicting which lion will consume which zebra (the phenomenological level), the apparent order contained within the statement disappears into a form of randomness.

By changing levels of abstraction and treating these levels as levels of scale, we can (as does Miller) define every type of living object from the individual cell to the supranational (global system) as systems (Miller, 1978). The trick involved is to ignore the lack of specific ties among the particular units that are defined at the lower level of scale when a higher level of scale is conceptualized using similarity among objects as the basis for creating a categorical construct, a species, for example. The appearance is thus created that there is an object that "exists in nature" that corresponds to the name of a class or category of individuals (species). For example, lions as a class recognized as being a species and given their own place in a linguistic code, are thought of as a larger entity than a single individual lion. Thus, species are as "real" as the individual organisms that belong to them.

Once this is done, "species" as real objects are treated as the parts of a "higher order" system called an *ecosystem*. This mental "slight of hand" does not occur at each transition point in a hierarchical ordering of systems, however. For example, if we use Miller's "eight levels of living systems" (Miller, 1978), the conceptual hiatus comes between the organizational and community level. Starting at the lower level of scale, the individual organs of an organism are comprised of particular, exact cells at any particular moment and not of categories of cells. Similarly, the whole organism is comprised of its own particular organs (heart, liver, lungs, etc.) and not categories of organs. So, too, can a social group be comprised of particular organisms that are differentiated according to the roles they play, and thus the group may be regarded as a larger object than its individual members, as can an organization that is made up of particular groups (see also Bates and Harvey, 1975).

The problem arises at the transition from the level of the multigroup organization to the community level. At the community level, we are dealing with the relationships among autonomous systems that are not tied to each other in stable, unit-specific relationships. In communities, categories of groups and organizations, the members of which, in the traditional view, are regarded as systems in their own right, are differentiated into a categorical (ecological) division of labor. Within the context of a community-level division of labor, the groups and the organizations interacting at any given moment change constantly as time progresses. Which particular ones are interacting at any given time is contingent upon conditions in the ecological field at that moment. As time progresses, the units that are actually interacting change moment by moment, so to speak. It is here that randomness enters the picture and, as a consequence, makes it ill-advised to think of a community as a system. The relationship among the parts of a community at the level of the individual groups and organizations is probabilistic rather than "organic" or "mechanistic." Communities simply lack the defining characteristics of a system, in particular the presence of unit-specific attachments in a systemic mechanism that operates as a single "machine" to generate the behavior of the parts of the system. Communities are nonsystems; or as I have said earlier, they are ecological subfields. If we accept this argument, the last three levels in Miller's hierarchy of systems become progressively broader and broader ecological fields.

It is the contention of this book that we have not lost anything by this act of reconceptualizing communities as ecological fields; instead, we have gained the capacity to create theories that can represent evolution and change more adequately, and allow us to see ways of understanding better how they are produced. The selection of species of systems for survival takes place at the level of the ecological field, as does the ultimate selection of systemic traits that allow us to see morphogenesis in systems. It is in being able to see interaction between and among bounded, autonomous systems rather than within them, more precisely, that promises to yield the benefit of a truly ecological ecology in contrast to an ecosystemic ecology. It is probably also true that sociopolitical ecology has the potential to be more useful in understanding market phenomena at the societal and global level, as well as politics within societies and between them in international affairs.

Sociopolitical ecology does not require us to impose the characteristics of a system on human communities, societies, or the global sociopolitical order. We can see this order through the medium of a new kind of ecology that seems to fit the economics and politics of the late 20th century.

It is important at this point to remind ourselves that we cannot say that the Miller or Bates perspectives are wrong or right in the sense that they correspond or do not correspond to the truth in nature. The two perspectives yield different realities when applied as cognitive machines used for the purpose of constructing mental images of a world that can only be imagined through cognitive action. Each perspective has its own value relative to itself and appears to solve the intellectual problems it poses. Only time and use in problem solving will determine which is more useful for particular purposes.

11.10   Worldview of Sociopolitical Ecology

Sociopolitical ecology, by using the cognitive machine presented in this book, constructs a particular type of reality and thereby presents a "world view" peculiar to itself. Although this reality is similar in some particulars to other well-known perspectives, the whole "cognitive package" represented by sociopolitical ecology differs from the usual way social scientists and biological ecologists have conceptualized the world of man and nature at the global or planetary level. For the sake of clarity, it will be useful in this summary chapter to point out the most important differences between it and more customary modes of thought.

The world, according to sociopolitical ecology, is populated by active, self-referential systems that operate as automatons in an environment that contains physical resources and conditions that, although defined by each system for itself, operate along with the impact of systems upon each other to select systems for survival. In this respect, sociopolitical ecology is similar to and draws upon evolutionary theory and upon biological ecology. It differs from biological ecology and from social ecology in that it envisions a world (planet Earth) that is neither an ecosystem, nor is it defined as a world-level geopolitical economic system. Instead, it is constructed as an ecological field in which the relationships among systems are probabilistic and cannot be accounted for by a set of causal relationships embedded in a nonrandom, nonentropotic order.

Sociopolitical ecology (by use of its own cognitive tools) creates a reality in which autonomous systems (socially detached individual actors and social systems) are the significant players, and in which human societies are seen as ecological fields rather than as systems. This leads to the conceptualization of the world as a global-sized economic, political, and sociocultural marketplace in which systems at the level of individual actors and social systems of group or organizational scale interact, impact upon, and draw resources from each other and, in the process, change their environments for better or worse.

In the world of sociopolitical ecology, nation-states and their governments are no longer the principal components of conceptualization. Nation-states dissolve into subpopulations of bounded, self-referential systems and therefore into ecological subfields. Governments fall apart conceptually into their institutionalized bureaucratic components that in sociopolitical ecology become separate, bounded, self-referential social systems in and of themselves. Thus, legislative and judicial bodies, along with the various components of the executive or administrative branch of government, are viewed as separate, systemic actors in the ecological field, just as separate economic organizations constitute such systems in the economic marketplace.

In the worldview of sociopolitical ecology, there is no one in control of a society, nor is there a control mechanism or steering device such as a command or authority structure. Governmental units as bounded, self-referential systems act as autonomous actors, and nongovernmental units respond in a similar autonomous fashion. If this is true within society, then certainly it is true at the intersocietal level. On the global stage, the political, economic, and social units usually thought of as the parts of separate societies interact in global markets as self-referential entities in a global division of labor, and the outcomes of this interaction are the products of uncontrolled ecological processes.

These ecological processes and their environmental consequences can be comprehended only through the use of metaphenomenological concepts that supply the basis for using probability theory to predict the outcomes of global-ecological interaction. The apparent order seen by observers at the global-ecological level is a stability produced by the use of metaphenomeno-logical constructs employed by observers to construct an image of a global-level set of relationships. This world-level order has not been discovered, but is constructed, by cognitive action.

12

Epilogue

12.1   *Structuralism and Sociology*

This book argues in favor of a cognitive-systems-theory, constructivist view of social structure and social organization that clearly separates the conceptual apparatuses employed in structural studies in sociology from that centered upon individual actors in the social-psychological sense or upon the relationship of the individual to society in the sense of social stratification. The objective has been to allow the structure of society to stand out as a distinct reality from the population of actors who people that structure and execute the transpiring events that constitute society as an emergent behavioral phenomenon. The point has been made repeatedly that to see any of these "realities," it is necessary for the observer to use an organized cognitive system to construct a cognitively comprehensible model. This means that an approach that uses self-referential systems theory and a structural strategy will construct a different reality than that produced by symbolic interactionism or by the Marxian stratification perspective.

It has also been one of the objectives of this book to distinguish between the structure of society and the processes that allocate people to that structure. This has required sharp distinctions among concepts that are ordinarily blurred by overlapping meanings in the everyday vocabulary of sociologists. For example, the logic of the argument presented here has required that the distinction between social organization and social structure made by Firth (1963) and others to be resurrected and, to some extent, redefined, so that structure can be viewed in a longitudinal perspective as an enduring pattern of social relationships and, at the same time, be used in connection with a theory of morphogenesis. This, in turn, has led to the use of self-referential systems theory as a means, first, of conceptualizing social structure as a phenomenon separate from the organized behavior that emerges as social organization, and second, as a vehicle through which to deal with stability and change. It was also the objective of this book to create a cognitive apparatus that would allow social scientists to construct images of global social structure and of the relationship of human systems to the global environment in the context of such structure.

12.2   The Utility of Self-Referential Systems Theory

For a number of reasons, self-referential systems theory, using a cognitive systems approach, when applied to social systems, seems eminently appropriate for these purposes. First, it takes as its target phenomena, systems of cognitively encoded information, thought of as interrelated sets of cognitive rules, capable of handling information and rendering it comprehensible to those employing the rules. In this case, the systems of rules are themselves rules for social behavior, which store a repertoire of behavioral responses that reproduce networks of social relationships. As a consequence, this theoretical approach offers an avenue through which to deal with social structure in the sense of an enduring, stable, repetitive set of socially organized behavior patterns stored in the form of culture. Culture itself may be dealt with as an ecological field consisting of a population of cultural patterns stored as cognitive systems. A cognitive science (constructivist) view of self-referential systems theory thereby offers a means of dealing with the episodic nature of social behavior and, at the same time, with the stability of behavior patterns through time by joining the idea of social structure with the idea of culture.

A second reason for turning to self-referential systems theory is that it offers a means of dealing with morphogenesis. By allowing the mating of "learning theory" with self-referential systems theory, it provides a framework for positing the conditions under which structural change will or will not occur. Self-referential systems theory, in the case of social systems, includes the idea that such systems develop in order to provide a set of actors with adaptive behavior patterns that render their collective relationships to their environment routine, predictable, and adaptive. By this, I mean that the patterns of behavior provided by the self-referential systems furnish a satisfactory set of input–output relations between the actors practicing them and their environment.

Beyond this, it is proposed that when conditions arise either internally within a network of actors or externally in its environment that lower the adaptive or predictive value of the system of rules, the system of rules will tend to be forced open to permit adaptive change or, as an alternative, be threatened with collapse because the rules fail to maintain an adaptive relationship between the population of actors practicing them and their environment. Furthermore, it posits the idea that the system of cognitive rules will become closed and therefore stable when such a relationship is achieved, thus fixing, for a period of time, a structural pattern.

These propositions form the foundation of a kind of ecological theory of morphogenesis. It is ecological in the sense that each self-referential system is seen as occupying a "niche" in an ecological field to which its sets of cognitive rules constitutes an adaptation. Because the environment itself is capable of changing independently of the system, and because the self-referential systems occupying niches in an ecological field are also capable of impacting upon the field and changing it, the relationship between systems and their environment is seen as a source of morphogenesis. The rules constituting such systems are the consequences of the learning that occur when actors practicing behavioral patterns in the context of a social system interact with each other and with the surrounding environment. That environment includes other human systems as well as other biological systems and the inorganic substratum upon which they depend.

12.3   View of Society and Social Change Produced by This Use of Self-Referential Systems Theory

The use of self-referential systems theory as a guide to building this model of social structure leads to consideration of a number of interesting questions concerning the nature of society and of its various parts and their relationships to each other, which do not occur in most discussions of social structure. It also leads to questions concerning social evolution that are not ordinary in discussions of social change. For example, we are forced to ask the question, "Can the structure of a whole society be regarded as a single, self-referential system or must we take a different view?" There is, of course, no definitive answer for this question, given the constructivist approach used in this book because all realities are relativistic and autoconstructed.

Nevertheless, in this book, a reasonable argument has been developed in favor of the position that modern societies, especially capitalist ones, can be usefully viewed as networks of separately evolving, self-referential systems that lack sufficient integration under an autonomous structural mechanism to constitute a system in and of themselves. Such a view has led to an examination of the linkage between the various units comprising modern social structures and has resulted in the conclusion that, at least in modern capitalistic societies, it is useful to regard structural conflict as the dominant relationship that connects the separate elements in the division of labor within an ecological field containing autonomous human systems as the units of structure. This structural conflict arises out of the contingent linkages and the resulting separate morphogenic processes that transpire in the multitude of specialized social units comprising the division of labor characteristic of urban–industrial societies under democratic capitalism.

At the same time that this conception seems descriptive of the late 20th century, it also appears possible that some societies, in earlier periods, and perhaps some smaller, simpler societies at present, can be usefully assumed to have achieved a level of integration approaching the point at which we would be justified in viewing them as under the control of a single, self-referential cultural structure. This means that perhaps long-range social evolution in the structural sense can be conceptualized as waves of fluctuating integration under systems of rules that make life in society almost totally routine, predictable, and stable during one period, followed by periods of disorganization, disorder, and, morphogenic, autopoietic development and change as the system breaks apart and then reorganizes itself.

12.4   The Future of the Modern World

A question arises as to the significance of this view for how we see the future of the modern world. It appears that the sociocultural integration achieved during the Middle Ages, which led to the formation of many separate, small societies, was shattered by the industrial revolution and by the events that led up to it and have transpired after it. Although the network of relations among separate societies has broadened constantly and nation-states have grown in magnitude and complexity, according to the traditional view of the world order, their structures have broken apart into many separately evolving, autonomous self-referential economic, governmental, and social systems. According to the ecological viewpoint of this book, this has resulted in the formation of a global network that has been increasingly characterized by growing alienation between separately evolving, self-referential systems that constitute the elements of the international division of labor characteristic of the modern world. In this new world order, neither societies nor sovereign nation-states are the units of structure in the global ecological field but instead, large, complex multinational conglomerates interacting in a global marketplace.

The Humpty-Dumpty of small, agrarian, self-referential societies was forced off the wall of medieval feudalism by industrialization, and as industrialism and now postindustrialism have move on to maturity and beyond into senescence, it is at least questionable whether he can ever be put back together again to form a single, integrated structural pattern of bonded, stable social relationships. To use Braudel's metaphor, the ship of medieval social structure crashed on the rocks of industrialized modernity, but instead of morphogenic processes constructing a single substitute ship to represent the modern social order, a whole fleet of smaller craft emerged that, instead of sailing majestically down the river of time, following a single course, are scampering hither and thither, crashing on separate rocks or, for that matter, into each other as they drift in the general direction of the future (Braudel, 1982–1984). Following this metaphor, it appears that social scientists must now construct many separate models of social structure, each with its own morphogenic processes if we are to understand much about the modern world. Our new view of society and of the structure of the global network must deal with the relationships among a multitude of separately evolving systems, changing in interaction with one another rather than together as an integrated whole. It is as if we need to understand the dynamics of a whole fleet of ships sailing toward individual objectives in an enclosed and crowded sea, where the individual vessels must take each other into account in order to obtain provisions and also to avoid crashing, but in which there are no rules to govern navigation.

12.5   The State and the Social Network

Taking this view requires a new perspective on the vaguest of all concepts in the social sciences, *the state*. This concept has always been employed in such a way as to imply some deeply embedded unity lying below the surface of social structure, imbuing a society with an essentially political character, and government with a special role in binding together a population of people and the institutions that constitute their social order. The idea of the state simultaneously adds sovereignty to the notion of society and along with it, the conception that through governmental actors, entire societies can act upon or interrelate to each other as if they were unified systems. At the same time, the idea of the state carries along with it a constitutional conception of the social order, as well as the notion that constitutions may be designed and redesigned at will.

If, however, we take the position that modern societies are uncoordinated networks of separate and conflicting systems, each with a degree of autonomy that stems from the structure of the division of labor, what then becomes of the idea of the state and of its associated concept, government? It is immediately apparent that we cannot view government as being in control of a society in the sense that the chief executive officer and the board of directors are in charge of a corporation, or the commanding officer and general staff are in control of an army. The government must, instead, be viewed as a subset of organizations with specialized functions, capable of exercising limited powers in relation to other organizations through a highly differentiated network of specialized relationships. Governmental bureaus are self-referential systems but they are *not* automatically, by definition, the managing directorate of a single system called the society or the state. From the perspective presented in this book, governmental units are treated like any separate structural element in the social network by other units that are part of the same societal network, that is, as being part of the environment to which nongovernmental units must adapt.

The systems of self-referential rules that apply to governmental institutions evolve separately, even though in interaction with other institutions, as these institutions adapt to each other as parts of the division of labor in society. It follows also that structural conflict is the dominant form of relationships that exist among governmental units and the multitude of separately evolving, nongovernmental units of such societies. The fact that government may create rules designed to regulate or control the actions of other units is not sufficient to warrant the assumption that a whole society is, in fact, controlled by an integrated set of rules. Instead, such governmental actions may be treated as environmental conditions to which nongovernmental units must adapt. But the separate adaptive processes of the differentiated parts of society continue to generate separate self-referential systems.

12.6   The Global Network

At the global level, the relationships among societies have been blurred to such an extent by social change that, sociologically, it is no longer possible to draw sharp boundaries between them using the cognitive tools available from the social sciences. This is a natural, inevitable consequence of the lack of integration characteristic of separate societies in the modern world. As I have argued, capitalistic and perhaps even industrialized socialistic societies such as the former Soviet Union are now better regarded as loosely knit networks dominated by contingency relationships among separately evolving self-referential systems. Many of these systems spill over what are considered the boundaries of societies in the traditional, political sense. For example, multinational corporations, themselves self-referential systems, exist as parts of the networks of multiple societies (defined in political terms). Markets that relate separate self-referential systems in networks of contingency relationships are global, not national. There is, in fact, a global village, or at least only a few multinational networks that constitute the world economic, political, and social order (McLuhan, 1989; Wallerstein, 1974). In this network, corporations and other organizations, for example, voluntary agencies, even governmental institutions, are evolving separately from any effective or dominating control by nation-states. This is not to say that the residents of various countries share equally in either the benefits or costs of this evolutionary process. But it does suggest that global sociopolitical evolution is occurring in a process that is dominated by the contingent relationships characteristic of the structural conflict that has emerged unplanned and unanticipated from the division of labor typical of the advanced industrialism found in some areas of the world as it exists side by side with preindustrialism, even tribalism in other parts. In the global network the conception of a multitude of separately evolving, yet society transcending self-referential systems is even more applicable.

12.7   Personal Conjectures and Commentaries

A writer hoping to make a contribution to the fundamental theoretical underpinning of a field should be careful to make his or her reasoning as clear
and as concise as possible. At the same time, there is an obligation to push
the theoretical argument to its logical conclusion and, if possible, to go beyond this, and to reveal whatever additional hunches and insights have
emerged, even if they are beyond the limits of traceable logical connections
to the main argument. These more speculative insights should, however, be
clearly set off from others for which the author claims a firmer foundation.
On the basis of this conviction, I have the following more speculative and
more personal thoughts to offer.

In developing the language of this book and in working out the logical
connections that weld it into a theoretical scheme, a number of highly speculative ideas have emerged, which intuition tells me are related to the main argument, but for which I cannot present a step-by-step logical argument of
the same degree of rigor used to formulate the central ideas presented previously. Nevertheless, I feel compelled to present a few of them for whatever
they may be worth. One possible value of such a venture is that they may reveal a hidden bias on my part, or perhaps an unstated set of underlying assumptions concerning the subject matter I have presumed to address in
earlier chapters. Another value might be that someone else may perceive a
better way of linking them to the core of my argument. Allow me, therefore,
to address the reader in a more personal vein concerning these matters.

12.8   A Pessimistic View of Man's Future in Society

My friend Aydin Germen, a Turkish scholar who read and insightfully criticized a much earlier version of this book, pointed out in his detailed commentary the essentially optimistic view of social evolution presented by Karl
Marx. After all, despite his dark allusions to the coming class struggle and
the presumed revolution to follow, he concluded that social progress is possible, perhaps even inevitable, and that the ills of capitalism and of advanced
industrialism in general are correctable. To him, there is a road that man can
take toward the perfection of social life. Not only was he optimistic about the
economic life of man in society, but also about political life, for he was also as
much in favor of political as economic freedom and equality. He even went
so far as to forecast the "withering away of the state" and the achievement of
an idyllic state of "pure communism."

In contrast to Marx, I am an extreme pessimist, as is my friend Aydin.
Neither the further development of capitalism nor of socialism seems to me

to hold much hope for more than a temporary and relatively elusive improvement in physical or material well-being for mankind. There seems also to be little promise of either an elevation in human reason to a higher level of general wisdom or a constant improvement in social justice. Both capitalism and socialism, along with their associates industrialism and urbanism, seem outmoded and inhuman and, in the long run, doomed to collapse of their own inflexible ideological weights. This conviction does not stem alone from my personal values or from my personal experience, which has exposed me over the past 70 years to much of the misery found in both the first and the third world, but it seems also to be a logical extension of the arguments concerning social structure I have presented in this book. Consider the following associated thoughts.

Suppose for purposes of argument we accept the grand view found among evolutionary systems theorists that the universe is evolving toward "higher," more "complex" levels of structure, and therefore away from the chaos implied by the "big bang" with which it all began, and with which it is foretold by cosmologists it will all end, presumably only to begin again. Under such a perspective, societies are merely the latest level of order to emerge out of the original chaos. But according to the arguments I have presented here, all "true systems" are examples of entities that have evolved a structure and therefore an internal order. Even so, the relations among such ordered systems remain a part of the original chaos until the separate systems themselves evolve a level of order that places all of them within and under the domination of a larger systemic mechanism. In the case of society and of social life in general, I have posited the existence of systems but have been forced by my own logic to deny the existence of any overall system, sometimes even at the level of a single community, and certainly at the level of society, at least in the case of industrial capitalism as I know it. I cannot even consider seriously the proposition that there is a "world system." Instead, my views have led me to the conclusion that relations among separate social systems are contingent and therefore, to an extent, random and chaotic. Furthermore, the randomness is a randomness of conflict and competition for survival among separately evolving systems and not merely a matter of unrelatedness and nonpredictability.

Yet logic also seems to compel me to conclude that perhaps a larger, more comprehensive social order is in the process of evolving. This is not only an extension of the notion of movement away from the original "big bang" and toward the next one but also is at the very core of self-referential systems theory as it applies to societies. It even seems to me that the notion of the universe collapsing into an ultimate explosion implies, among other things, that the collapse is somehow related to the process of structuring that, when near completion, results in a loss of randomness and a near static order.

This, too, seems compatible with the notion that self-referential systems become closed and fixed, and therefore inflexible, once they achieve a high level of adaptation to an existing set of conditions. Without the existence of some degree of chaos and randomness, it is apparent that there is no room for change and therefore no room for further creative adjustments among the parts of a now totally deterministic system. This seems to foretell a sudden decline into ultimate structural entropy, once the system closes, since it appears reasonable to think that systems avoid entropy only by taking in resources, primarily energy, from their environment, and when there is a completely structured universal system, there is no environment from which energy can be obtained.

Of course I am, as a sociologist, ill-prepared to really understand the esoteric theories and concepts of physical cosmologists, but what I have said here has application to social life. It seems to me that societies and intersocietal networks can only evolve toward a wider social order by doing something akin to what, I am sure, Max Weber would have called organizing and bureaucratizing the world under a common authority structure. In other words, the only route toward the elimination of chaos in social affairs and toward overcoming the cruelty of the marketplace, and at the same time to foster technological advance and improvement in human physical well-being, not to mention the elevation of human understanding, is to further structure societies into deterministic, self-referential systems. In the same vein, it appears to me that to eliminate international conflict and to eliminate cross-societal inequities in physical and social well-being, however defined, the only road open is to structure the world into a more deterministic, less random, global social system. This structuring implies the imposition of severe constraints on the independence of the various component parts of the system, and by implication, on the people who carry out the behavior that constitutes the system as an operating entity. In other words, order in social affairs can only be achieved at the sacrifice of what we have called "political freedom and independence." But worse than this, if order were ever achieved it would be, like the total order in the physical universe, doomed to collapse of its own structural weight, because it would have no source for its most vital adaptive resource, new information upon which more adaptive rules could rest.

It seems apparent to me that a tightly organized world order would have the effect of eliminating completely the social environment upon which current systems depend for adaptive resources. Parenthetically, it seems obvious to me that at present, the thing we see as progress and as political freedom in the developed world is dependent on a chaotic world system in which units from one society exploit units in another to achieve a temporary economic and political advantage. It is not that American and other relatively affluent societies as integrated systems exploit less fortunate societies as units, but separate organizations from the advanced industrial powers, as bounded, uncontrolled, evolving entities, exploit similar units in other societies, and as a consequence, appear temporarily to develop beyond their competitors.

Late 20th-century Americans judge their society to be "more advanced" than societies of the third world on the basis of the capacity of the many separate and structurally unintegrated economic and political enterprises that constitute the American social network to produce, or more accurately, overproduce physical products. But all of this is a consequence of a lack of order in the world political and economic system. This lack of integration permits units in societies that are well positioned geographically and with respect to natural resources and historical circumstances, to be a few steps ahead technologically and to enjoy a higher standard of living than less fortunate neighbors. For the United States, Western Europe, and the developed nations of Asia to remain ahead, it appears to be absolutely necessary for them to be free to exploit the rest of the world.

This is best achieved either under a system of colonialized empires, as in the 19th and early 20th centuries or under its successor, a world capitalistic marketplace. The first implies the creation of a multinational system with political and military domination from a central power, and the second implies the continued chaotic state of world relations characteristic of the present economic relations between nations, which themselves lack internal integration. This latter situation, of course, presages continued economic and political inequality between the so-called advanced industrial powers and the poor, unindustrialized societies of the world, a condition that seems to me morally and ethically unacceptable.

But if this exploitation ceased and all units in all societies were integrated into a set of bonded, rule-guided "bureaucratic-like relationships," eventually the whole global system would be homogenized under a common set of rules, and developmental change would be likely to cease. This, I believe, would lead in the very short run to rapid depletion of physical resources if the homogenization were at a high level of consumption, or to a gradual decline in consumption and a slower rate of resource depletion if the general level of consumption were lowered. Even so, without the generation of innovation through the random variation provided by the modicum of chaos left between social units, adaptation would be too slow to avoid the collapse of social life in the form that we now know it.

Thus, to me, Marx's optimism is unwarranted. To put it in the Southern vernacular, we are between a rock and a hard place. The rock represents the cruelties and the savage and profligate excesses of the global capitalistic free market, and the hard place is the mind-numbing, self-defeating ultraconservative excesses of a centrally managed world state. This is the ultimate contradiction of modern times.

I must add that despite recent events in the socialist world, I believe, with Marx, that history is moving us toward a centrally managed economy and toward a world political order but, unlike him, I view this as the prelude to catastrophe instead of the opening scene of the millennium to be played out in a new political and economic Eden. At the same time, I cannot accept the view that capitalism offers a brighter alternative. Adam Smith was obviously wrong in holding that it "offers the greatest good for the greatest number" if one considers the whole world, because it appears that the greatest good is for those at the core of the world economy, and the greatest numbers are at the periphery.

To those who think that all of this can be saved by achieving some kind of humanistic consensus, and by substituting new values and beliefs for old, I have little to say other than to remark that they do not understand social structure and have a naive conception of social systems and a defective, myopic view of the social and economic conditions that prevail in the world today. Whatever the ideological climate, even though humanitarian and equalitarian, the mind will be just as numbed by the homogeneity and regularity of a new world order. But without it, we are doomed to the chaos in which the strong exploit the weak, and power accumulates according to the roll of the geopolitical dice.

12.9   A Word on Chaos and Self-Referential Systems

One of the propositions of self-referential systems theory is that they move toward closure, which is reached when their rules provide an almost machinelike precision in predicting their relationship to their environments. This proposition implies that until closure is reached, there is a degree of randomness internal to such systems. In other words, their processes of morphogenesis are incomplete and the relationships among their parts, as well as between them and their environment, are "partially chaotic." Closure, and therefore the end of morphogenesis, is achieved when all internal relations are predictable, and when their relationship to their environment is therefore under complete control by the rules of the system. When and if this happens, the system ceases to change and adapt. I believe that this also is likely to mean that such systems may often fail to open in time to make new adaptive adjustments as their environments change. This is true partially because the system itself defines its own environment and therefore may be internally incapable of admitting completely new types of information for which its rules do not prepare it.

I say this despite the popular faith in human creativity and in the capacity of the human mind to invent symbolic means of dealing with previously unknown phenomena. It is my belief that this creative capacity, if it indeed exists in any real sense, does not often take quantum leaps and is more likely to make a small step forward only under relatively chaotic conditions. When already accepted, and well-practiced ideas are available, innovation is unlikely. Besides this, the acceptance and institutionalization of innovation are dependent on more than the innovator and upon more than the apparent practical advantages of the innovation. Its persistence and adaptation are dependent on the structure of the system into which it is introduced, and if that structure is closed, where can it fit?

For these reasons, I hold a pessimistic view concerning the capacity of self-referential systems, once near closure, to survive environmental changes. It is really upon this logic that my pessimism about the viability of a world social order rests. It rests, furthermore, on the belief that individual human beings as thinking organisms are themselves self-referential systems, programmed by their experience, which inevitably embeds them in self-referential social systems that exercise severe constraints on individual creativity and innovation.

My final comment is on the use of deterministic and probabilistic theories in the social sciences and, because of this, on chaos, randomness, and indeterminism as ideas. I strongly believe that indeterminism, and the consequent use of probability theory, is made inevitable by our abysmal ignorance and not by the ultimate nature of things. But, after all, ignorance is a permanent and inevitable human condition. The world, both physical and social, is not so much indeterminate and random as it is infinitely complex and therefore beyond human comprehension. Sheer complexity alone ensures permanent human ignorance.

There are many potential problems of explanation that we have either never conceived of or are beyond our most optimistic reach, because to comprehend them we would have to know so much from observation that it is beyond our information-processing capacity. In a state of complete ignorance, all things appear chaotic and random. This does not mean that they are not ordered, but that we cannot comprehend, the order present in them, either because it is so complex or because we have not yet developed the cognitive capacity to unravel a part of that complexity.

In such a state, we have no alternative other than to treat many problems stochastically. I must confess that I think a belief in "free will" in the case of human beings is a concept made necessary by our ignorance of the order in human affairs. It is because the behavior of human beings is so complex that we cannot perceive order in all aspects of it, that we sometimes posit a kind of random independence for the individual, calling it free will. Of course, the more intellectual among us prefer the term *creativity*, but it is all the same. The concept, *self-referentiality*, in what is written here, takes over some of the ideological burden borne by the concept *free will*. It, however, lacks the connotation of self-control in the sense of willed action and uses the concept of an automaton as its control metaphor. Through using it and the concept *metaphenomenon* to conceptualize the structure of ecological fields, we have pushed back the frontier of complete chaos, creating instead a kind of bounded indeterminacy.

In this book, I have talked a great deal about structure and about systems, both of which are obviously related to the notion of order, and therefore to determinism. But at the same time, I have talked about chaos and randomness, and about contingent relationships among independent systems. I believe that we must use deterministic, and therefore structural and systematic reasoning when dealing with certain aspects of social life, namely self-referential social systems, but because of the complexities introduced by categorical (metaphenomenological), contingent linkages and the results of the division of labor and the conflict it engenders, we must fall back on probabilistic theories to deal with between- and among-system relationships.

I will go one step further and say that we are likewise compelled in this direction if we attempt to deal with the relationship between categories of individuals, or perhaps even the relationship of a single person to the structure of society. Although it seems apparent to me that where a given person ends up in the social structure is completely determined, the elements involved in the determination are so complex that we are forced to view the problem in probabilistic rather than deterministic terms. This all leads me to the conclusion that causal reasoning based an a "deterministic view" is appropriate when dealing with systems, but that probabilistic, correlational, actuarial reasoning is appropriate for dealing with the contingent relationships among structurally separate systems.

This is the message I found hidden beneath the surface of Popper's (1972) discussion of "clouds and clocks." Clouds, and cloudlike phenomena are best approached stochastically, but clocks and clocklike phenomena are understood best as determinant systems. To me, this means that groups and organizations, being self-referential systems, should be approached using deterministic, causal reasoning, but communities, societies, and world systems, being contingency networks, should be approached stochastically, using probabilistic reasoning and an indeterminacy framework.

References

Ashby, W. R., 1956, *Design for a Brain*. (2nd ed.). London: Chapman & Hall.

Alexander, J. C., 1984, "Social-Structural Analysis: Some Notes on Its History and Prospects," *Sociological Quarterly*, 25: 5–26.

Barker, R., 1963, *The Stream of Behavior*, New York: Appleton-Century-Crofts.

Bates, F. L., 1956, "Position, Status and Role," *Social Forces*, 34: 313–321.

Bates, F. L., 1957, "A Conceptual Analysis of Group Structure," *Social Forces*, 36: 103–111.

Bates, F. L., 1960, "Institutions. Organizations and Communities: A General Theory of Complex Structures," *Pacific Sociological Review*, 3(2): 59–70.

Bates, F. L., 1962., "Some Observations Concerning the Structural Aspects of Role Conflict," *Pacific Sociological Review*, 5(2): 59–70.

Bates, F. L., and L. Bacon, 1972, "The Community as a Social System," *Social Forces*, 50(3): 371–379.

Bates, F. L., and C. Harvey, 1975, *The Structure of Social Systems*, New York: Gardner Press.

Bates, F. L., and J. D. Kelley, "A Station Centered Approach to the Study of Social Stratification," *LSU Journal of Sociology*, 2(2): 22–47.

Bates. F. L., and W. G. Peacock, 1989, "Conceptualizing Social Structure: The Misuse of Classification in Structural Modeling," *American Sociological Review*, 54: 565–577.

Bateson, G., 1972, "Metalogue: What Is an Instinct?" in *Steps to an Ecology of the Mind*. San Francisco: Chandler.

Bateson, G., 1972, *Steps to an Ecology of Mind; Collected Essays on Anthropology, Psychiatry, Evolution and Epistemology*. San Francisco: Chandler.

Bateson, G., 1979, *Mind and Nature: A Necessary Unity*, New York: Dutton.

Berger, L., 1966, *The Social Construction of Reality*. New York: Doubleday.

Bertalanffy, L. von, 1968, *General Systems Theory: Foundations, Development and Applications*. New York: Braziller.

Biddle, B. J., and Thomas, E. J. (eds.), 1966, *Role Theory*. New York: Wiley.

Blau, P. M., and R. K. Merton, (eds.) 1981, *Continuities in Structural Inquiry*. London: Sage.

Blumer, H., 1969, *Symbolic Interactionism*, Englewood Cliffs, NJ: Prentice-Hall.

Blumer, H., and G. H. Mead, 1980, "The Convergent Methodological Perspective of Social Behaviorism and Symbolic Interactionism," *American Sociological Review*, 45: 409–419.

Boulding, K., 1968, "General System Theory: The Skeleton of Science," in W. Buckley (ed.), *Modern System Research for the Behavioral Scientist*, pp. 3–11. Chicago: Aldine.

Buckley, W., 1967, *Sociology and Modern System Theory*, Englewood Cliffs, NJ: Prentice-Hall.

Catton, W. R. Jr., and R. E. Dunlop, 1978, "Environmental Sociology: A New Paradigm." *American Sociologist*, 13: 41–49.

Churchman, C. W. 1979, *The Systems Approach and Its Enemies*. New York: Basic Books.

Comte, A., 1893, *The Positive Philosophy of Auguste Comte*. London: Kegan Paul, French and Trubner.

Davis, K., 1949, *Human Society*. New York: Macmillan.

Ehrlich, P. R., A. H. Ehrlich, and J. P. Holdren, 1977, *Population, Resources, Environment*. San Francisco: W. H. Freeman.

Fine, G. A., 1993, "The Sad Demise, Mysterious Disappearance, and Glorious Triumph of Symbolic Interactionism," *Annual Review of Sociology*, 19: 61–87.

Firth, R. W., 1963, *Elements of Social Organization*. Boston: Beacon Press.

Flood, R. L., 1990, *Liberating Systems Theory*. New York: Plenum Press.

Fortes, M., 1963, *Social Structure: Studies Presented to A. R. Radcliffe-Brown*. New York: Russell and Russell.

Geyer, F., and J. Van Der Zouwen (eds.), 1986, *Sociocybernetic Paradoxes: Observation, Control, and Evolution of Self-Steering Systems*. London: Sage.

Gleick, J., 1987, *Chaos: Making a New Science*. New York: Penguin Books.

Goffman, E., 1974, *Frame Analysis*, Cambridge, MA: Harvard University Press.

Goffman, E., 1983, "The Interaction Order," *American Sociological Review*, 48:1–17.

Golley, F. B., 1991, "The Ecosystem Concept: A Search for Order," *Ecological Research*, 6: 129–138.

Goodman, N., and C. Z. Elgin, 1988, *Reconceptions in Philosophy and Other Arts*. Indianapolis, IN: Hackett.

Gross, N., W. S. Mason, and A. W. McEachern, 1958, *Explorations in Role Analysis*. New York: Wiley.

Hawley, A. H., 1968, "Human Ecology," in *The International Encyclopedia of the Social Sciences*, 13: 328–337. New York: Macmillan.

Hempel, C. G., 1952, *Fundamentals of Concept Formation in Empirical Science*. Chicago: University of Chicago Press.

Hiller, E. T., 1962, *Social Relations and Structure*: New York: Harper & Row.

Jantsch, E., 1980, *The Self-Organizing Universe*. New York: Pergamon.

Kant, I., 1943, *Critique of Pure Reason*, J. M. D. Meiklejohn (trans.). New York: Wiley.

Katz, F. E., 1976, *Structuralism in Sociology*, Albany: State University of New York Press.

Katz, D., and R. L. Kahn, 1978, *The Social Psychology of Organizations* (2nd ed.). New York: Wiley.

Klier, G., 1969, *An Approach to General System Theory*. New York: Van Nostrand.

Koestler, A., 1967, *The Ghost in the Machine*. London: Hutchinson.

Korzybski, A., 1941, *Science and Sanity*. New York: Science Press.

Lazlo, E., 1972, *Introduction to Systems Philosophy: Toward a New Paradigm of Contemporary Thought*. New York: Gordon and Breach.

Lazlo, E., 1986, "Systems and Societies: The Basic Cybernetics of Social Evolution," in F. Geyer and J. Van der Zouwen (eds.), *Sociocybernetic Paradoxes*. London: Sage, pp. 145–172.

Leach, E., and S. H. Udy, 1968, "Social Structure," in *International Encyclopedia of the Social Sciences*, 14: 482–495. New York: Macmillan.

Lilienfeld, L., 1978, *The Rise of System Theory: An Ideological Analysis*. New York: Wiley.

Linton R., 1936, *The Study of Man*. New York: Appleton-Century-Crofts.

Luhmann, N., 1984, *Die Soziale Systeme*. Frankfurt, Germany: Suhrkamp.

Luhmann, N., 1986, "The Autopoiesis of Social Systems," in R. Geyer & J. Van Der Zouwen (eds.), *Sociocybernetic Paradoxes: Observation, Control and Evolution of Self-Steering Systems*, Beverly Hills: Sage, pp. 172–193.

Malinowski, B., 1944, *A Scientific Theory of Culture*. Chapel Hill: University of North Carolina Press.

Marchal, H., 1975, "On the Concept System," *Philosophy of Science*, 42: 448–468.

Maturana, H., and F. Varella, 1980, *Autopoiesis and Cognition: The Realization of the Living, Studies in the Philosophy of Science*, Boston: Reidel.

McLuhan, M., 1989, *The Global Village*. New York: Oxford University Press.

Maturana, H., and F. Varela, 1987, *The Tree of Knowledge: The Biological Roots of Human Understanding*. Boston: New Science Library.

Merton, R. K., 1968, *Social Theory and Social Structure*. New York: Free Press.

Miller, J. G., 1978, *Living Systems*. New York: McGraw-Hill.

Mingers, J., 1995, *Self-Producing Systems*. New York: Plenum Press.

Nadel, S. F., 1957, The Theory of Social Structure. London: Choen and West.

Odum, E. P., 1953, *Fundamentals of Ecology*. Philadelphia: W. B. Saunders.

Odum, H. T., 1971, *Environment, Power, and Society*. New York: Wiley.

Parsons, T,. 1951, *The Social System*. Glencoe, IL: The Free Press.

Parsons, T., and E. A. Shils, 1951, *Toward a General Theory of Action*. Cambridge, MA: Harvard University Press.

Pelanda, C., 1989, *Cognitive Neo-Systemics: Theory of "Artificial Observers."* Athens, GA: INTERLAB Monograph, The University of Georgia.

Piaget. J., 1967, *Biologie et Conoissance*. Paris: Gallimand.

Pondy, L. R., and I. Mitroff, 1979, "Beyond Open System Models of Organization" in B. Staw and L. L. Cummings (eds.), *Research in Organizational Behavior, 1:* 3–39. Greenwich, CT: J.A.I. Press.

Popper, K., 1972, "Of Clouds and Clocks: An Approach to the Problem of Rationality and the Freedom of Man," in *Objective Knowledge: An Evolutionary Approach*. Oxford: Clarendon Press, pp. 206–255.

Putnam, H., 1981, *Reason, Truth, and History*. New York: Cambridge University Press.

Radcliffe-Brown, A. R., 1977, *The Social Anthropology of Radcliffe-Brown*. London: Rutledge & Kegan Paul.

Rappoport, A., 1968, "General Systems Theory," in *International Encylopedia of the Social Sciences*, Vo. 15, pp. 452–458. New York: Macmillan.

Skinner, B. F., 1971, *Beyond Freedom and Dignity*. New York: Knopf.

Spencer, H., 1900, *First Principles*. New York: A. L. Fowle.

Smith, Adam, 1910, *The Wealth of Nations*. New York: Dutton.

Varela, Francisco J., 1979, *Principles of Biological Autonomy*. Amsterdam: Elsevier.

von Foerster, H. M., 1984, "On Constructing a Reality," in P. Watzlawick (ed.), *The Invented Reality*. New York: Norton.

von Glasersfeld, E., 1987, "An Introduction to Radical Constructivism," in P. Watzlawick (ed.), *The Invented Reality*, New York: Norton.

Wallerstein, I. M., 1974, *The Modern World System*. New York: Academic Press.

Watson, C., F. L. Bates, and A. P. Garbin, 1989, *Rethinking Social Structure: A Commentary on the Use of Classification and Modeling in Sociology*. Athens, GA: INTERLAB monograph, The University of Georgia.

Zeleny, M. (ed.), 1981, *Autopoiesis: A Theory of Living Organisms*. New York: North Holland-Elsevier.

Index